'Are you there, God?'

Thirty
Searching Sermons
for
Puzzled People

Edward Hulme

Dedicated to my family, friends, the churches
where I preach and all sincere searchers.

FRONT COVER by the author who has tried to suggest the
human search for meaning in the awesome mystery of Creation.
The colours represent the setting and main features of planet
Earth's fragile splendour – the infinity of space; the enveloping
atmosphere; the land, fair as it should be; the ocean depths;
the mineral-rich rock, in places penetrated by the fiery magma
beneath, reminding us that creation continues.

ISBN 978-0-9561363-0-5

Published by Hensley Publications
10 Hensley Raod
Bath
BA2 2DR

Book designed by Michael Walsh at
The Better Book Company

A division of
RPM Print & Design
2-3 Spur Road
Chichester
West Sussex
PO19 8PR

The illustrations have been designed by the author in consultation with the artists, Diane Holness for the Introduction, Geraldine Marchand for the sermons (except those marked EH)

CONTENTS

ABOUT THE AUTHOR

Edward Hulme was born in Sale, Cheshire, and brought up in Bowdon a few miles to the south, attending Union Church (Baptist and Congregational), Stretford. For his secondary education he went to Wrekin College, Shropshire, where he learnt to appreciate the dignity and beauty of Anglican worship and music.

Following his baptism by immersion at 16, he became a full member of his family church and, shortly after, felt called to become a Christian minister. He trained at the then Manchester Baptist College, gaining a Bachelor of Arts degree in 1959, and a post-graduate Bachelor of Divinity degree in 1962, both at Manchester University.

In the same year, he was ordained and appointed to the pastorates of Cottingham Road and Priory Road Baptist churches, Hull, serving concurrently as a part-time chaplain at the university. In 1969 he became minister of Oldfield Park Baptist Church, Bath.

Always drawn to the teaching side of his ministry, in 1975 Edward spent a year at St Matthias College, Bristol, taking a P.G.C.E. course and specializing in Religious Education. His first school appointment was as an assistant teacher at John of Gaunt comprehensive school, Trowbridge. In 1980 he became Head of Religious Studies at Bristol Grammar School where he was also responsible for the management of twice-weekly religious assemblies and shared in the leadership of special services.

Since retirement in 1996, he has led day and evening courses on Ethics, Religions and Ideologies, and Credible Faith for the University of Bath Lifelong Learning Division. Throughout his teaching career and subsequently he has regularly taken services in local Free Churches. For relaxation, he enjoys gardening, cycling, music and his model railway.

Edward has a wife, Mary, who works as a braillist, a daughter, Philippa, a son, Marcus, and two grandchildren, Catherine and Sarah.

ABOUT THE ARTISTS

Diane Holness, illustrator for the introduction, graduated in Fine Arts. She worked as a professional artist for ten years and as a model-maker for a further ten. She has recently qualified as a landscape architect.

Geraldine Marchand, illustrator for the sermons (except where marked 'EH'), is a freelance fashion lecturer, illustrator and painter/printer. She trained at Hornsey College of Art, London and has a Master of Philosophy degree with the Open University. In recent years, she has taught sculpture at St Gregory's School, Bath, and led courses in art appreciation for the Lifelong Learning Division of the University of Bath.

PREFACE

"What's the point of life?" "How can God allow so much suffering?" "When I die, what will happen to me?" Even in our overtly materialistic times, people still ask age-old questions such as these. Or they express their innermost concerns in statements. "I can't get my head round miracles". "Climate change frightens me". "I just want to be happy".

In short, many people – churchgoers among them – are profoundly puzzled as they make life's journey. And at least some of them search seriously for enlightenment. If you are one of them, I invite you to read this book in the hope it will provide at least a little help in your quest.

When I first prepared these sermons, I did not expect to publish them. I have done so, however, because, in recent years, I have had a markedly positive response to my preaching. People have made comments like these: "You have given us so much to think about", "I'd like a copy of your sermon so I can reflect on what you said" or "That sermon really should be put into print!"

Of course, the written word lacks the gestures, facial expressions and spontaneous adaptability of the spoken word. But it does give people an opportunity to mull things over in their own time and at their own pace.

Some things I say are bound to spark off very different reactions. For some readers, an idea will provide relief and even liberation. For others, the same idea may cause irritation or even distress. Unless a preacher's policy is to keep the peace at all costs, an element of controversy is inevitable. All I will say is that I never preach simply to 'stir it up'. My sole aim is to do what every minister is called to do: to share what I honestly believe is true and should help people to grow spiritually.

widely varying themes

As the Contents page shows, the themes in this collection vary widely. Some sermons focus on matters of conduct and attitude – like how to keep sane in a crazy world or coping with worry. Others are about social issues, such as the challenge of climate change or our responsibility to the animal kingdom. Yet others focus on great Biblical themes like holiness and compassion or the dangers of idolatry. There are no joke-a-minute sermons but you will find lighter patches in my collection, not least in the two playlets.

Many of my sermons tackle, head-on, a range of intellectually and spiritually 'tough' questions. These include the most difficult ones of all – belief in God and the problem of suffering – and some probably very rarely considered, such as those I have titled 'Sometimes or Always' and 'Poles and Axes'. Being intrinsically complex and enigmatic, such topics deserve as thorough investigation as is reasonably possible. In such cases, the sermon is likely to take between twenty and thirty minutes to deliver. To help concentration, however, I invariably present it in two or three stages interspersed with appropriate hymns, readings or CD excerpts.

key convictions

The conviction that underpins all my preaching is that what Jesus of Nazareth offered the world two thousand years ago is as vital to its well-being as ever. But readers will soon become aware of two further strong convictions.

One is that our quest for meaning requires intellectual rigour. I believe the reluctance of many Christians to talk openly about their beliefs is partly because they find much of the faith they have inherited intellectually wanting. As the United Reformed Church theologian, David Peel, has observed in his book 'Reforming Theology': *"The church has lost its intellectual credibility in the eyes of many people, but if we do not have a credible belief system we will not cut ice in the modern world".*

The other strong conviction is that, since we live in what we call a *uni*verse, all avenues to truth (such as science, logic and religious faith) must ultimately cohere and that where they appear not to, it is our perception that is at fault.

an entertaining and illuminating Introduction!

Introductions to books can be tedious. I hope mine is not! In fact I hope readers will find much of it entertaining and all of it illuminating. It starts with my experiences and training as a 'theolog' in the very different world of Manchester in the late Fifties and early Sixties. Then it focuses on the problems and challenges facing both preachers and congregations. It concludes with some further personal thoughts about preaching. The Introduction is, I believe, an important complement to the collection of sermons that follow – which, I hope, you really will find 'searching' in more ways than one.

Edward Hulme, Autumn 2008

ACKNOWLEDGEMENTS

I am grateful first to **my parents**, for their Christian values and example, and to **my home church** for its loving support and the intellectual rigour of its minister and Sunday School teachers.

I am especially indebted to: **Mary**, **my wife**, for her constant encouragement and unflagging help in checking scripts, searching the web and making numerous suggestions on matters of detail; **my illustrators**, **Diane Holness** (the Introduction) and **Geraldine Marchand** (the sermons, except those marked EH), for their expertise and patience with my quirky ideas; **Simon Carter** for his computing skills and hands-on guidance in preparing material for the printer; **The Better Book Company** for final editing, printing and binding of the book.

I am indirectly indebted to countless people including: my lecturers, tutors and fellow students at Manchester University and the former Manchester Baptist College; my long-suffering congregations in Hull and Bath; my colleagues and pupils at John of Gaunt, Trowbridge and Bristol Grammar schools; and a great range of academic and general writers and journalists whose knowledge and wisdom I have imbibed over the last fifty or so years.

Since the great majority of the sermons in this collection were originally prepared without any intention of their being published, my record of sources is limited. While apologizing to anyone whom I have inadvertently overlooked or have not been able to identify, those authors and books I do know I have used are named in the text or in the following list, or in both where I supply additional details. Where legally necessary, I have sought permission to quote.

Preface: Dr David Peel, 'Reforming Theology', published by United Reformed Church.
Introduction: Dr Mary Ede, 'The Chapel in Argyle Street, Bath, 1789-1989', published by Central United Reformed Church, Bath; Philip Richter and Leslie J. Francis, 'Gone but not forgotten', published by Darton, Longman and Todd Ltd.

Sermon 1: Professor Paul Davies, theoretical physicist and cosmologist, newspaper article and 'The Mind of God', published by Simon and Schuster UK Ltd. Keith Ward, Regius Professor of Divinity Emeritus, Oxford University, and Fellow of the British Academy.

Sermon 3: Professor Samuel P. Huntington, 'The Clash of Civilizations', published by Simon and Schuster UK Ltd.

Sermon 5: Dr Theresa Carino, Co-ordinator, Amity Foundation Hong Kong office, Friends of the Church in China Newsletter Spring 2008; Neal Lawson in The Guardian 'Debate', 3/1/07; Simon Jenkins in The Guardian 'Comment', 2/5/08.

Sermon 6: Dr Andrew Weller, University of Bath, Bath Chronicle report, 8/12/06.

Sermon 10: Professor A. C. Grayling, philosopher, The Guardian, 25/3/00, reprinted by personal permission.

Sermon 11: The Chief Rabbi, Sir Jonathan Sacks, newspaper report.

Sermon 13: Pope Benedict XVI, address to the Ecclesiastical Diocesan Convention of Rome, at the Basilica of St John Lateran, 6/6/05.

Sermon 14: A range of theologians including Bishop John Shelby Spong, 'Jesus for the Non-Religious', published by Harper San Fransisco.

Sermon 15: Susan Howatch. 'A Question of Integrity', published by Little, Brown Book Group.

Sermon 20: Annals of the Rheumatic Diseases, May 2008.

Sermon 21: Drs. Paul Hawken, Amory B and L. Hunter Lovins, 'Natural Capitalism', published 1999 by Earthscan Publications Ltd. (extracts from pages XIV, 1, 321 and 322): reproduced by permission of Earthscan Ltd.

Sermon 30: Carl Dudley, quoted in 'Gone but not forgotten', Darton, Longman and Todd Ltd.

Very nearly all scripture quotations in this publication are from the Good News Bible, 2nd edition copyright 1992 by the American Bible Society and used by permission (September 2008).

INTRODUCTION

This introduction starts by focusing on the author's preaching background, in particular his experiences and training as a Baptist theological student in Manchester between 1956 and 1962. Then it considers the problems and challenges preachers and congregations face. It concludes with a few further, personal thoughts about preaching.

"What title should I give my introduction?" I asked myself as I set about writing it. "'Pulpit and pew?' That's snappy, but it's hardly accurate. Nowadays, as often as not, the preacher propounds from somewhere less lofty". "The minister uses the lectern", the duty steward explains. "Then I will, too", you reply, as you contemplate squeezing Bible, hymn book, prayers and sermon script onto a slippery slope no larger than a laptop.

As for pews, they are rapidly migrating to secular pastures, like trendy restaurants or posh barn conversions. Recognizing that being comfortable isn't really such a sin, more and more churches are replacing their pews with chairs, some of them with arms. "You see, many of us have worn-out knees and hips, so we need a little help when it comes to standing up".

I thought again about a title and came up with 'Preacher and People'. "It's more personal", I mused, "and it gets round the furniture changes… though it might suggest the preacher, coming first, is more important – which would never do, even if some of us do speak more about ourselves than God!"

Of course, preachers do have a special role. Supremely, this is to help worshippers recognize their spiritual need and to help them grow in faith and character. The special role of preachers is symbolized by their physical elevation, whether they are perched on the rostrum, a mere foot higher than their flock, or in a pulpit, 'six feet above contradiction'.

Or even twelve feet, as in one church I used to visit as a student. Leaving college before the crack of dawn, usually in the depths of winter, I would make my way (or feel it, if the fog was thick) to the No 53 bus. After a dismal trip through the then drab Manchester suburbs, I would reach the stop where I could catch another double-decker to the town at the end of the route. Then, a steep walk up took me to a grimy barn of a church built to impress approaching worshippers and, it seemed to raw students like myself, to intimidate those invited to mount its massive pulpit.

That west Pennine church contrasted starkly with one of several homely chapels in rural Cheshire whose diaconates were magnanimous enough to give learner-ministers a chance to practise. One sandstone gem boasted an elegant, thoroughly High Church, style of pulpit. Getting into it, however, was a risky business. For the preacher entered through a narrow, five-feet-six-inches high doorway, direct from the vestry behind. "Now *do* mind your head", the kindly vestry deacon advised the trembling student. "I will, thank you", he distractedly replied, only to forget seconds later, as cranium cracked against the hostile apex. "Owwh!" he exclaimed, hoping his added expletive hadn't actually escaped his lips!

Still scrabbling around for a suitable title, I momentarily considered 'Preaching in Principle and Practice', and then 'Preaching Then and Now'. But I rejected both because I am not, in fact, offering either a manual or a history of the sacred art, even if I do share my thoughts and briefly trace the changing status of preaching. So, in the end I scrapped the idea of a title altogether. Instead, I would help the reader by providing sub-titles.

The changing status of preaching

I have not done any systematic research into the subject, but my impression is that, over time, the status of preaching fluctuates. Compare, for example, the preaching climate of the years when Argyle Church, Bath, was founded with that of its successor today, Central United Reformed Church. The Reverend William Jay, minister from 1790 to 1853, usually preached for a mere 45 minutes, short by the standards of his day! Now, the norm is nearer 15 minutes so if preachers wish to expound more fully, they know it is wiser to deliver their sermon in two or three stages, with a hymn slotted between each section. Even in historically 'word-orientated' denominations, the sermon doesn't appear to enjoy the prestige it once did.

As relatively recently as the 1950s, there was still a handful of preachers of whom any reasonably informed person would at least have heard. Dubbed 'great divines', it was believed they were outstandingly skilled at divining and communicating 'the mind of God'. They attracted large congregations in their own churches and as guest preachers. The mid-week, lunchtime services held in central Manchester, pulled in punters by the hundred. I well remember being wowed by such men as Leslie Weatherhead, Donald Soper and William Sangster. Sadly, and perhaps a sign of society's wholesale secularization, the latest edition of Chambers Biographical Dictionary doesn't mention any of them, the only Sangster deemed worthy of inclusion being a racehorse breeder!

If it is broadly true that sermons commanded greater respect fifty years ago than today, one reason could be the quality of both the producers and their product. Of course, there were good, bad and mediocre preachers, as there were sermons. The 1950s and 1960s certainly weren't a golden age for churches. Nevertheless, if you went to a service in a Baptist, Congregational, Methodist or any other mainstream Free Church at that time, I believe there was a greater chance than now that you would hear a good quality sermon given by a well qualified preacher. Today, for all sorts of reasons, a smaller proportion of full-time ministers have had the benefit of a long and rigorous theological training, a reality that has, I believe, had a detrimental effect on the overall standard of preaching. I use the phrase 'overall standard' advisedly because there are, most definitely, still plenty of able preachers around, doing an excellent job in often taxing circumstances.

There is certainly no need to include a full-blown sermon at every service, if only in order to reduce ministers' often cruelly excessive workload. As long as they are skilfully led and are not allowed to degenerate into embarrassing squabbles, 'conversations' between preacher and congregation can be enlightening and productive. Provided they are meticulously prepared and managed, high tech presentations can be extremely effective. But I am convinced it is shortsighted to bin sermons altogether. Carefully thought out and well delivered, they still have an important role in 21st century church life.

Learning to preach

Now I wish to say a little about my own ministerial training, even if some of the narrative might appear entertaining rather than illuminating, perhaps self-indulgent in places. I hope this excursion proves interesting, as well as instructive for both the content and style of my sermons.

Half a century ago, theological colleges and their students were fortunate. The social and political circumstances of the mid-twentieth century facilitated extended ministerial training. Local Education Authority grants were much more generous than today, enabling the great majority of students to cope financially for at least three years and many much longer. This meant it was perfectly possible for ordinands to take two three-year degree courses, with the broad and solid academic base this provided.

Though obviously presenting problems for the minority of students who were married, the obligation to reside in college during term time was, overall, hugely beneficial. Living in, weekdays and most weekends, facilitated all sorts of valuable courses and activities, as well as providing ample opportunity for students to interact intellectually. We regularly stayed up to the small hours discussing theological, philosophical, ethical and topical matters.

High jinks

But life was not all work. There was a big (thankfully alcohol-free) fun element. We particularly liked playing practical jokes or 'mickeys' as we called them.

A major 'mickey' – skip this and the next two paragraphs if you wish to keep to the serious stuff – took place each year shortly before our summer exams. It was played on the hapless candidates up for interview and entrance exam. The entire college, staff and students, sustained the charade from the moment prospective recruits arrived to the night before they left.

There were always several cranky individuals as well as eccentric groups, like the Jazz Club and their opposites, the Holy Club. The jazz types strutted round in casual garb, taking every opportunity to make an almighty racket. Meanwhile, the dour-faced 'holy' huddle, wearing black from neck to toes, paced round quoting absurdly obscure texts at the unsuspecting visitors. One year, the Holy Club leader, incensed by his antagonists' impiety, snatched an armful of 78 rpm records from them and triumphantly hurled the brittle booty from the top landing, down the well, and onto the hard tiles of the ground floor far below where they exploded with a mighty crash, to the alarm of the now thoroughly disconcerted visitors!

The wretched candidates also had to endure a mock sermon class and an interview with a 'mad' professor whose Greek and Hebrew graces were so long and so nonsensical that those of us 'in the know' found it all but impossible to stifle our mirth. All told, it was no wonder there was always at least one candidate who asked if he could pull out, only being restrained by the principal's assurance, 'I'm afraid the men', as he habitually called us, 'get rather tense before their exams'. It was a relief for everyone when the moment of denouement came and prospective students discovered the college wasn't quite such a madhouse after all!

Whether good and clean or cheap and mean, such high jinks proved a welcome change from the exacting pressures of degree work, college lectures, sermon writing and all the other duties preparation for Christian ministry entailed. At times, the

pressures imposed and the personal discipline required were all but overwhelming. So diversions were doubly important. As well as mickeys, these included football (played savagely against rival theological colleges), music of various kinds, walks round the local Platt Fields park, and nibbling our way through large tins of chocolate digestives. Girl friends, too, provided a blissful escape though you knew, when you brought in your latest for the first time, you would have to run the gauntlet of students ogling round every corner and pillar. Interestingly, unlike just about every other college in those days, the then Manchester Baptist College had no official 'girls out' deadline – just trust!

Rigorous courses
College and university courses alike were rigorous. Although our principal, the Rev Kenneth Dykes, prescribed courses geared in part to students' individual preferences and abilities, certain subjects were deemed essential. These included Biblical Studies, theology and the history of Christian doctrine. Biblical studies, based on modern scholarship with its scientific methodology, respected the scriptures but did not allow you to take them at their face value. The historic context, the writers' intentions, the process of compilation, the meaning of the original languages, and many other factors were explored.

Christian Doctrine involved a critical survey of belief from the days of Jesus's ministry to the 20th century. We studied the convictions of New Testament writers, the stormy evolution of the historic creeds, the great heresies, and many of the people and movements that shaped Christian faith down the centuries.

Ministerial training also included courses of a more general nature, such as English, where, at the first lecture, the tutor reeled off a list of eighteen classical and modern books he expected us to read and study by the summer exam, just nine months off. But that was child's play compared to the challenge of getting to grips with three subjects new to most of us – classical Greek, Hebrew, and philosophy.

The importance of English

These subjects proved their worth, not least English with its language as well as literature elements. Rightly, the college made mastery of our mother tongue a high priority. Any preacher worthy of the title must be able to express the obscurest of concepts and most difficult of arguments, concisely, clearly and cogently. As every sermon class made dauntingly clear, every word had to be chosen with care and scripts refined and re-refined until you said what you wished to say in the most efficient and effective way. "Mr Smith", the 'Boss' would challenge the victim as he recoiled from the ordeal of preaching to principal, tutor and thirty ultra-critical colleagues, "why did you use the word 'fructify'? I'm not sure what some people in your congregation would make of it... And if their concentration was wandering, they might even think you said something – er – unmentionable. Couldn't you find a simpler word?"

The great philosophers

Philosophy was another 'must'. For those of us on the two degrees programme, this involved a study of historic thinkers like Plato, Aristotle, Descartes, Leibniz, Locke, Berkeley, Hume, Kant, Hegel, and more recent figures like Bertrand Russell and A. J. Ayer. It incorporated a large slice of Philosophy of Religion where we probed questions like the existence of God, the problem of evil, the meaning of religious language, the problem of verifiability, and the significance of death. It introduced us to the psychology of religion, where we ploughed through such classics as William James' 'The varieties of religious experience' and Sigmund Freud's 'The Future of an Illusion'. By such exacting means, we examined both the notion and the practice of religion and, in the process, found our fragile faith well and truly put through the mill.

The value of logic

Then there was logic. This was largely formal logic, with its fearsomely abstruse formulae and equations. We burnt the midnight oil trying to make sense of its baffling language.

For me, it was not until a fortnight before the final exam that pennies dropped by the bagful and I began to grasp what it was all about. I have long since forgotten the formal processes but the course left me in no doubt about the crucial importance of logical thinking. How many opinions do you hear, see or read in the media, where even learned experts commit logical howlers! How many sermons have you sat through where preachers pull the rug from under their own feet, simply through their neglect of elementary logic?

It was probably the logic course more than any other that first prompted my dislike and distrust of paradoxes, not least the idea that Jesus was both fully human and fully divine at the same time. I believe a claim of this kind can be no more than a tentative statement of faith and one that Christians should therefore feel free to explore and express in fresh ways.

Over the years, I have also come to believe that logic is a medium – along with others like mathematics, science, philosophy, music, art and theology – which can give us glimpses of ultimate reality, of the way things essentially are. If it has this capacity, if it is one of the 'languages of God', I suggest logic may be used as a guide not only for reasoning but also for conduct.

The resulting conduct is likely to be at odds with what the world generally thinks is 'logical' behaviour. The world too often behaves as if going to war, getting your own back, breaking through the glass ceiling, making 'loadsa' money, and putting 'number one' first, are the logical things to do. Logic in tune with ultimate reality, however. in tune with the way things are 'meant to be', shows that love, forgiveness, service, giving and altruism are what actually make sense. Paul, I believe, reveals his knowledge of logic at its profoundest and truest, when he observes, "For what seems to be God's foolishness is wiser than human wisdom, and what seems to be God's weakness is stronger than human strength".

Ethics – another 'must'
Ethics – both general and Christian – was also a 'must'. This was a popular course, probably because its relevance was so obvious. True, we were enthralled by sexual ethics – after all,

we were young men mostly without personal sexual experience, sex in those days, certainly for Christians, being strictly reserved for marriage. But Ethics covered many areas of life, ranging from personal questions like 'should you always tell the truth?' to complex social issues like crime and punishment.

The dreaded sermon class
One final feature of my college days I have already touched on but wish to describe more fully, and is especially relevant to my preaching philosophy and style, is the dreaded sermon class. This took place every Friday evening soon after formal dinner. Each week one student would be 'in the dock' for up to two hours. He would conduct a service he had prepared and which included three or four hymns, Bible readings, prayers and, most importantly, a sermon of at least fifteen minutes.

After this trauma, the victim sat at a table, script at hand, while his fellows, initially invited by the principal and then in a free-for-all, questioned and mauled his efforts. The entire operation was ruthless and if, as a member of the congregation, you didn't find something to censure, you got a black mark yourself! To cap it all, a tape-recording was made to demonstrate the ill-chosen word or factual error or logical non sequitur or slipshod delivery. Eventually the ordeal ended with the principal giving his personal verdict. And all too often he would declare: "Mr Jones, you used *far* too many pious platitudes. Cut 'em out, say what you really want to, without all that holy froth!"

After sleepless nights leading up to your own sermon class and enduring the torment itself, you felt mentally, emotionally, physically and spiritually drained, truly thankful you were in the hot seat only once a year. If you were at college for six years, you attended around 180 classes altogether so ended up with a pretty fair idea of what a good service and a good sermon *should* be like. How far, over the years, I and my fellow students have actually lived up to the high standards college put before us is another matter!

I have highlighted certain aspects of my ministerial training partly to shed light on one major influence on the content and style of the sermons in this collection, and partly to mention some of the factors which I believe should shape all worthwhile preaching.

Preaching today

I wish every full-time minister today could have the depth and breadth of preparation that I and many other preachers received fifty years ago.

But my wish is unrealistic. Public bodies are far less supportive. Since most ministerial candidates now are ten or twenty years older than in my training days, and many of them have family commitments and mortgage payments to keep up, several years of full-time residential training could not be the norm.

Indisputably, older ordinands have a wealth of life experience that can greatly enrich their ministry and preaching. Even so, I maintain that a solid academic foundation is as desirable as ever, if the preacher is to win the ear, convince the mind and move the heart, of thinking younger and older people in the generally sceptical climate of today. Without such a foundation, preachers are likely to feel, and be, inadequately equipped to tackle the great intellectual questions and big ethical issues that confront their congregations.

As challenging as ever

But whatever academic training ordinands undergo, once qualified and in harness they will find preaching is as challenging as it has ever been. Probably saddled with several churches and facing an ever more exhausting workload, they will have less time to read and study, let alone prepare sermons on really difficult themes.

So, naturally, they look for help. Whereas their predecessors of the late 1960s might have eagerly responded to a Mr Thody's 'instant sermon service' advertised in the Church Times, with 'vitalising and challenging' scripts available at five shillings a time, preachers nowadays may well turn to the internet for such assistance.

The Lectionary: blessing or bane?

An increasing number of Free Church preachers seek refuge in The Lectionary. While basing sermons on lectionary readings may save them time searching for a theme and might even deter them from releasing any more of the same old bees from the same old bonnets, this potential blessing can easily become a curse. Worryingly, The Lectionary has become so dominating that some preachers feel obliged to use it, even when, on their own admission, none of the prescribed readings moved them!

So, if the allotted passage is a parable, they will tediously retell and fancifully embroider it, treating it as if it were an historical incident rather than a made-up story, and already 'known backwards' by most of the congregation. Or, taking the appointed scripture right out of context, they squeeze from it every possible and impossible truth. But even when preachers habitually use the appointed readings well, just by keeping slavishly to The Lectionary they shut out a huge range of relevant and urgent biblical and extra-biblical themes, such as many addressed in this collection. To put it bluntly, it could be argued that many churches and preachers would gain enormously if they gave The Lectionary a very long holiday!

Whether churches and preachers prefer prescription or freedom in their choice of theme, whether they are sacrament- or word-centred, I am convinced sermons still have an important role in shared spiritual nourishment. When sermons address people's deepest needs, are prepared with diligence, imagination and care, and are delivered with clarity, precision and empathy, people *will* listen and their souls, or innermost selves, *will* be fed.

Choosing hymns

Although I naturally focus on the preaching element of worship in this introduction, I believe every feature of a service is important and worthy of meticulous preparation. Hymns, for instance, need to be chosen with extreme care, a process that requires imagination, skilled judgment and time. Few things make me wince more than the idea that hymns can be chosen in the vestry just before the service.

The preacher, I submit, should choose hymns which make good theological sense, are of sound literary merit, contribute to the liturgical integrity of the service, and are appropriate to the particular congregation. There should be a balance between those that focus on the individual and those that focus on society. Ideally, they should vary in mood, length and metre.

And the preacher should beware of any that are excessively obscure or sentimental, let alone trite. While some hymn books make selecting a nightmare, others – like 'Rejoice and Sing' – make it a rewarding task.

The perils of preaching

Raw recruit or seasoned veteran, preachers face a frightening array of perils, some of them to do with attitude, others with content.

Perils of attitude

The supreme attitude type of peril is *to focus on oneself more than the message*, let alone God. Preachers can all too readily behave as if they were celebrities. And the trappings of the job can reinforce their vanity. While vestments – bright or sombre – lofty location, and official title, are all meant to elevate the preacher's *function*, there is always the danger they may boost the preacher's *ego*!

Facing the same temptation the greatest preacher of all confronted, when he fleetingly imagined himself jumping unscathed from the top of the temple, preachers ever since have been tempted *to win over their hearers by impressing them in some way.* They may 'speak to the gallery' or they crack a joke a minute. The galling thing is that preachers who put style before substance are often the ones who get the invitations to the big occasions! And there, in the melee afterwards, their adoring fans exclaim "Wasn't he brilliant?" even though their hero has done little more than 'tickle their ears', like the populist teachers Paul warned trainee pastor Timothy not to emulate. Preachers in a different league can take comfort from the fact they will never become victims of adulation! Because those who do rest on their laurels are likely to skimp their preparation and, sooner or later, atrophy.

If preachers resist populism, they may well try – knowingly or unknowingly – to impress their hearers by their erudition or eloquence. They choose words and phrases that sound learned, even esoteric, rather than those that most effectively convey their thoughts. A longer word may be more economical than a phrase but a shorter one may well be more appropriate.

Probably the greatest self-indulgence the preacher faces – and one to which I admit I yield – is to use the pulpit to get off your chest matters currently annoying or offending you, *to treat your congregation as a mental vomitorium!* There may be times when the preacher's 'wrath' *is* 'righteous' and needs to be vented. Generally, however, it is wiser to try and steer a course somewhere between the Scylla of insensitive bluntness and the Charybdis of cowardly timidity.

A further peril is *to become sanctimonious*. This may show in a preacher's voice or gestures. Or in the emulation of a particular hero's style – I remember one student at college who cultivated the breathy mannerism of the renowned Martin Lloyd-Jones, until finally teased out of it.

But religiosity may be more subtle, as when peripatetic preachers boast they never repeat a sermon, as if there were something intrinsically irreverent about doing so. Of course, a favourite sermon should be constantly updated and adapted for each congregation and always delivered as if totally fresh. That said, isn't it terribly wasteful of time, effort, and maybe inspiration, to ditch a 'good' sermon after a single airing? Personally, I find that further reflection, feedback from a congregation, and where possible listening to a tape recording, all make the second time through better than the first, and the third better still! True, excessive repetition produces staleness. Nevertheless, my dictum is: "If a sermon is worth preaching at all, it's worth preaching *more* than once; if it's worth preaching *only* once, it may not be worth preaching at all!"

Yet another peril is *to harangue the congregation*. Have you ever sat in the pew and felt the preacher was treating you as a naughty child or an army recruit? Resident ministers especially may feel like tearing their hair out because of the torpor of their flock. No one has come forward to be church secretary, only three people have offered to help with Christian Aid Week, there's been but a tiny increase in weekly giving in spite of a special appeal. Such unresponsiveness may be exasperating, and yet, apart from the fact there may be understandable reasons for the apparent apathy, bullying a congregation is likely to be counter-productive.

One final peril of attitude: *to patronize your congregation*. "They're all old dears at that church so I'll just tell them a story". In fact, those 'old dears' may well be just as bright and educated as anyone else. Appearances can be very deceptive. More to the point, they will certainly wonder, as much as everyone else, about the great questions and big issues of life. Every congregation should be treated with dignity and respect.

Perils of content

A common peril of content is *to confuse objective certainty and subjective certitude*, to treat 'fact' as 'faith' and 'faith' as 'fact'. But this won't do, for there is little, if anything, either material or spiritual, about which we can be unflinchingly definite. However passionately we believe something to be true in religion or any other realm, we cannot ever step beyond the frontier of faith. Theist, non-theist, and atheist alike, can never be other than, in the strict sense of the word, 'a-gnostic', 'not-knowing'. Absolute certainty is a will o' the wisp. "What we know now is only partial".

A second peril of content is *to abuse or overuse analogies*. They can certainly be helpful pointers to truth. They are an attractive, indeed, beguiling communicator's tool. Jesus used them (to good effect) as did Paul (often to good effect). Regrettably, however, too many preachers – even famous and popular ones – seem blissfully unaware that analogies can also be seriously misleading. For what may be perfectly valid in the adopted analogy may be quite false when applied to the point the preacher wishes to make. For instance, a favourite way of cheering up a church depressed by declining support or by the seemingly relentless growth in some social evil, is to promise "The tide *will* turn" or "The pendulum *will* swing back". But because we can be sure (as much as we can about anything) that after the sea ebbs it will flow, and that the swing of the clock's weight will return when it reaches each extremity, it doesn't follow we can be comparably confident that a change in the church's or society's circumstances will occur. Unless we can come up with a valid analogy, we should stick to straight, lucid argument.

Quotations, too, may be abused or overused. "As Shakespeare said", may lend gravitas but words from the bard or any other source only add weight if they are genuinely applicable. Words from biblical figures will often provide authoritative support but when preachers take them totally out of context, they cheat their listeners and use the Bible improperly. A well chosen quotation may clinch an argument but it is sometimes just as effective, and often quicker, to devise one's own 'quotation'.

Possibly the most grievous sin that can entrap the preacher is *to skimp preparation*. To be fair, resident ministers may sometimes be bombarded with unexpected demands on their time. Seven of their flock die in the same week instead of the customary one or two, an alcohol-sodden lout prangs their car, the children are off school with chicken-pox, an aging parent insists they take them to the superstore. I remember an horrendously busy week in my first pastorate when I couldn't even produce a third-rate sermon and instead resorted to someone's ready-made meditation. Yet not even a candid explanation and grovelling apology in the church porch afterwards, managed to assuage the anger of one lady who stormed out spluttering "I might just as well have stayed at home!" Most people in a congregation appreciate that crises happen and forgive the resultant prattle or sermon substitute. But preachers who habitually leave their preparation to Saturday evening risk cobbling together a shallow, ill thought out and unworthy sermon – gravy without the beef.

Pitfalls for people in the pew

If preachers face a legion of perils, people in the pew also face pitfalls.

Perhaps the number one pitfall is *to lose concentration!* Nodding off, mentally or physically, or both, may well be perfectly understandable. Life being generally frenetic, many people come to church tired and world-weary. The church may be stuffy and the preacher even stuffier. It is easy to daydream.

Though it's a good job our thoughts at such times don't suddenly materialize! Just imagine if all the objects floating around people's minds escaped and floated round the sanctuary, visible to all and sundry! The air would be filled with ovens roasting joints, weeds running rampant, leathers polishing cars, whirring computers, muddy mountain bikes, weekend magazines and, who knows, handsome hunks and nubile women! Letting our minds wander may sometimes be excusable, but is it so forgivable when it's the result of sheer laziness? Just as preachers should put mind, body, heart and soul into both preparation and delivery of their worship, shouldn't those of us in the pew discipline our response? After all, one hour is only one one-hundred-and-sixty-eighth of the week, about as long as it takes to eat a leisurely meal.

Then there's *clock-watching!* This can be painfully obvious. I remember how one 'pillar' of my home church invariably looked conspicuously at the clock on the side wall when the sermon started, and how a deacon in my second pastorate closed her spectacles case with a loud snap, when she thought it was time for the preacher to reach his destination! The trouble is, even when the glance at the clock is furtive and the yawn all but stifled, the preacher is almost bound to notice and, if nervous, be blown off course.

Thinking of clocks, some people have very definite views on the right length of sermons. "There's no subject that can't be covered in ten minutes", they declare. Ten minutes may well be enough for some topics. It's amazing how much of depth and worth can be packed into as little as three minutes, as any listener to Radio Four's 'Thought for Today' slot knows. Yet some questions and issues are so intrinsically complex and problematic, that even the most carefully constructed and fluently delivered half-hour sermon cannot do justice to them.

A final pitfall for people in the pew is *to nit-pick*. Of course, listeners should be alert to preachers' faux pas, illogical arguments, inaudible speaking and any other correctable failing and gently put them right. But patience and empathy are always desirable. For a resident minister may be monstrously overloaded having to prepare and give a hundred or more new sermons or addresses, year in and year out. And unforeseen emergencies can play havoc with the intentions of even the most organized of preachers. They really do need their congregation's support.

My preaching rationale

I wish to conclude this introduction by making a few further points about my personal preaching rationale.

Like every preacher, the aim of my pulpit ministry is to help people grow in faith, intellectually and spiritually. Ideally, this should be achieved with absolute honesty and openness. In reality, preachers minister under certain constraints, supremely the doctrinal assumptions of their particular denomination or congregation. For resident ministers especially, such constraints may be inescapable, if they are to keep their job.

Free to believe
In my own case, I have belonged to a tradition wherein you are free to believe only whatever you can sincerely accept. I have never been obliged to consent to an elaborate creed. All I have had to affirm is my conviction that, in the words of the earliest Christian statement of belief, 'Jesus is Lord' and that God, in some sense, is tri-une. For Christians of this persuasion, faith is more 'fiducia' in nature (believing *in*) rather than 'credo' (believing *that*).

A free outlook clearly demands intellectual openness. Such openness, however, means that Christians of this ilk, although normally inclusive in spirit and in practice, eschew the dogmatism and literalism characteristic of 'fundamentalist' circles.

The dangers of 'fundamentalism' – religious *and* secular

I am fully aware that the term 'fundamentalist' goes back to the years between 1910 and 1915 when a group of conservative Christians published a series of pamphlets under the title 'The Fundamentals'. These were five doctrines they claimed represented the quintessence of Christianity and to deny the truth of even one of them was not just heresy but apostasy. But the term 'fundamentalism' now refers to an attitude, and one that is totally opposed to the notion of a faith which may be questioned and understood in new ways.

Christians of my persuasion are equally disturbed by secular fundamentalism which, in its attitude, mirrors its religious counterpart. So the dogmatism of certain eminent biologists, for instance, is also deemed objectionable. Dismissing all religious metaphysical affirmations with the mantra 'There is not a shred of evidence to support your claims', these biologists not only arrogantly assume that they alone can define what counts as 'evidence' but also illogically exclude the possibility of evidence emerging in the future. While slamming religion for allegedly treating concepts of faith as proven fact, they themselves treat at least one totally speculative theory as virtual fact! I have in mind their reply to those cosmologists who argue that the astoundingly 'fine-tuned' orderliness of creation justifies belief in the possibility of a Cosmic Intelligence. The reply of these biologists, to the effect that such a universe as ours is statistically inevitable since we almost certainly live in a '*multi*verse', is actually one hundred per cent speculation, there being, as yet, no evidence whatever to support the assertion!

Fundamentalism, religious or secular, is, I submit, an enemy of knowledge, understanding and faith. In Christianity, it engenders the mindset which treats the entire Bible as if its contents were all of equal validity and merit. It fails to recognize the possibility of 'progressive revelation' whereby human understanding of truth is believed to develop. As a result, fundamentalists cling to all sorts of Old Testament theological and ethical notions that mainstream Christians believe have been superseded by the teaching and example of Jesus. Their whole approach, I believe, can only alienate anyone seriously eager to discover the 'real' Jesus.

Preachers never 'arrive'
I do not for one moment imagine the sermons in this collection are model ones for preachers can never be fully satisfied with their efforts: we never 'arrive'. But my sermons are sincere, thoughtful and thorough attempts to probe the great questions and big issues as well as important but more straightforward themes. Like all genuine sermons, they are, I believe, partly the result of inspiration – which really may come 'out of the blue' (when I'm shaving, or in the bath, or at dead of night) – and partly the result of perspiration – strenuous mental and spiritual effort.

Although tweaked for written presentation, the thirty sermons are substantially as preached. I have added headings and sub-headings, as well as the occasional extra explanation which would normally go on the day's service paper. I hope you find them worth reading.

Some questions for churches
I conclude with a particularly relevant extract from 'Gone but not forgotten', a book which considers both the reasons for leaving church and the factors that are most likely to retain and attract people in today's intellectual and social climate:

"If churches are to retain their members they need to take account of the difficulties people face in maintaining their faith. Churches need to ask whether they are devoting enough energy to the task of apologetics. Are churches taking seriously the actual questions people are asking in late-modern society? Have churches equipped themselves to meet the questions of an increasingly well-educated population? Do churches encourage their members to express doubts and to ask hard-hitting questions? Do churches truly cater for those who are struggling with their faith?"

xxx

A PREACHER'S PRAYER

Lord, I would like to be a worthier and better preacher.

By your grace, help me:
to study diligently and read widely;
to reflect carefully on both 'word' and 'world';
to use judiciously any genuine source of enlightenment;
to prepare my sermons thoroughly;
and to deliver them clearly and sensitively.

By your grace, save me:
from patronizing or haranguing my congregations;
from courting popularity or any other form of self-indulgence.

By your grace, give me:
the courage to tackle difficult themes and share unwelcome truths;
the integrity to resist entertaining but misleading illustrations;
the honesty to be tentative rather than dogmatic;
the love to be positive and encouraging whenever I can.

Grant me, most of all, the discipline to practise what I preach!

Amen

Five 'R's of Preaching

READ widely
REFLECT carefully
WRESTLE bravely
WRITE clearly
REFINE thoroughly

1   *"ARE YOU THERE,* GOD?"

An enquiry into the existence,
nature and significance of God

"God, ANOTHER Monday!"... "Thank God it's FRIDAY!"... Curse or cliché, a superficial notion of God remains popular. If the prevalence of religious faith is a fair guide, a profound notion of God is also popular, not so much in Europe as it once was but certainly on the world stage.

Now most of the time, people who use the word 'God', whether superficially or profoundly – and there's often a subconscious depth even when it's used trivially – most of the time, such people are either too busy, too confused, or too confident, to stop and think whether the God they address actually exists. But, I submit, most people, perhaps just once, maybe from time to time, or even frequently, do ask the mega question: 'Does God exist?' They mean, of course, outside their own minds.

Well, as you've guessed, it's this very question I wish to tackle now. You certainly won't expect a definitive answer from me or anyone else! All I shall do is offer a few thoughts about the

1

existence, nature and significance of God. I hope they will help you in your personal, spiritual quest.

So: "*Are you there*, God?"

Let's feel at ease

Before I go any further, I appreciate that posing *this* question, of all questions, may make you feel uncomfortable. Surely, a service is the one occasion when we *assume* God is 'present and correct'! We feel, with ex-Catholic priest Donald Harper, that 'God is not a problem to be solved, but a mystery to be enjoyed'. Maybe; but the reality is that virtually every day we are exposed to the contemporary climate of scepticism or atheism and are not immune to its questions and doubts, uncertainties the responsible preacher should face.

But need we ever shrink from this question? Because, whatever you, I, or anyone else, believes or says about God, won't actually affect, one whit, the *reality* of God.

By talking about God we can certainly affect other people's *perception* of God, something which may influence them for either good or evil: think how many kind actions and social reforms have been initiated by people convinced God is compassionate and inclusive; conversely, think how much violence has been committed because people were persuaded to think of God as a ruthless, partisan warrior. But talking about God won't change God's actual nature.

That said, the philosophical 'you' may well wonder: how far *can* you distinguish between subjective perception and objective reality? Even the professors couldn't decide whether the tree in the quad remained a *tree* (as opposed to an organized collection of molecules in dynamic relationship) when no one was looking at it! We cannot dismiss that philosophical chestnut – or was it an oak? – yet, intuitively, we sense we really cannot change the objective essence or truth about God.

(This, incidentally, is why I don't see any sense in getting too worked-up about blasphemy. It is hurtful to believers and therefore unkind but it won't damage, let alone destroy, God, as some objectors appear to fear)

So let's feel at ease, as we utter our cri de coeur *"Are you there, God?"*

It all depends
Not surprisingly, when I was teaching Religious Studies at secondary school level, I was regularly asked: "Sir, do *you* believe in God?" Sometimes experience told me it was a trap question but mostly it would be a sincere one. Contrary to what many students expected, however, I didn't jump in with a "Yes, of course I do – I wouldn't be in this job if I didn't". I invariably paused and answered, *"It all depends on what you mean by 'God'"*.

This would still be my reply. Before we can offer a sensible, though necessarily tentative, answer to our mega question, we need to think about what sort of God we have in mind. Because there's a vast number of different notions, judging from the variety of names or images claimed to represent the essence, or some facet, of God's nature.

God's many names
Hindus have thought up countless deities in their attempt to portray their understanding of Brahman, as they call God. When teaching Religious Studies in Bristol, I took children to a local temple. There, at the front of the sanctuary, they saw images representing gods like Lakshmi the god of beauty and Ganesh the god of wisdom. Every day, the images are washed and symbolically fed, worshippers finding their presence spiritually enriching. Visually, the images didn't appeal to me, but I recognized them as sincere attempts to probe the mystery of the one God we all share.

The ninety-nine beads on a Muslim necklace represent the ninety-nine names of the incomprehensible Allah.

In the Hebrew-Jewish tradition, as we know from the scriptures Christians call the Old Testament, God is known, among other names, as Rock, Shepherd, Shield, Light, Fountain, Redeemer, King, Father, Husband, Helper, The Most High, The Almighty.

The Christian New Testament contains a great variety of names for Jesus, each historically believed to represent a truth not only about Jesus but about God's nature, too. Such as Son of God, Son

3

of Man, Son of David, Messiah, Saviour, Good Shepherd, Bread of Life, Light of the World, the Door, the Vine, the Lamb, the Great High Priest, the Alpha and Omega, the Way, the Truth, the Life, the Word.

Honest perplexity

Rip off the veneer of dogma, and you find, in the world's religions, a healthily honest perplexity about God's nature. You find hundreds, if not thousands, of different ideas of God all shaped by people's religious, cultural, philosophical, psychological and personal circumstances.

But is it any wonder there's such diversity, when you remember these faiths are all trying to conceptualize nothing less than what they believe is the Source and Sustainer of ALL-THAT-IS? Who, however, is to say which of these ideas might point to *some*, or *the*, truth about God?

Christian notions of God

Jumping now to today, what's the 'state of play' in Christian theology? In broad terms, Christians belonging to mainstream denominations hold two notions of God.

We are all familiar with the 'conventional' notion. Though partly rooted in ancient Hebrew belief, it evolved in the early Christian era until it was formalized in the historic creeds, particularly the one hammered out in the Council of Nicaea in 325.

...the 'conventional'

This claims that God is a Holy Trinity of three 'Persons' in one Being. The first 'Person' is God the Father, or Creator, who exists outside the material universe yet is responsible for its creation and sustenance. As a psalmist puts it: "The Lord rules supreme in heaven" (Psalm 93:4). The second 'Person' is the Son, Jesus, whom, as the Fourth Gospel explains, God "sent into the world to be its saviour" (John 3:17). The third 'Person' is the Holy Spirit who, according to the same Gospel, Jesus promised would lead his disciples "into all the truth" (John 16:13).

According to this 'conventional' notion, God intermittently intervenes in human matters, such as when he sent Jesus or in response to those prayers he chooses to answer favourably.

...the 'progressive'
Now this familiar notion of God is the norm both in Britain and worldwide. But an increasing number of Christians – particularly in the US and UK but elsewhere too – are unpersuaded by 'conventional' theology. Such Christians – sometimes calling themselves 'progressives' – are asking, in the light of modern knowledge, searching but sincere questions, not least about the nature of God. Can we any longer characterize God as an eternal, triune being? Did Christ really exist before becoming Jesus? Even though God surely was present in Jesus to a unique degree because Jesus himself so completely opened his soul to the divine spirit, wasn't Jesus essentially human? Most radically of all, should we still think of God as a Being 'out there' – who may sometimes lovingly intervene yet too often seems to ignore humanity's desperate pleas?

More positively, Christians of this persuasion identify God more as a 'universal presence', the source of life and love, the reality undergirding everything that is. And, insofar as anyone persistently opens their innermost self to this ubiquitous spirit, they become truly human, much closer to what they are 'meant' to be.

Having touched on a range of names and notions of God, I hope you'll agree that belief in God's existence really does depend on what we mean by 'God'.

So, "*are you there* God? We really would like to know!"

No place for dogmatism
Put prosaically, is there objective evidence for God's existence?

Clearly, any response to this question must be tentative. There can be no place for dogmatism. Logic will not permit even the most ardent believer to point to the astounding diversity, intricacy and cohesion of life on Earth and pronounce it as proof of a Cosmic Designer, God. Scientists such as Charles Darwin and A. R. Wallace have shown that the complexity of life could actually arise from the physical process of natural selection among replicators. Later, James Watson and Francis Crick showed how replication itself could be understood in physical terms. That said, it could be pointed out that the very existence of the evolutionary process

– governed by laws and processes operating from the very first millisecond of creation – certainly doesn't annul the possibility of a Cosmic Intelligence being the overall instigator.

Because our question is a metaphysical one – literally 'beyond nature' – scientists, too, must not be dogmatic. Unfortunately, this is just what the popular and immensely influential biologist, Richard Dawkins, is. His favourite mantra is 'there is no evidence whatever for God'. But whenever he repeats it, he seems oblivious of the logical fallacy he commits. This is that it is impermissible to make a universal deduction from a necessarily limited set of particular statements. In other words, until we know everything there is to know about the universe (and perhaps beyond it), we logically cannot conclude there is no possible evidence for God – or for anything else. What's more, it may be that we cannot tell whether certain data is or is not evidence, or that the evidence still awaits discovery.

(As a footnote to my comments about Richard Dawkins, I wonder how far he is aware of the own-goal that he has scored in his enthusiastic support for a campaign purportedly promoting atheism. I refer to the slogan, appearing on central London buses during January 2009, "THERE IS PROBABLY NO GOD. NOW STOP WORRYING AND ENJOY YOUR LIFE". For the opening statement is unequivocally *agnostic!* Is he *really* admitting that the only intelligent philosophical response to the question of God's existence is that we really cannot *know* one way or the other?)

There are questions in both the material and conceptual spheres where all we can do is make provisional statements based on the balance of probability. Whether we are inclined to be 'for' or 'against' God's existence, there can be no room for dogmatism. *Any* statement or conclusion is made in *faith.*

Arguments for God

That said, over the centuries, many theologians, philosophers and cosmologists have come up with arguments in favour of belief in some concept of God – in some Being or Entity or Spirit somehow vital to the existence and well-being of the cosmic order and everything in it, including the human world. Taken as a whole and brought up to date, I believe these arguments still make a strong case for the possibility and desirability of a transcendent Ultimate Reality.

It would take too long now to name, describe and evaluate all the traditional arguments. So I will touch on the one that I personally believe is the most appealing, namely, the centuries-old teleological argument.

...from the nature of the physical world
If you can't remember how it goes, it claims that the universe – and particularly planet Earth – provides evidence of design and, on the analogy of human artefacts, a cosmic designer.

In recent decades, this argument has been refined by a number of theoretical physicists. One of them is Professor Paul Davies. He is a top rank cosmologist, a skilled philosopher and well versed in theology. I have found his articles and books, particularly 'The Mind of God', accessible and convincing.

Professor Davies rejects the conclusion that the universe is a result of purely accidental processes. The "physical world is not arbitrary and absurd but ordered in a rational and intelligible way", he claims. So the concept of a 'purposeful intelligence' to explain the universe's structure, intricacy, balance and cohesion is a plausible one. "I am impressed", he says "by the extraordinary ingenuity, felicity and harmony of the laws of physics. It is hard to accept that something so elegantly clever exists without a deeper reason or purpose". For Davies, the 'deeper reason and purpose' could derive from a source we may call 'God', as long as we think of God as more like a 'timeless abstract principle' than a 'personal' being.

Support for the notion of 'purposeful intelligence' lies in one version of the anthropic principle. This claims that, from the first microsecond of the 'Big Bang', there appears to have been the potential for intelligent life – life which would eventually be able to study and harness the very cosmos it came from. Indeed, without such capacity the universe's structure would be unrecognized and many of its resources unused. If this understanding is correct, it is reasonable to infer 'design' and 'foresight' were involved which, in turn, suggest a 'purposeful intelligence' – God – was responsible, rather than mind-less chance.

In an article in 'Reform', October 2008, eminent scientist and theologian Keith Ward acknowledges that we cannot prove the existence of a Creator God. But he goes on to observe: "The way in which the fundamental forces of nature need to interlock in a large number of very precise ways before humans can exist is a very strong confirmation that some vast cosmic intelligence exists and has designed the universe to produce life… The universe shows a beauty and a deep mathematical structure that strongly suggests an underlying mind, the mind of God".

…from the wisdom and life of Jesus
If a refined 'design' argument makes belief in at least a 'Creative Intelligence' 'respectable', are there rational grounds for believing God is *also more* than a distant, abstract entity? What evidence might there be that God is also involved with the human situation and experiencable? It cannot be proved but it is surely honourable to believe the wisdom and life of Jesus of Nazareth are evidence. What he said and did have been so universally and persistently applicable, so individually and communally transformative, that it is surely reasonable to believe he was externally empowered. To believe, in other words, that Jesus allowed his soul, or innermost self, to be fully infused with the Presence of God.

…from the human conscience
My third argument for the existence of God is an extension of the second. It centres on the human conscience. Felt by people the world over and for as long as humanity has been around, the human conscience, I submit, points to the same spiritual resource which empowered Jesus. The 'voice of conscience' can be so strong and persistent, sometimes lifting people above self-serving instincts and tawdry conventions, that it cannot surely be dismissed merely as a 'genetic or social mechanism'. Could it not, in truth, derive from a beneficent Presence – 'God'?

"What I know now is only partial"
"*Are you there*, God?" Philosophizing may give us a provisional answer. But it won't give us God 'on a plate'! By definition, God is a mystery beyond human comprehension. As the apostle Paul concluded: "What I see now is like a dim image… what I know now is only partial." To be personally confident that God IS 'there' we must rely on our individual spiritual experience.

8

"I am who I am"
Finally, does belief in God *really matter?*

I believe there's a crucial pointer to the answer in the Call of Moses. Precise history or not, the occasion described represents a moment when Moses sensed the 'Mysterium Tremendum' and a truly amazing name for this awesome Presence flashed to his mind. It was, in transliterated Hebrew: "eh'yeh asher eh'yeh" and means, literally, "I AM WHO I AM".

As a child, I thought the name was potty but now I think it's brilliant! Because it can encompass a whole bundle of notions, suggesting God is unique, unchangeable, uncaused… the Ground of all that is… the Ultimate Reality.

Faith in God crucial
Does it matter whether we believe in God? If God *is* the Ultimate Reality, the Source and Sustainer of ALL THAT IS, logic answers: that Planet Earth, and everything in it, will only flourish insofar as its most powerful species takes God with the utmost seriousness. And it is Jesus, Christians affirm, who best shows us what that means.

2   TRUE HAPPINESS

Jesus and the appeal, meaning and possession of 'happiness'

What is it that everybody wants yet nobody knows what 'it' is? To put my riddle more accurately, what is it that it seems everybody wants yet nobody quite knows what it is they so desire?

One answer could be 'happiness'.

For, sooner of later, whenever you leave your personal mental or physical space and join the world around you, you find people, generally subconsciously, engaged in the quest for what may loosely be called 'happiness'.

And 'happiness' is the subject of my sermon. We shall consider the appeal, meaning and possession of it, drawing especially on the teaching of Jesus.

The appeal of happiness
First, then, the appeal of happiness. There's no doubt it is a powerful attractant, the desire to possess and enjoy it being one of life's strongest motivators, often impelling people to keep going even in their toughest moments. You can pick up signals showing the appeal of happiness all over the place.

"Happy Days!" proclaims a slogan on a fence surrounding a huge building site in Bath, "Happy Days! 400,000 square feet of new retail space". The rash of new shops, it is assumed, will give residents and visitors alike a fresh chance to savour the happiness they constantly seek.

Emblazoned across one of my recent Cycle magazines were the words: "Happy families: the best way to go cycling with kids", a claim supported by an article on the joys and benefits of two-wheel family outings.

A flyer dropped on my doormat announcing 'The Bristol Happiness Lectures', just one example of an apparently burgeoning market for talks and courses about the nature and acquisition of happiness.

At pretty well the same time, I read that the tiny Himalayan kingdom of Bhutan had held its first parliamentary election. The winner was the Bhutan United party. And its intellectual basis? The Buddhist idea that economic growth alone does not bring contentment, an idea compressed into the party's slogan 'Gross National Happiness'.

In one of a succession of his great speeches, Barack Obama said: 'Tonight, we gather to affirm the greatness of our nation – not because of the height of our skyscrapers, or the power of our military, or the size of our economy. Our pride is based on a very simple premise, summed up in a declaration made over two hundred years ago: "We hold these truths to be self-evident, that all men are created equal. That they are endowed by their Creator with certain inalienable rights. That among these are life, liberty, and the pursuit of happiness".'

Jesus and the quest
So happiness does seem to be something 'everybody wants'. True, a minority of religious adherents – some Christians among them – value *misery*, in the form of extreme self-denial or even painful self-mortification, but even that is a form of holy happiness. And Jesus, I submit, strongly backed the happiness goal.

I haven't time to support my conviction with chapters and verses. But, if happiness embraces such things as freedom from oppression, release from compassion-stifling legalism and religiosity, mental and physical health, the possession of basic needs (like food, shelter and clothing), economic justice, personal integrity, receiving and giving love, ethnic and social harmony, living a purposeful and fulfilled life – if happiness embraces such things as these, then, as all four gospels show, Jesus *was* consistently and profoundly in favour of satisfying people's yearning for it.

But isn't this what we should expect? For, as I see it, the 'happiness quest' is a secular way of describing the human search for the 'Something More' which religious believers identify as God. In other words, people's longing for happiness is actually nothing less than an unrecognized hunger for God, and one which Jesus committed his life to identify, foster and satisfy.

Happiness dissected

But just what *is* this happiness everyone craves? Let me now try to dissect it.

Philosophers have always been fascinated by happiness. Two in particular come to my mind, the 4th century BC Greek, Aristotle, and the 18th century Briton, Jeremy Bentham.

An intellectual condition

In his treatise on Ethics, Aristotle asserts that the possession of true happiness is the only proper and worthy goal of life, the supreme good. But it is not to be equated with bodily pleasure or with any form of amusement. No, it has to do with the training and discipline of the intellect. At its noblest, happiness is to be found in what he describes as 'contemplative speculation'. And, because scientists in the ancient world spent their time contemplating and speculating (rather than experimenting and verifying as in modern science), they are likely to be the happiest of people! Be that as it may, intellectual satisfaction surely is extremely important to our well-being. This will include gaining knowledge and skills but the supreme goal of education must always be the nourishment of the mind with the satisfaction, or happiness, this yields.

An emotional state

Jeremy Bentham argued that happiness was primarily an emotional state, more to do with feeling than thinking and therefore attainable through the pursuit of pleasure. Of course, some types of pleasure are damaging and morally wrong but we all know there are also plenty of pleasures offering an honourable route to happiness.

What's more, Bentham claimed, everyone has a right to 'feel happy'. In his treatise 'Introduction to the Principles of Morals and Legislation', he went so far as to say that the aim of all actions and law making should be "the greatest happiness of the greatest number", an ideal ever since dubbed 'utilitarianism'.

Between them, Aristotle and Bentham have profoundly influenced moral values and political programmes. They have both shed light on the nature of happiness and its role in a civilized society.

13

A physical matter

Personal experience and observation tell us that happiness is also closely connected with physical well-being. It's difficult to smile when you've got raging toothache, let alone really serious pain or illness. We usually feel happier after rather than before an operation. Of course, it's possible to be happy in spite of disability or disease; we all know people who show remarkable serenity and cheerfulness in the most trying of physical circumstances. But they would still dearly like to be free of their limitation or distress. Being well and fit most certainly can contribute to our happiness. And there's ample evidence in the gospels that Jesus fully recognized the desirability of physical health for personal contentment.

The wealth factor

While mental, emotional and physical factors undoubtedly affect our level of happiness, how far do you think our material or economic state should do so?

Massively, contemporary culture shouts! Our whole global economy is based on the principle of relentlessly expanding consumerism. And in order to promote this raw capitalism, people must be persuaded not only of their genuine but also their imaginary needs. 'The more you buy or borrow, the happier you will be!'

But *are* we?

No, a string of serious journalists argue. "Economic growth is seen as good", notes one, "yet it makes many in the rich world miserable". "Consumer capitalism is making us ill", laments another. "Shopping until you drop leads to debt and misery", observes a third. "A love of money can make us antisocial and mean", warns a fourth. "The popular idea of happiness as hedonistic is misleading – the good life can't be purchased", concludes a fifth, supporting his statement, like the others, with solid evidence. And, according to a study by Girlguiding UK and the Mental Health Foundation, "teenage girls feel under increasing pressure from magazines and websites to live up to material and sexual 'ideals', leaving them vulnerable and unhappy".

However, the penny just may be beginning to drop that unlimited material growth is neither possible nor desirable in a finite planet.

Certainly at the personal level, more and more people are recognizing the down side of rampant consumerism. According to analyst Datamonitor, over three million people are fed up with long working hours, fed up with information overload and the pressure to reach ridiculous targets, fed up with always being short of time for the family or to enjoy the house and possessions their good income has provided – and so fed up that they are 'downshifting', swapping wealth for quality of life. Probably few of them realize it, but in switching their values, they are actually heeding the way and words of Jesus.

One of the BBC series 'Tribal Wives' told the story of a workaholic British businesswoman who spent a month with an Ecuadorian tribe. She immersed herself in their community life, joining in hunts, bathing in piranha-infested rivers, sharing in their social

15

customs. Her recurring impression? That those people, with their simple, money- and mortgage-free lifestyle, were far happier than the hectic, competitive, consumerist society back home.

Now Jesus certainly didn't propose that asceticism – extreme material self-denial – should be the norm. Caring passionately about poverty and economic justice, he clearly favoured the principle of material sufficiency. What *did* worry him were the temptations of excessive wealth and the unhappiness that unbridled consumerism could produce. Refusing to be drawn into a row about family property, he warned the gathered crowd: "Watch out and guard yourselves from every kind of greed; because a person's true life is not made up of the things he owns, no matter how rich he may be" (Luke 12:15). If ever there were a timely message!

The social dimension
If intellect, feelings, health, and material condition all have a bearing on happiness, what about the social dimension? Personal experience tells us that relationships are hugely significant to our morale. We don't feel happy when we're cross with or have upset someone – and the greater the tension or rift, the unhappier we are.

Once again, we find Jesus 'on target', stressing the vital contribution of good relationships to personal contentment. Consider the Sermon on the Mount anthology. Here, among other down-to-earth advice, he urges families to sort out differences sooner rather than later; he recommends generous forgiveness when we are wronged; and he claims that true love extends even to enemies!

And Jesus practised what he preached. Whoever he met – including those society marginalized – he accepted, respecting their social or ethnic background, and according them the dignity they deserved and was vital to their self-esteem and happiness.

Treating people with dignity... what a difference this can make! How much better we feel when shopkeepers, cashiers, train staff, receptionists, nurses and all the other individuals we might come across in the course of our day, treat us with respect and courtesy! Treating people with dignity should be the bedrock on which everything from daily life to politics, law making, democracy, civilization indeed, are based for doing so is crucial to people's happiness.

The spiritual facet

Yes, happiness is a complex concept subject to mental, emotional, physical, material and social factors! But there's one more facet of our being that's pivotal to our possession of not just 'happiness' but TRUE happiness. You've been waiting for it! The spiritual. This is so central that we are bound to wonder: can anyone be genuinely happy – happy in the deepest and strongest sense – unless the spiritual facet is taken seriously and kept in good working order?

Professionally, over the years I have read and studied a good deal of philosophy, theology and other material relating to the enlightenment and nourishment of the human spirit. But I can honestly say, I have never come across ideas and teaching about it put as clearly, convincingly and as comprehensively as those offered by Jesus, not least what he said about real happiness.

As I suggested earlier, a huge swathe of Jesus's teaching and ministry could be said to illuminate what real happiness is and how you acquire it. But Jesus did sometimes expound on it explicitly.

True happiness

As we well know, Matthew opens his great collection of Jesus's teaching, known as the Sermon on the Mount, with the familiar sayings called The Beatitudes. These may originally have been isolated statements which, because of their common opening word and form, the evangelist grouped together. Whatever the story behind them, the Greek 'makarioi' is not easy to translate today. The traditional translation 'blessed' no longer packs the punch it once did, nowadays perhaps suggesting a rather intimidating piety. But modern versions which simply use the word 'happy' also won't do, I submit, because they fail to convey the profundity of the condition Jesus was defining, the bare word 'happy' too often referring to the flossy jollity of the kind TV commercials dream up. So I personally prefer to render the Greek with the phrase 'truly happy'. But whatever word or phrase we prefer, these sayings of Jesus provide the world with a monumental and timeless Charter of Happiness.

Jesus's Charter

As you'll be so familiar with the Beatitudes, I won't simply repeat them but will dare to try and distil their essence. Here goes!

> You will be truly happy (Jesus promises):
> when you realize your spiritual weakness and need;
> when you accept God's help in times of distress;
> when you humbly open your soul to God;
> when you put God's way first;
> when you are generous and forgiving;
> when your intentions are pure;
> when you work for peace;
> when you are willing to suffer on God's behalf.

To sum up

To sum up. Happiness does seem to be something 'everybody wants'. The quest for it may well be an unrecognized search for God. Happiness involves every facet of our being. But, to discover and possess *true* happiness – a quality of happiness far removed from the cheap and false alternatives currently on offer – to discover and possess true happiness, we have to choose the way of Jesus; the way eloquently expressed in his beatitudes and lovingly shown in his life.

3   WHO ARE WE?

Some reflections on the subject of personal identity

Who are we? Who am I? Who are you?

The immediate answer to the question, in its singular form, is a straightforward matter. Unless we're suffering from some temporary memory loss, we all know our names. I am Edward Hulme. You are Phil Archer, Bianca Jackson, Zak Dingle, Peggy Armstrong, Sir or Lady Hinton Blewitt or whatever your name really is!

A bundle of selves

Thinking about the question more carefully, we soon realise we are several people all at the same time or, rather, one person at the centre of a web of relationships. As well as being either a son or daughter, we are almost certainly someone's close friend. We may be a wife or husband or partner. Many of us may also

be fortunate enough to be a parent or grandparent or great-grandparent. We may well be a brother or sister. We are quite likely to be an aunt or uncle, at the same time as being a niece or nephew ourselves. Perhaps we are a cousin or first cousin or second cousin twice removed or all three. It's more than likely we are someone's – or several persons' – neighbour. Even if we think of ourselves primarily as Welsh, Scottish, Irish or English, we are

19

also British – or of some other nationality. But that's not all: we encompass a range of *other* selves. We belong to this or another church, to this or that club or voluntary group. Some of us have a job and fulfil various roles in that capacity. Yes, each of us has a range of identities; each of us is a bundle of selves. And juggling our different duties and loyalties can sometimes be a tricky business.

For some people, managing their various selves can be extremely taxing. Caring for an aged, ailing parent while looking after a family, or holding down a job while bringing up a child on your own, can be physically, mentally and spiritually debilitating.

Identity problems

Now many people face the problem of deciding exactly who they are at some stage in their life. In my own case, the only personal problem of identity I can recollect was a minor one. It happened when I went to theological college and university at the age of 18. I had been brought up and educated in a strongly right-wing climate (incidentally, in the Tatton constituency where Martin Bell the white-suited Independent candidate ousted the notorious Neil Hamilton in 1997). On going to college, however, I found myself in an avowedly left-wing climate. Suddenly, I felt torn between the old and the new influences: where did I now stand? Who was the true 'me'?

But *my* identity problem was trivial in comparison with what many people in society today suffer. For some people the problem is a very serious one. They themselves may not be aware of the label given to their condition but their sense of confusion and feeling of alienation show they are suffering what is often called an 'identity crisis'. Such people include children whose parents have divorced and whose apparently strong network of family ties has collapsed or been superseded by a new set of relationships, as Mum or Dad or both find a new partner or spouse. Who are their parents now? What surname do they use? Who *are* they?

Then, there are unknown numbers of people in Britain – and in other countries – who live in our midst (to be precise, usually in run-down urban or rural areas) yet feel they do not 'belong'.

Sadly, they may indeed be shunned by so-called mainstream society, perhaps deliberately harassed or persecuted. Among such people are refugees and asylum-seekers – or, as I *should* say, men and women who happen to be refugees or asylum-seekers (we really shouldn't identify people by their status or even physical condition – too many people, who ought to know better, still refer to people with leprosy as 'lepers'). Sadly, and increasingly, people on the margins tend to be lumped together in popular thinking, regarded as generally inferior, if not suspect. Of course, a fraction of them *will* be cheats and rogues (as in society generally) but many others are honest people, perhàps highly qualified, just desperate to escape a brutal regime. Where *do* they 'belong'? For them, the problem of identity may be grimly serious.

So the question 'Who am I?' or 'Who are we?' is an important one, directly or indirectly affecting us all.

Insights from the Bible
Like everything basic to human nature and conduct, problems of identity have been around a long time. Not surprisingly, we come across them in the Bible.

Take the Old Testament. You will be well aware it was written, compiled and edited with the supreme purpose of telling the story of a particular people's spiritual pilgrimage. It therefore describes 'sacred' rather than 'secular' history, even if the two strands are normally intertwined.

So, on the one hand, we find graphic descriptions of the interaction of fiercely proud regional tribes, stories about Moabites, Hittites, Jebusites, Amorites and lots of other 'ites'. As these diverse identities clash, all too often there is horrific carnage. Woven into this largely secular drama, however, is the spiritually-focused story of the tribes that coalesced into the Hebrew-Jewish faith community and identified itself as God's special people.

As the scriptures reveal, to their credit, the people of Israel repeatedly shirked their calling. They turned to other gods, compromised their ethical ideals, defied the prophets who, in their wiser moments, they recognised as God's 'prefects'.

They frequently scorned, fought and tried to wipe out those they regarded as 'impure' or rivals. In large measure, the Old Testament is a story about clashes of identity.

But these historic clashes continued into New Testament times, even if held at bay by Roman imperial might. The Twelve, most of them brought up as Jews, a faith-culture which claimed to be unique and superior, understandably found the transition to Jesus's massively wider, inclusive way of thinking extraordinarily difficult.

Three incidents in Luke chapter 9 starkly illustrate their problem. In an argument about which of them is the greatest, they identify with worldly power. Complaining about a man driving out demons in the Master's name, they exhibit a jealous, 'dog in the manger' elitism. When some Samaritan villagers give them the cold shoulder, they retort with a narrow, belligerent nationalism. But on each occasion, Jesus firmly urges them to broaden their perception and attitude.

Not many years after those three incidents, we find members of the primal Church falling prey to narrow, partisan thinking and dividing into cliques identified with particular leaders. This happened, as strikingly as anywhere, at Corinth where one member claims "I follow Paul", another counters "I follow Apollos" and another declares "I follow Peter", while a fourth boasts "I follow Christ". Not surprisingly, Paul exhorts them all to focus on Jesus and his crucifixion with its inclusive implications.

Tragically, the ancient clash of identities – grimly evident in so much of the Old Testament but lurking in the background in the New – continues to this day, as conflicts in the 'Holy Land' region regularly and shockingly remind us, the adversaries paying a terrible price for their myopic cultural self-perception. We can but grieve for citizens, on both sides, who have a vastly broader sense of identity and who long to smash down the mental and physical barriers. Oh for leaders with the vision, courage and internationalism of musician Daniel Barenboim whose Divan orchestra draws from both main cultures and offers a glimpse of a happier, united Holy Land!

A deeper kind of identity

The Barenboim enterprise provides a natural link with the New Testament and indeed the best of the Old. There's no evidence that Jesus ever wished to belittle people's differentness. But doesn't his message, echoed throughout the pages of the New Testament, extol a deeper, all-embracing kind of identity – one that transcends people's subsidiary identities, one which enables people in all their diversity nevertheless to live contentedly together?

As we well know, many members of the earliest Church, brought up as Jews with their notions of cultural purity, simply couldn't stomach the idea of accepting Gentiles. So rows erupted, some wanting to slam the Church door in the Gentiles' face, others wanting to fling it wide open. From the outset, the Church had an identity problem: was it to be a spruced-up brand of Judaism with a restricted membership, or a model community open to the whole human family?

'Top brass' Peter and Paul came down decisively in favour of an inclusive Church, Peter persuaded by his extraordinary dream and its aftermath, Paul by his momentous Damascus-road switch from Christian terminator to Christian ambassador. As he explained to the church at Philippi: "I am an Israelite by birth, of the tribe of Benjamin, a pure-blooded Hebrew... a Pharisee" – I may claim all these elite identities – but, he goes on, "For Christ's sake, I have thrown them all away" – old world view, old priorities, old status, even old name Saul (Philippians 3:5 and 8). But just as *he* had changed, so must God's People. As disciples of Jesus the Christ, they should welcome Jew and Gentile, men and women, free people and slave, rich and poor, well and ill – everyone, whatever their lesser identities.

Some positive suggestions

Having shared some of my reflections on the question of identity and considered some of the vital insights presented in the Bible, I must now draw our thoughts together by offering a few positive suggestions.

Our personal and church roles

Firstly, about our personal and church roles. Like any organisation, churches require a range of people to run them and, sooner or later, an office or responsibility becomes vacant, so able and willing replacements are sought. In our laudable zeal to find someone, however, isn't there a danger that we put undue, if not unfair, moral pressure on apparent candidates? By all means, let us invite and encourage people to say 'yes' but don't we also need to bear in mind a person's total life situation? If we badger them into submission, might we not cause them to withdraw from some vital niche in the wider community they are particularly well equipped to fill?

If we need to be cautious in making demands on fellow church members, how much more should we be mindful of our ministers' well-being? Most pastors are under immense pressure, especially now that so many have more than one church in their charge. At the same time, their flocks – surrounded as they are by a sceptical, secularised society – more than ever need solid, mature, intellectual and spiritual nurture. But if ministers are to provide thoughtful, relevant and mature worship, they need ample time and energy to think, to study, to research, and to prepare. Which means – I am confident you'll agree – we need to be extremely restrained in the demands we put on them!

Our role as British and world citizens
Secondly, a thought about our role as British citizens. There are so many identity matters that should concern us. Such as the complex and thorny matter of identity cards – just how do you achieve a practicable balance between security and liberty? Or questions raised by ever-advancing biotechnology – to what extent should society allow people to design the identity of their babies? Or problems raised by the very diversity of British citizens – just how do we reconcile the interests of our various cultural groups with a sense of national unity? (Supposing, for example, a Muslim woman believes she should cover all but her eyes whenever she is out: should she be allowed to conceal her identity when doing so might make others feel threatened?) These are big issues I can only mention now – but they all relate to the underlying question: 'who are we?'

Thirdly, one or two thoughts about our role as world citizens. For a start, I believe we need to be aware of how, in so many parts of the world, people's perceptions have changed. According to Harvard Professor Samuel Huntington, author of the acclaimed book 'The Clash of Civilizations', the question 'Who are we?' is the most basic one humans can face.' But since the end of the Cold War, he argues, people are identifying far less 'with ideological, political or economic distinctions and far more with cultural groups, such as tribes, religious communities, nations and, at the broadest level, civilizations'. In other words, since 1990 there's been a major shift in the way great numbers of people perceive themselves and a whole series of what are increasingly termed 'identity wars'. So, if we are to develop sound strategies for preserving world order, governments must take on board these changes of perception and attitude.

The truth is, as the faith community at the heart of the Old Testament only haltingly discovered, and many of their successors in the New only painfully grasped, the one identity that counts way above the myriad lesser identities, is that of the human family. Didn't Jesus make it plain, by precept and example, that the whole world is our neighbour? This is familiar stuff but that doesn't make it any less revolutionary or crucial!

Our identity with all Creation
Lastly, shouldn't we now, albeit frighteningly late in the day, take far more seriously than hitherto, our identity with *all* Creation? For the great bulk of their history, Jews and Christians have focused on that verse in the Genesis story where God is said to give humanity control over the natural world. There *is* a vital truth in that theology but, sadly, it has habitually been interpreted as giving the green light to an exploitative, often ruthless, attitude to the natural world. But now humanity is paying the price for its rapacious greed, evident in the global decline of wildlife and the alarming acceleration of climate change. While acknowledging our role as *managers* of our natural habitat, we sorely need to focus on the prior truth to which both Creation stories testify, namely, that human beings are nevertheless *part* of Creation, one species among millions which share and depend on the same Planet Earth for their very existence. Humankind needs to identify far more closely with other forms of life, for we sink or swim *together!*

Who are we? We are a bundle of often conflicting and pressured selves. We are also members of a particular local community and nation, and of one of the (arguably eight) global civilizations.

Supremely, as Jesus so bravely and momentously testified, we are members of the one, worldwide human family. To this we must now add: while called to manage Planet Earth, we are an integral part of it. May God help us carry out our various roles with empathy, vision and courage!

4   HEAVENLY HOPES
and EARTHLY EXPECTATIONS

How to keep sane in a crazy world!

Who of us, over the years, has not been shocked by the vicious mutual hostility of so many Israelis and Palestinians? People the world over have been appalled, in particular by the callous conduct of the Palestinian suicide bombers and the brutal reprisals of the Israeli army. Latterly, we have been disgusted by the building and rapid extension of the hideous separation wall with its debilitating and humiliating impact on the men, women and children of the weaker power.

Dreams and reality today

With indisputable justification, modern Israel is proud of what, as a small nation, it has achieved since its establishment as a modern state shortly after the Second World War. Out of a conglomeration of immigrants from all over the world, they have built a nation with a strong identity. They have developed thriving industries and made the desert bloom. In the kibbutz movement, they have shown that alternative social systems are possible. In calmer areas, the visitor – as you may have discovered for yourself – can fully appreciate why Israeli citizens are so proud.

You can also understand why they are so defensive, so quick to explain why they have to take up a rigorous if not aggressive posture, so touchy if they sense you may be criticising them. The reason is, of course, that even before the modern state was set up, there were those who did not want it to exist at all and who, once it was founded, vowed to wipe it off the map.

In short, modern Israel has great aspirations which are, nevertheless, tempered by the surrounding international realities. So its motto could be: 'We have heavenly hopes but earthly expectations'. This ambivalence towards the outside world and towards the future is evident in all sorts of ways but no more strikingly so than in the Golan Heights, that wedge of country formerly belonging to Syria but now occupied by Israel. There are military installations all over the place but perched on a promontory overlooking a road close to the frontier is a poignant sculpture which I, for one, will never forget. It is of a tank part of which has been turned into a plough. The barbed wire, armoured vehicles and soldiers in the vicinity represent the nation's 'earthly expectations' but the sculpture symbolises its 'heavenly hopes'.

God's goodness and human weakness
The idea expressed in the sculpture, you know full well, harks back to the prophet Micah who looked forward to the day when nations would hammer their swords into ploughs and their spears into pruning-knives. But the weaponry close by could be said to represent the lesser-known words of another prophet, Joel. He urged his people do just the opposite: 'Prepare for war. Hammer the points of your ploughs into swords and your pruning-knives into spears. Even the weak must fight' (Joel 3:10). Diametrically opposed messages within the same body of sacred writings do cause problems, but in this case they honestly expose ancient Israel's struggle to discern and do God's will. Like their modern counterparts, the people of early Israel were torn between their ideals and by the realities of the moment, between 'heavenly hopes' and 'earthly expectations'.

But isn't this tension between what is believed to be *God's* will and *human* inclinations at the very heart of the Old Testament?

The tug-of-war between divine goodness and human weakness is no more eloquently expressed than in the book of Hosea. The prophet, you'll recall, was deeply concerned about his people's idolatry and their faithlessness towards God. Their waywardness, he told them, paralleled his own disastrous marriage. Just as his wife, Gomer, turned out to be unfaithful to him, so God's people had deserted their Lord. Yet, even as Hosea still loved his wife, so, he believed, God still loved his people: "How can I give you up, Israel? How can I abandon you? ... My heart will not let me! My love for you is too strong!" (Hosea 11:8)

The hopes and tears of Jesus
Centuries later, wasn't the same tender, constant love evident when Jesus stood on the Mount of Olives and beheld Jerusalem? If you have visited the city, you will probably agree that one of the most stirring moments is when you look down from that

28

selfsame hill, over the Garden of Gethsemane with its venerable olive trees, on to the Kidron valley below, then up to the hallowed city walls and the Temple mount itself. Jerusalem is obviously far bigger now, yet from that vantage-point you can readily appreciate Jesus's elation.

However, could any traveller in that spot also adequately appreciate Jesus's deepest feelings – his sadness, his disappointment, his frustration, his grief, as he realised the city was about to throw away its greatest ever chance of renewal and that its futile attempts to overthrow its Roman masters were doomed? 'Jesus came closer to the city, and when he saw it, he wept over it, saying, "If you only knew today what is needed for peace! But now you cannot see it! Yet the time will come... when your enemies will completely destroy you and the people within your walls... because you did not recognise the time when God came to save you!"' (Luke 20:41-44) At that moment, it was Jesus's earthly expectations rather than his heavenly hopes which prevailed.

Taking the ministry of Jesus as a whole, however, hopes and expectations constantly interact.

Lofty goals, limited prospects
Consider the Sermon on the Mount. This anthology of wisdom shows Jesus commending all sorts of *apparently* way-out ideas and attitudes. Whoever so much as looks at a woman and desires her as good as commits adultery! *Ideally*, we should: 'offer the other cheek' rather than seek revenge; love rather than hate our enemies; 'keep mum' about our good deeds; stop worrying about material essentials and beware of judging others hypocritically! If this momentous collection of teaching is a blueprint for the Kingdom of God, then its specifications are truly daunting. Jesus most emphatically DID cherish heavenly hopes for humanity.

Mercifully, the gospels also show us a realistic and kindly Jesus – one who, through family and business experience, knew well the demands of life; who knew the all-but-overwhelming power of temptation; who characterised his ministry as one of 'bringing good news to the poor, liberty to captives, relief to the oppressed'; who understood and befriended outcasts and sinners. Jesus certainly did offer humanity lofty goals but he also recognised people's weaknesses and limitations. His hopes for God's world were undoubtedly heavenly while his expectations were mercifully earthly!

So in both Old and New Testaments, not least in the attitude and teaching of Jesus, we find a dynamic tension between heavenly hopes and earthly expectations. But isn't this dynamic tension intrinsic to the life of faith?

I have myself found awareness of this tension extraordinarily helpful. I can honestly say that in the ten or so years since I dreamt up the slogan 'Have heavenly hopes but earthly expectations', it has helped me keep calm and positive in the face of all sorts of personal and public situations. On the one hand, it has helped me keep hopeful, to visualise, and do my bit for, a better world. On the other hand, it has helped me to be realistic and not to get too downhearted when human failings impede the realisation of my hopes and visions. It has helped me keep sane in a crazy world!

Personal hopes and expectations
So now let me suggest what bearing the slogan 'Have heavenly hopes but earthly expectations' might have on our lives, starting at the personal level.

Hasn't it got something to say about our perception of marriage or 'committed partnerships'? The wedding service and its parallel rituals are full of 'heavenly hopes'. In the more traditional Christian marriage ceremony, the couple pledge to 'have and to hold' each other 'for better for worse, for richer for poorer, in sickness and in health *until death*' – a truly awesome promise! So awesome, in fact, that many couples fail to keep it while many others feel unable to make it in the first place. Now the reasons for the retreat from lifelong commitment are diverse and complex, but I do wonder whether the witnesses to the promises – family and in-laws in particular – sometimes expect too much, putting unfair, albeit subtle pressure, on the couple. Perhaps a little more empathy and patience, more 'earthly expectations', would be more Christlike and more fruitful. As relatives and friends, we naturally hope and pray for a strong and lasting partnership, but don't we also need to be aware of the immense pressures and temptations people face in the current cultural climate?

Isn't another area in which it's important to temper one's honourable heavenly hopes with earthly expectations, the bringing-up of children? Of course we have high aspirations for our sons and daughters, grand- or great-grandchildren. We love them and want them to flourish mentally and physically, to develop academically, to get a fulfilling job, to find the right partner, above all, to grow in character. But might not parents' and grandparents' hopes just sometimes be overbearing, even perhaps a projection of their own thwarted ambitions, making their children or grandchildren feel inadequate or hedged-in, unable truly to be themselves?

Yes, at the personal level, there are circumstance when we need to temper our wholly natural and laudable heavenly hopes with more earthly expectations – preferably before learning to do so the hard way!

The wider world
Turning to the wider world, how might our slogan apply there?

In a world whose very survival remains threatened by humanity's technological power and indulgent materialism, I believe that selfsame humanity needs heavenly hopes, as much as ever. For a start, we need visionary leaders with visionary policies, such as former Soviet President Mikhail Gorbachev. Probably more than any other leader of the time, he articulated the world's ordinary people's 'heavenly hopes'. He recognised, in the bleak and terrifying early 1980s, that if the human species was to survive, let alone thrive, a new era had to be conceived, born and nurtured – an era in which nations everywhere recognised and promoted 'common human values'. But what ARE such 'common human values' if not those of empathy, tolerance, reconciliation, compassion, and 'agape' love – the very qualities and aspirations Jesus practised and extolled?

Thank God, in spite of what the cynics claim, in all sorts of ways the world community does, to a notable extent, recognise and express these common human values. The constant flow of international conferences, agreements and conventions, on a vast range of human and environmental issues, would not happen without such recognition and expression. In spite of all the conflict and immense problems facing the human family, it nevertheless co-operates to a degree only dreamt of half a century ago. There's ample evidence that leaders and people the world over DO have 'heavenly hopes'

And yet, only a Utopian dreamer would be blind to the limitations of the EU, UN and any international organisation. For, however noble its purpose, any human institution is only as effective as its members allow it to be and, since 'all have sinned and fall short of the glory of God', human weakness and selfishness tarnish and limit every human aspiration. So, when great gatherings of world leaders take place, on debt or poverty or trade or disease or climate change or any other big issue, let's have our heavenly hopes and do our bit to encourage agreement and progress, but don't let us ever expect too much, so that we become downhearted, cynical and negative.

The same is true at national level. Politicians share their vision of a better Britain, particularly at Party conference time and especially when a general election approaches. As people practising a vision-based faith, shouldn't we welcome their fine, and may well be sincere, aspirations? At the same time, we know we should never expect all that much to be actually achieved. We are also people with a realistic faith, acutely aware of the human condition. In one form or another, like a series of bumpy sleeping policemen (or should that be officers?), selfishness always puts a brake on progress. Politicians and public alike definitely should have heavenly hopes but they should also be canny enough to have earthly expectations.

The example of Jesus
In conclusion, may I draw your attention to that highly-charged scene described only in the Fourth Gospel, a scene so disquieting that many early manuscripts omitted it altogether. I refer, of course, to the one where teachers of the Law brought to Jesus a woman caught committing adultery. Contrary, however, to what the bystanders expected, Jesus simply invited "whoever was sin*less* to throw the first stone". After a silence you could cut with a knife, he then said to the woman herself: "I don't condemn you either. Go, but don't sin again" (John 8:11). In his brief but unforgettable response, Jesus offered both earthly empathy and heavenly aspiration.

By word and example, Jesus showed that civilised living requires both lofty ideals and compassionate realism... *both* **heavenly hopes** *and* **earthly expectations**!

5   CRAZY OR CRUCIAL?

Religion in the dock!

Religion... Is it CRAZY... or is it CRUCIAL?

You and I, presumably, would not be here if we thought religion were *totally* crazy! Yet plenty of people 'out there' DO dismiss religion, most vigorously of all the 'militant atheists'. Judging from the continuing national decline in church attendance, huge numbers of people, whilst not rejecting it out of hand, no longer think religion is crucial. And, honesty bids us admit, many regular worshippers are confused, feeling in their hearts their faith makes sense but wondering in their minds if it really does.

Religions and religion

Before we go any further, we need to remember that the word 'religion' is ambiguous. It can refer to a *particular* set of beliefs encompassed by a particular faith like Judaism, Islam or Christianity. Or, it can have a *general* application referring to the function of every specific religion, namely, the evocation and nourishment of human spirituality. It's important we make this distinction because there are people 'out there' who, whilst having no time for specific religions – viewing them as odd, irrelevant and even crazy – are, at least subconsciously, hungry for what religion in the broader sense has to offer; there are people who never darken the doors of their local temple, synagogue, mosque or church yet who *are*, albeit dimly, aware of their spiritual need.

Is religion *crazy?*

With the difference between religions and religion in mind, let's think about the first option: Is religion *crazy?*

Its record...

There's no doubt many people think it is. They deem it crazy partly because of its RECORD.

...in stoking-up conflict

"'But Sir", many a student has said to me "religion has caused more wars than anything else!" And I have always conceded that religion has been a significant contributory factor in the history of warfare, from the Old Testament genocides, through the intervening centuries, right up to present times, as conflicts in Northern Ireland, the Balkans, Kashmir, Sudan, Israel-Palestine and elsewhere exemplify. I have not, for one moment, defended what happens when religions get hi-jacked by extremists whether they are militant Muslims, ultra-orthodox Jews or fanatical Christians – extremists not only contradict all that is good and noble in their own religions but incalculably damage the *entire* religious quest. Having shamefully acknowledged the violent element in the story of religion, I have also pointed out that other factors – such as economic greed, national aggrandisement, megalomania and political expediency have actually proved even greater causes of conflict. I have further suggested that for every burning of a heretic, the secular world (through men such as Hitler, Stalin and Pol Pot) has murdered may be ten, perhaps many more, people simply because they belonged to the wrong ethnic, political or national group. That said, who of us would deny religion *is* crazy when it uses violence to achieve its goals?

...in supporting injustice

Some people damn religion because of its social record. They accuse it of keeping the rich, rich and the poor, poor, thereby perpetuating injustice. To some extent, that's a fair indictment. For several centuries, a succession of rich and influential Christians were heavily involved in the slave trade and, today, in America, many on the so-called 'religious right' oppose policies designed to make the world more equitable. When religion, supremely the faith supposedly based on the teaching and example of Jesus, behaves like that, who of us would deny it *is* crazy?

Yes, there *is* plenty that's crazy in religion's record – though there's also much that is sane and good, as I shall later remind you.

Its claims...

Some people, today as in previous eras, deem religion to be crazy because of its CLAIMS. Among them, perhaps for understandable reasons, there are those who have a chip on the shoulder and are therefore so prejudiced against anything with a religious 'smell' that they reject religious claims outright.

...about a metaphysical world

Others, however, quite sincerely cannot accept the idea of a *meta*physical world, of any genuine existence outside the physical world knowable by our five senses – the world we can explore, measure and predict by scientific methods. They just cannot believe in such alleged concepts as God or an afterlife. They may even think such notions are crazy.

Now some religious extremists (Christian and non-Christian) respond bluntly to such sceptics, telling them their unbelief amounts to a one-way ticket to hell. But mainstream Christians, like you and me, prefer to engage in dialogue, to show such doubters that we do actually have reasonable grounds (though not proof) for our beliefs. And, since *any* belief about life's meaning is necessarily based on faith rather than certainty, we are happy exploring life's mysteries with any genuine searcher.

...about its holy writings

As well as questioning religion's metaphysical claims, many people question the claims it apparently makes for its holy writings. "How can you believe that?" they exclaim. Assuming all believers take the entire Bible at its face value, they fail to appreciate many of us make the vital distinction between factual and figurative texts.

Quite frankly, I reckon religion would well deserve to be labelled 'crazy' if it really did mean taking stories like the one about Noah 100% literally. Where, I ask, did enough H2O to raise the sea level by five miles in forty days come from? How could you collect, let alone house, 14 million creatures (two of every species)? What sort of human leader, never mind divinity, would commit virtual speciocide, simply because one particular tribe had behaved violently? No, you and I know the Bible deserves respectful but intelligent treatment. For it transmits – sometimes directly, sometimes through picture language – events, experiences, insights and wisdom of crucial value to the human condition; most vital of all, it tells of the potentially world-transforming life and love of Jesus.

Its demands

Thirdly, some people deem religion is crazy because of its DEMANDS. They see religion as something essentially restrictive and threatening. "Why shouldn't I do what I like?" I've had students exclaim, not that they're alone in their views. "What's wrong with getting drunk if I want to?" "Keep to one partner for life? You must be joking!" How many radio and TV programmes have you heard, or articles have you read, where a speaker or writer rubbishes religion as prudish or spoil-sporty, out of touch and unrealistic! Others concede that religion does have a residual function – helpful at times of communal anguish to help people come to terms with some tragedy – but in the normal run of life to be kept at arm's length, lest it disturb one's indulgent, materialistic life-style.

To those who dismiss religion because of its demands, we surely have to reply that it *does* make demands, Christianity as much as any faith. But these demands, we should add, though sometimes *appearing* negative and limiting, in the long term are actually liberating and life-enhancing. We could do worse than point to the rich and influential young man who, turning to Jesus for the clue to happiness, discovered there was a price to pay for inner peace – in his case saying good-bye to his wealth. Not prepared to pay it, he drifted sadly away. Christian discipleship *does* make demands but sooner or later they yield true happiness and are worth their cost.

'Offensive to Jews and nonsense to Gentiles'

In the eyes and experience of many people then, religion is deemed to be closer to the *crazy* end of the spectrum than the *crucial*. It is thought to be crazy because of its *record*, its *claims* and its *demands*. So, if you've got your wits about you, you don't get entangled in its web!

Of course, in one sense, people who think religion is near enough crazy are right! Christianity, for one, does to some degree fly in the face of what is usually thought logical and normal. The idea of worshipping and following a world-saver who was crucified in the process was, as Paul observed, 'offensive to Jews and nonsense to Gentiles', absurd two thousand years ago, and, on the face of it, crazy still!

Or is it *crucial?*

Yet Christianity claims that such craziness is, in truth, crucial to the well-being of humanity and its planet! Why?

Social problems and the human spirit
Consider a few down-to-earth questions... Why are so many public toilets filthy and horrible to use? Why is there so much litter and gum and graffiti along our streets? Why do so many people ignore speed limits? Why is there so much fouling in sport? Why is there so much bullying in the workplace? Why is there so much sleaze in public life? Why do children growing up in the UK suffer greater deprivation, worse relationships with their parents and are exposed to more risks from alcohol, drugs and unsafe sex than those in any other wealthy country? Why have wild flowers and birds in Britain (such as sparrows), forests and animals all over the world, and so *many* features of Nature, taken such a battering? Why do giant financial systems collapse? Why has there been and is there still so much hatred and conflict in the world?

Is it simply because cleaners, sweepers, police officers, referees, managers, teachers, parents, social workers, civic and business leaders, farmers and foresters, financiers, politicians, diplomats and spies, aren't very efficient or as vigilant as they should be? Obviously they're involved in the problems, for good or ill.

But isn't the *root* cause behind these and all social and environmental problems, personal selfishness – and, therefore, the malfunctioning of the human spirit? Of course we should monitor those responsible for society's institutions and tackle any injustices which exacerbate the evils. At the same time, we must never lose sight of the basic truth that both the cause and the solution of every human problem are inextricably bound up with the spiritual condition of the individual.

A crucial source of spiritual nurture
But what is to evoke and nourish the spiritual within us?

Moral education is important, in schools and in every sector of society. As we all know, however, it's one thing to declare an intention, quite another to carry it out! One of the greatest of philosophers ever, Aristotle, confessed he simply couldn't work out how to make people good. The apostle Paul admitted that he found doing what he knew he should do, was invariably frustrating.

But Paul also discovered the *answer* – to allow the spirit of Jesus to dwell within him; only then was he able to live as his conscience prompted. So religion – and supremely the Christian faith – is crucial because it gets to the heart of things, the *human condition*. It is religion, furthermore, that openly and systematically offers the **spiritual nurture** that is vital to personal fulfilment and communal integrity.

A crucial source of timeless wisdom
If religion is a major source of spiritual nurture, isn't it also a major source of wisdom? The 20th Century witnessed an unprecedented number of ideological experiments but they all proved inadequate to the human condition. Galloping through them, Communism, more accurately called Marxism-Leninism, has had it positive achievements but its excessive collectivism has ridden roughshod over individual rights. Traditional Socialism has its merits but too often it has been perverted, as in Sweden, for instance, where it once initiated a cruel eugenics programme. Conservatism, historically the watchdog of individual liberty, degenerated in the 1980s into what the Tory author Alan Clark called 'ruthless economic Darwinism', encouraging personal greed and a callous contempt for those with weaker elbows. Unbridled Capitalism, based as it is on the idea of infinite economic expansion, has done shocking damage to our finite planet. I need hardly remind you how Nazism proved a grotesque disaster.

Isms come and go... but religion persists and, *at its best*, provides a source of **timeless wisdom**, promoting principles, values and conduct of truly abiding worth – these, Christians claim, being presented sublimely in the life and teaching of Jesus.

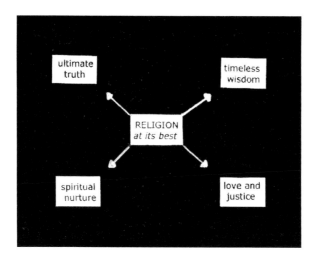

A crucial source of ultimate truth

If religion is a crucial source of *spiritual nourishment* and *timeless wisdom*, isn't it also a crucial source of **ultimate truth**? Of course, its teaching – and for you and me this means primarily that of Christianity – demands a leap of faith, faith which takes us beyond the realm of certainty. But we may confidently trust that it does give us glimpses of ultimate truth about the universe around us and about our special role within the tiny planet we inhabit. Whatever the physical processes – probably involving an explosion of unimaginable magnitude around fourteen billion years ago, and so far as life is concerned, a truly amazing evolutionary sequence – religious faiths agree that creation *does* have meaning and life *does* matter, for both, they believe, derive from a ubiquitous and beneficent Cosmic Intelligence commonly called God.

A crucial source of love and justice

Finally, if religion is a crucial source of *spiritual nourishment, timeless wisdom* and *ultimate truth*, isn't it also a crucial source of **love and justice**? Yes, religion has too often stoked-up conflict and backed injustice. But that's far from the whole story. Religion, not least the Christian faith, has also been a massive force for love and justice.

From the Early Church onwards, countless disciples of Jesus have lived and died championing the poor and oppressed. Resisting the so-called divine right of the Stuarts, 18th century Quakers led a cluster of progressive movements. The anti-slavery pioneers in America were churchgoers, roused by speeches from the pulpit. In the 19th and 20th centuries, Christians initiated a myriad of social reforms and charities.

And that passion for a fairer, freer world has continued in recent years. The Reformed Church, in what was East Germany, played a decisive role in the collapse of the GDR dictatorship in 1989.

The presiding minister of the St Nicholas church in Leipzig described the momentous climax in these words: "On October 9th, the prayers for peace ended with the bishop's blessing and the urgent call for non-violence. More than two thousand people leaving the church were welcomed by ten thousand waiting outside with candles in their hands… Jesus's spirit of non-violence seized the masses and became a material, peaceful power… causing the party and ideological dictatorship to collapse". Later, a member of the Central Committee of the GDR admitted: "We had planned everything. We were prepared for everything. But not for candles and prayers". Shortly after that, in South Africa, the Church played a comparably central role in the movingly successful Truth and Reconciliation Commission. In 2008, at its 17th Party Congress, the Chinese government, for the first time since the Party's foundation, formally accepted that "religion is not only here to stay but can make valuable contributions to building a harmonious society".

Nearer home, the Church has fostered love and justice. Up and down the country, local churches have initiated and run a huge range of organisations. They have taken a lead in campaigns – to drop the chains of debt or promote trade justice, for instance – and arranged pre-election forums or debates on issues like going to war in Iraq and climate change. Atheist news commentator Neal Lawson has observed: "Religious communities are among the increasingly few places that bring people together as citizens rather than consumers". Local churches have provided meals, accommodation, support services and friendly contact for homeless people. They have adapted their premises making rooms and halls available, at a payable price, to all sorts of worthwhile community groups. Sane and decent journalist Simon Jenkins wrote of the redeveloped St Martin-in-the-Fields church: "Even an atheist can marvel at this exquisite refuge for the urban poor".

Religion crucial for people and planet
So may we assert that religion, however mysterious and even odd it may sometimes appear, however fallible its institutions and individual members, is actually anything but crazy? I submit that religion – *at its best*, I repeat, *at its best* – is the *supreme* source of **spiritual nurture, timeless wisdom, ultimate truth** and **love and justice.** It *is* therefore **crucial** to both the well-being of humanity and the health of planet Earth.

6   CURIOSITY AND CONSCIENCE

The role of religion in the quest for knowledge

Do you remember Dolly? Not Dolly Parton, though she may well be memorable, probably more to men than women! No, the one who, whenever her photo appeared in the papers, always bore the same, sheepish expression. You've got it! I have in mind, Dolly, who, just before the turn of the century, was the woolly wonder of the world, the first sheep to be produced by cloning. Unlike every other lamb born since her species was domesticated, she could never be called Dolly Mixture for she had no father, just a mother!

Whatever our moral opinions about the method of her creation and that of creatures similarly produced since, the cloning process has increased our knowledge about human and animal physiology – knowledge that appears to be already helping in the treatment of inherited diseases.

Shooing Dolly aside for a while, the kind of bold scientific curiosity which produced her has, down the centuries, undoubtedly generated a myriad useful things.

The benefits of science

Probably most of us came to this service by car: but our quick and comfortable journey could not have happened unless someone had invented the wheel and someone else the internal combustion engine. What's more, we shall only be able to justify this convenient mode of transport in the future, if scientists and technologists continue to be curious. Thankfully, a group of scientists at Bath University has recently taken the development of unpolluting, hydrogen-powered cars a step further. Announcing their success, spokesman Dr Weller observed: "The fact that we discovered material for storing hydrogen safely, *by chance*, is a fantastic advertisement for the benefits of curiosity-driven research".

You probably wouldn't be enduring this particular sermon had not Alexander Fleming's curiosity led him to discover penicillin which almost certainly saved my life as a little boy, only a few months after the resultant medication was first prescribed.

The world might not be enjoying the benefits of the amazing Internet had not *Homo sapiens* found how to defy Earth's gravity and reach into space.

What a debt we owe scientists, technologists and inventors, for their dogged curiosity!

Our debt to art and music

Curiosity has yielded a bumper harvest in the field of culture. For instance, in the 16th century, Venetian painter Titian played about with the new medium of oils, making a lasting impact on the evolution of painting. In the early 20th Century, Picasso, whose attempts to portray the passing of time and the changing moods of a subject all in one picture, sparked off further innovation. A little over two hundred years ago, Beethoven's radical inventiveness produced some of the finest piano sonatas. Those of us with sparse or grey 'thatch' will recall how the Beatles took the world by storm through their novel style of popular music. What a debt we owe artists and musicians for their bold curiosity!

Our debt to thinkers

Civilization owes a massive debt, too, to original thinkers like philosophers, theologians and writers who have tried to make sense of the human condition and wrestled with the great riddles of life.

Thinkers like Mr. Job, the Bill Gates of his day, even if the only computer he owned was the one he stored in the space between his ears.

Rightly or wrongly taking the story at its face value, all went well at first. Job married, had a large family, owned a huge estate, and was popular. What's more, he was a truly decent sort of bloke. Suddenly though, his life turned sour. Robbers rustled his cattle, bandits mugged his staff, freak storms destroyed his house and family and, to cap it all, he caught a gruesome skin disease. No wonder he cried out: "Why should this happen to *me*?" As the Bible book of his name reveals, Job never found the definitive answer to the age-old question of the innocent sufferer. But his – or the author's – intense search for an answer, his penetrating intellectual curiosity, gave humanity literature of profound and lasting worth.

Turning to the great New Testament theologian, Paul, we find a man who refused to let thorny issues barricade his quest for an understanding of the Jesus Event. The result? A testimony of monumental importance.

In the centuries since, theologians and philosophers have explored the dense intellectual and existential jungles of life and shared the riches they discovered. What a debt we owe to thinkers for their dauntless curiosity!

Rooting for the truth takes all sorts of forms. Ever since the invention of radio and television, there have been programmes designed to probe and discover. In recent years, Crimewatch and Watchdog have invited the entire nation to sniff out criminals and expose racketeers. Top-notch reporters risk their lives investigating every sort of evil from corruption to genocide. What a debt we owe them for their courageous curiosity!

Curiosity could be providential
I am not aware of geneticists identifying a 'curiosity' gene, or cluster of genes. Judging from the universal habit of toddlers 'to get into everything' (now putting a finger into the squishy gravy, now biting the corner of the table), I wouldn't be surprised if it were shown that we are biologically programmed to be curious. Certainly the anthropic principle implies that curiosity is vital to our survival as a species. Just think how much vital knowledge and how many natural resources would remain hidden and unused, were it not for people's curiosity! It seems our species really is crucial to the realization of planet Earth's potential; that curiosity is not a luxury but a necessity.

In theological terms, inquisitiveness seems to be a gift of God, essential to the well-being, if not survival, of humanity. If so, isn't it our duty, our sacred calling, to understand as much as we possibly can about our planet? Down the centuries – may the bigoted secularist note – religious faiths, especially Christianity and Islam, have encouraged and sponsored agents of curiosity like maths, astronomy and science in general, even if such enthusiasm has sometimes backfired on traditional belief, as in the case of Galileo or Darwin.

So: let research and exploration, experimentation and innovation, flourish – in science, technology, culture, thought and education! May Christians welcome and support a *spirit of enquiry*. With all the threats facing the human family, not least climate change, it could be providential.

Not an unalloyed 'good'

That said, my mind's ears hear alarm bells ringing. As this sermon has developed, you have probably kept saying to yourself 'humph!' or its modern equivalent. You know full well that curiosity is not an unalloyed 'good'.

Yes, Dolly's production may indeed have provided crucial knowledge in the battle against inheritable diseases and the ground-breaking curiosity she symbolized could well lead to all sorts of wonderful developments. But it *could* turn out that future generations will look back and ask why people, on the threshold of the 21st century, were so blind to the dangers of biotechnology. They might say: "Pity they didn't call the wretched animal, *Folly*!" The poor creature could turn out to be the precursor of human cloning with its dreadful possibilities: would the world *really* be a better place with Big Brother replicas scattered around?

Maybe human cloning won't happen. But we already *do* have godlike clout. Thanks to the nature of modern warfare, people slaughtered around one hundred million of their fellow humans in the 20th Century. But that's nothing to what would happen if all the nuclear missiles now around were unleashed. Modern curiosity has endowed humanity with prodigious knowledge. Has the world community, however, truly grasped the apocalyptic possibilities of such knowledge?

A lesson from Eden

Though the degree of human knowledge and therefore power was minuscule in comparison with today, those who put the second creation story into Jewish scripture were, it seems, fully aware of the power and danger of knowledge, especially of moral knowledge. "God", the myth asserts, "planted a garden in Eden...

in which stood the tree that gives life and the tree that gives knowledge of good and evil" (Genesis 2:8-9). The parable that follows is a graphic tale but it's a timeless warning that knowledge can be used for evil as well as good. But if knowledge is a mixed blessing, then its progenitor, curiosity, is also an ambivalent attribute.

The conflict within

Thankfully, there's something else in our psyche just as vital to human well-being as curiosity. You can't smell or see or touch it. But you can, in a sense, feel and hear it. In fact, some people describe it as a kind of voice in their head which tells them they should or should not say or do something. I refer, of course, to conscience.

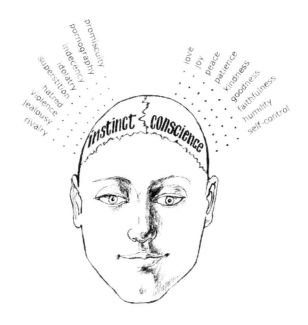

As Paul might, today, have expressed the tension between
"human nature" and "God's Spirit"

The apostle Paul was keenly aware of this aspect of human experience. Part of his innermost self wanted to ignore it, another part to go along with it. In his letter to the Galatian churches, he depicts this tension as a conflict between human nature and God's Spirit: "What human nature does is quite plain. It shows itself in immoral, filthy, and indecent actions; in worship of idols and witchcraft. People become enemies and they fight; they become jealous, angry, and ambitious. They separate into parties and groups; they are envious, get drunk, have orgies, and do others things like these". Whereas, Paul continues, "the Spirit produces love, joy, peace, patience, kindness, goodness, faithfulness, humility, and self-control" (Galatians 5:19-23).

Curiosity shorn of conscience

When the conscience – perceived by religious faiths as a universal agent of the Spirit of God – when the conscience is ignored, every sort of mean and rotten thing happens. Not least when curiosity gets detached from conscience.

Understandably, Albert Einstein felt bitter when the results of his genius were used to make atom bombs and their horrific successors. Reflecting on what happens when curiosity and conscience are divorced, pioneer radio astronomer, Sir Bernard Lovell, said: "The simple belief in automatic material progress by means of scientific discovery and application is a tragic myth of our age".

We can all think of examples where experiments have been made without moral constraints. Such as Hitler's brutal eugenics programme. Or how, back in the 'forties, the U.S. government withheld life-saving treatment from an entire black community in order to find out more about the effects of syphilis. Or how, in recent years, the search for fossil fuels has caused terrible ecological damage. In so many areas of life, channels of curiosity – like exploration, research and innovation – too often produce harmful, if not evil results. Why? They do so when let off the leash of conscience.

I believe Hans Holbein's familiar but always startling painting called 'The Ambassadors' eloquently portrays the truth I'm driving at. The expressions and clothes of both figures, you may recall, exude wealth and success. On two shelves between them are all manner of symbols, the lower ones representing Man's study of the Earth, the upper ones his study of the sky. The whole scene portrays humanity's self-confidence as its knowledge and power expand. However, just visible, top left, is a crucifix, and slashed across the foreground is a very strange shape which careful inspection reveals is a human skull. Curiosity shorn of conscience, the picture could be saying, is highly dangerous!

The decisive role of conscience

A novel whose entire plot centres on the challenge of the conscience is Anthony Trollope's 'Cousin Henry'. At one point, the author observes: "We are too apt to forget, when we think of the sins and faults of men, how keen may be their conscience in spite of their sins". Deep within even the worst of rogues, you will find at least faint signs of a stunted conscience.

It may be true that Jesus gave little specific teaching about the role of conscience. But he did utter frequent warnings about the sins of greed, vanity and arrogance, those very attitudes which corrupt curiosity and entice people to apply its fruits malevolently. Isn't his observation that "a good person brings good out of the treasure of good things in his heart" and "a bad person brings bad out of his treasure of bad things" a veiled reference to the decisive role of conscience? (Luke 6:45)

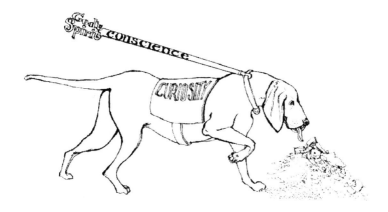

And what a difference it makes when people *do* foster and obey their conscience! They use their knowledge, skills, time, power and money wisely and generously. They are more considerate, more forgiving, more compassionate, more concerned about justice and peace.

Seek, mindful of God

"Ask, and you will receive; seek, and you will find; knock, and the door will be opened to you". Jesus surely had in mind the spiritual quest. Since, however, as both religious faith and modern physics claim, the spiritual and material are inextricably related, may we not apply his words to *all* forms of curiosity?

If so, the message of Jesus is: be curious, search on...

But the seeking should be done mindful of God and God's rule. Then, like the truly caring human father, who gives his children only presents which are good for them, so God – we may deduce – will reward our curiosity, giving us *not just* knowledge and power, *but also* the moral will and discernment to use these gifts beneficially.

With the crises we face – rampant disease, ceaseless conflict, climate change and many more – people the world over need *to apply their innate curiosity* as keenly as ever. Even more though, as people of religious faith should patiently and persistently urge, we must all *heed the 'still, small voice' of conscience.*

7 WASPS ARE GOD'S CREATURES TOO!

A playlet about our personal care for the natural world

This playlet formed part of a Harvest service and incorporated thoughts previously submitted by the congregation. Ernest Hope, Mona Gloom, Faith Wise and Frank Talker are enjoying their regular afternoon tea at the River Gardens café.

The four walk in, one holding a tray with pot of tea, crockery, scones, jam, cream, and cake

Ernest Hope That table's empty – and it's in the sunshine. All agreed?

Mona Gloom It'll be too hot for me, Ernest. And that blob of jam will attract the wasps – which I *hate*. Let's sit *here*.

Faith Wise Wasps are God's creatures too, Mona – a part of 'nature's balance'.

Frank Talker That's funny, the other day me and my neighbour

MG 'My neighbour and I' – didn't they teach you English at your school, Frank?

FT My neighbour and I were chatting over the fence about 'Nature's balance' after a crow had waded into her pond and caught a newt, eating it live before our very eyes – you could see the little thing writhing in agony!

MG Not a pretty sight – 'nature red in tooth and claw', as they say.

FW And not easy to square with the notion of God as Love... I mean, why *does* God allow such suffering in Creation?

EH That's a big issue, Faith!

FT I get the Big Issue every Friday – and now I've started reading it, I find there's a lot of worthwhile stuff in it. It's quite meaty sometimes – I get it on my way to my super butcher in Green Street – coo, that beef last Sunday melted in your mouth!

MG Can we get back to the question, please: why does God allow such suffering in Creation?

FW We could be here 'til midnight discussing this one, just as thinkers and theologians have for centuries. It worried Job two-and-a-half millennia ago, and Paul talked about 'all Creation groaning'. No, it's one of those very puzzling metaphysical questions... but I'm sure there must be *some* worthy reason... Mind you, I sometimes wonder if we'd see things differently if we didn't think of God so anthropomorphically.

MG Anthro-WHAT?

FW Anthropomorphically, Mona – thinking of God as a sort of man, albeit a superman...

FT That reminds me, there's a new Superman film coming out soon – can't wait to see it – er, take my grandson to see it.

FW Thank you, Frank. As I was saying, may be we should think of God more as an infinitely great Spiritual Presence whose nature and ways we can only glimpse, but whose involvement with Creation is evident in its physical laws... in its astoundingly intricate and integrated forces and systems... in the way living species, by and large, evolve and improve... in its staggering variety of plants and creatures – in its, its, its – sorry, a senior moment – its

EH 'Biodiversity'?

FW That's the word!

EH Certainly, over all, Creation *is* truly amazing – surely, the work of an almighty God! But I'm still not really happy about the crow eating the newt.

FT Or the newt eating the tadpole.

FW Or that sparrow eating a moth.

MG Or you eating your beef, Frank!

EH Seeing that sparrow [*he points*] – and its mates by that table – really gladdens my heart, because I hardly see any at home – nothing like as many as when we moved to Bath twenty odd years ago.

FW They're certainly not as common as they were in New Testament times either, when, as Jesus noted, you could buy five for just tuppence!

FT Personally, I'm very, very worried about the decline in so many so-called 'common' birds – not only sparrows but starlings, too – and I don't know when I last saw a thrush in my garden.

FW I'm worried, too... But it's probably *our* fault – Man's fault, oops, 'Humanity's' fault... We want cheap food but that means factory farming... with its herbicides and pesticides and goodness knows what else. They kill off the weeds and insects vital to birds… It boils down to the fact that people are just too keen on a bargain, too *greedy*.

FT [*holding up a plate of scones*] Anyone for another scone? Mona?

MG Not for me – they're not exactly fresh. Nor's the cream. And the jam isn't up to much.

FW But there's no point in simply wringing our hands in sorrow and shame over the crash in bird populations. If God cares for every single sparrow, even every single *hair*.

FT And every single *rabbit*? Ha ha!

FW I'll ignore that one, Frank. Now Jesus was exaggerating – that was his style – when he said every hair on your head is numbered, but the point he was making was that God really does care for *everything*. And if *God* cares, surely we should, too!

EH I couldn't agree more… Now the RSPB…

MG I wish people wouldn't use initials – I forget what they stand for, half the time.

EH Sorry, Mona, I thought everyone knew RSPB stands for The Royal Society for the Protection of Birds. Anyhow, the RSPB has saved all sorts of species from virtual or actual extinction. Like red kites. A few years ago, there were just a dozen or so pairs left, in Wales. Now they've been reintroduced in various parts of the country and their numbers are, like the kites themselves, soaring. Many rivers, across the length and breadth of Britain, have been dramatically cleaned up, so that fish have returned along with fish-eating birds, not to mention otters.

FT Yes, in fact, the other day, I read that more fish are now found in greater numbers in rivers, lakes and canals in England and Wales than at any time since the 19th Century! Thousands of salmon are caught in the Tyne each year whereas only 40 years ago there were zilch. Rivers which were sterile now teem with life. Why, it was only a few years ago you could sometimes see raw sewage floating down the Avon, just over that railing!

MG Do you mind, Frank, you're putting me off my cake!

FT Talking of cake, have you heard the one about the two Eskimos? They were sitting in a Kayak and were feeling rather chilly. So they lit a fire in the craft, but it sank. Which proves you can't have your kayak and heat it, too!

FW Can we get back to what we were talking about, please? We *were* discussing what we can *do* to help God care for the planet.

MG All people ever care about is themselves!

EH That's rather a gloomy, one-sided view, Mona! My Bible, my reading of history, my observation of the world today, all show me people *do* have immense potential for *evil*, yes, but that they *also* have huge possibilities for *good.*

FT Even *governments*, Ernest?

EH Even *governments*... international conferences on biodiversity have produced all sorts of agreements and actions... Mind you, they could do a lot more.

FT Such as?

EH For a start, they could double the price of petrol and other fossil fuels – stop people using their cars so much, or at least strictly limit their size – I mean the size of the *cars*, not the people [*he scoffs another scone*]

MG *You'll* need to limit your size, Ernest, if you eat any more scones!

EH D'you know, a Japanese lady told me the other day that in Tokyo, each Wednesday, motorists are asked to use public transport, and what's more, many people do – not least business people... Nearer home, I really wish people wouldn't use their cars for short trips – journeys under a mile – unless they *really can't* walk or've got a heavy load.

FT *I'd* like the government to introduce a law insisting that all new buildings of a certain size – supermarkets, warehouses, airport buildings and so on – have solar cell roof tiles.

FW To provide electricity for their users?

FT Yes, and any surplus goes into the National Grid.

EH Talking of electricity, *I* think we should adopt a more rational, less prejudiced attitude towards nuclear power. If we used it more, we'd produce fewer greenhouse gases.

MG As well as save increasingly scarce fossil fuels, I suppose.

FT Well, I know modern nuclear power stations are tons safer than the old ones – but what worries me is they're a sitting target for terrorists, and where on earth do you put all the dangerous waste they produce?

EH Thinking of waste,

FT [*Whispering and looking somewhat furtively*] I say, Ernest, that girl clearing up the table's got a tidy little waist!

EH *As I was saying*, thinking of waste, *I'd* like the government to ban the use of plastic bottles and anything that's not bio-degradable.

FW What *I* want to know is, what can *ordinary* people – like the four of us round this table – do?

FT For a start, we could recycle more, especially household items – after all it's so *easy* now, with the green boxes.

FW But how can we care for sparrows and all the other animals and plants of God's Creation?

MG [*Slapping a fly on her forearm*] Got you! That's one less fly to plague us.

FT We're talking about *caring* for God's creatures, not *killing* them! We're far too ready to destroy *every*thing – from bluebottles to elephants – to suit our purposes, too ready to ravage the world for short-term gain.

EH So why not make our gardens wildlife friendly? We could cut down on chemicals like slug pellets – delphiniums and suchlike may not survive but what thrushes there are will have a better chance. We could give a decent space to wildflowers – with minimal management they can give you as much pleasure as their posher cousins. We could feed birds all through the year, following RSPB guidelines, of course. We could plant native species of shrubs and trees which produce berries or nuts and are good for butterflies. We could put up nest boxes – and bat boxes.

MG Not ME, bats make me *shudder* [*she shudders*] – I don't want them getting caught in my hair, *thank you very much*!

FT That's an *old wives'* tale, Mona!

EH We might dig a pond – an informal, natural one that encourages newts, frogs, toads, dragonflies and so on to breed… Gardens are now a major habitat for all sorts of threatened creatures. *Twenty million* pairs of birds now breed in Britain's homes and gardens!

FW But it's not only private gardens that matter. We have to work together, by joining environmental organisations like the Woodland Trust, or the Worldwide Fund for Nature or Plantlife International that's saved all sorts of wild plants from extinction. I support all of these… and yet, funnily enough, I still haven't plucked up courage to ask my neighbour to stop using peat!

EH   Well, folks, I've enjoyed our chat – and the goodies – but I really *must* be on my way... We've certainly got a *lot* to chew over.

MG   Like the scones.

EH   *And* much to *regret*. But if we get off our backsides [*he stands slowly and stiffly*], if we just get off our backsides and *do* something, individually and together, we *can* change things for the better... In fact, I think there's *real hope* for the future, *real hope*... Bye!

FT   And I must take this book back [*he picks it up*] to my church library – it's called 'Natural Capitalism', by the way, and it actually ties in with what we've been discussing, claiming that if even *existing* scientific and technological know-how were generously and justly applied by the 'have nations' it would make a *huge* difference to Earth's health... Come to think of it, its message is a very hopeful one... I found the chapter on biomimicry absolutely fascinating... [*He walks off*] See you next week!

MG   What's 'biomimicry', when it's at home?

FW   It's about applying nature's methods to technology. In religious language, learning God's methods.

MG   There are certainly lots of proverbs in the Bible advising us to learn from the natural world – like, 'Go to the ant, sluggard, and learn her ways!'

FW   Of course, the writer had in mind *spiritual* lessons... but it seems we also need to learn some *practical* lessons from God's genius... Well, we've had a good natter... and all about things that *matter*... You know, faithwise, we *ought* to be *hopeful* – we *can't* go wrong if we *really* take the loving, caring way of Jesus ... It's not *all* gloom and doom, Mona dear!

MG   [*smiling for the first time but hardly noticing Faith go*] You know, I don't feel as fed up as I did... Gosh, must hurry if I'm to catch the Number 14 and feed those birds...

8   LAW, LIBERTY, and LOVE

Three pillars of civilised living

Speed cameras!
What do you think of speed cameras? In the community at large, opinions range from outright opposition to wholehearted support. Some citizens cynically dismiss them as an easy way of funding the police, while others claim they save lives, grief and public money. Some people see cameras as an effective way of enforcing the law, others see them as an unnecessary restriction on personal liberty.

The question of 'speed' or, according to your point of view, 'safety' cameras is an important issue in itself. I refer to it, however, because it provides a time*ly* example of the time*less* tension between law and liberty civilised living invariably involves. The recurring camera debate also shows how slow people are to recognise that both the fundamental *reason* and *remedy* for excessive speed lie in the attitude of the individual driver. In short, the camera debate highlights three pillars of civilised living, namely: LAW, LIBERTY and LOVE.

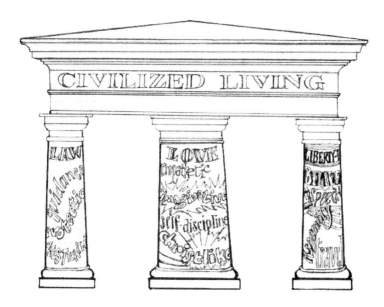

Let's now, in three stages, focus on each concept, beginning with *law*.

LAW

The Notion of Law

At every level of human society – from the nuclear to the global family – we find law, in the broadest sense, operating. It may not always be systematic, let alone written down. It may often function in the form of expectations rather than formal rules. But, in one way or another, institutions (like clubs, schools, churches and companies), local authorities, nations, international organisations, all run according to the notion of law.

What's more, I hardly need remind you, the notion of law has been around a very long time, and is probably as old as humanity. Tribes could not flourish, let alone survive, without rules and their enforcement. Early, historic communities were knit together by precepts and regulations, not least that of the ancient Hebrews.

Hebrew-Jewish law

We find *their* amazing range of sacred rules in the Old Testament books of Exodus, Leviticus, Numbers and Deuteronomy. Some of these regulations focus on worship and ritual, while vast numbers deal with the minutiae of daily life. Some are now redundant, others – like those concerning property and boundaries – remain the foundation of modern society. We may smile at some and wince at those now deemed sexist, but probably all of them were agreed for what was thought to be a good reason at the time.

To mention a few, there are laws about which animals may or may not be eaten. "You may eat any land animal that has divided hooves and that also chews the cud, but you must not eat camels, badgers or rabbits..." (Leviticus 11:2-4) (So choose extra carefully next time you go to the butcher's!)... There are laws defining what a woman must do after childbirth, detailed regulations about treating skin-diseases, rules about dealing with mildew on clothes and rot in houses, intimate guidance about personal hygiene. There's a huge list of forbidden sexual practices – which, incidentally, shows us there's nothing new about casual, obsessive or way-out sexual conduct!

Four vital Commandments

But the essence of these five or six hundred ancient Hebrew laws is, of course, summed up in the Ten Commandments. As pointed out by the American scholar Huston Smith, four in particular touch on matters of universal relevance. What, he asks are the four greatest powers and therefore 'danger zones' in human life? How we use: *force, possessions*, *speech* and *sex*. Let loose, each can wreak havoc.

In recent years, terrorist attacks – perpetrated in widely scattered countries, such as the USA, the UK, Australia, India and Kenya – have reminded us what devastation *force* can inflict. It's a sobering thought that humanity now has the power to blast all life on Earth into dust.

Our passion for *possessions* causes shocking injustice and poses a major threat to the environment, directly or indirectly accelerating climate change.

Our misuse of *speech* leads to domestic rows, miscarriages of justice, wrecked reputations and much more.

Our abuse of *sex* leads to personal misery, unwanted children, killer diseases like AIDS.

So, it seems those who produced the ancient prohibitions – Do not kill, covet, lie, or commit adultery – really *did* know what they were talking about! Yes, there are those, Christians among them, who make light of the notion of law. They are, for instance, content to use a bus lane to get past a queue of traffic, if they think they can get away with it. Realists, however, know civilised living is impossible without the guidance, restraints and protection law provides.

The limitations of law

That said, who of us would give law, both as a concept and a social institution, ten marks out of ten? We well know law has its limitations.

For a start, lawmakers can never keep up with changing circumstances. When a migrant society becomes a settled community – as happened with the Israelites – established laws have to be modified and new laws formulated. At a time of rapidly developing technology, such as we live in now, not least in medical matters, knowledge and power overtake our ability to devise a just and protective legal framework.

It's notoriously difficult to produce laws which foil those extra clever lawyers and accountants employed to find and exploit loopholes. Where laws burgeon in numbers and complexity, they are difficult to enforce and may thereby lose public respect (as Charles Dickens' novel Bleak House graphically demonstrates).

Laws can be excessively harsh. They certainly were in Britain less than two centuries ago, judging from a Guardian newspaper report of 1st December, 1821. Early that day, a crowd gathered to witness the execution of three citizens, one for robbery, one for burglary, and a 17 year old youth for using a forged £10 note! They can be brutal today, sometimes restricting people's freedom to travel or work where they wish (currently the case for Arabs in Israel-Palestine) or, in totalitarian regimes, deterring citizens from believing, speaking or acting according to conscience. Recent UK laws devised to combat terrorism and improve security also threaten many cherished liberties.

Worst of all – as the apostle Paul so shrewdly observed – such is human perversity, that the very existence of certain laws can make us wish to break them! "It was the Law that made me know what sin is", he confesses in his letter to the Roman Christians, "If the Law had not said 'Do not desire what belongs to someone else', I may not have known such a desire. By means of that commandment sin found its chance to stir up all kinds of selfish desires in me" (Romans 7:7-8).

When I see the words 'Wet Paint' chalked or scribbled next to a fence or doorway, I still have an almost irresistible urge to touch it and see if it really is wet! Children, if not adults, dare each other to trespass: I can vividly remember the thrill of 'Bury-baiting', a game in which my friend and I saw how far we could get into Mr Bury's big garden next door before he or his gardener chased us off. Many apparently 'respectable' people get a kick out of cheating the tax inspector or 'pulling a fast one' on the traffic warden or getting away with an inflated insurance claim.

Just as it did for Paul, law – whether rules, regulations or statutes – can still prove provocative. As he conceded in his letter to the Christians of Galatia, law has a vital purpose: it shows us what wrongdoing is; it's a valuable 'tutor', pointing to what is socially beneficial; it's a necessary means of guiding, restraining and protecting individual and community alike. Yet it remains fundamentally inadequate. Something else is needed too: *liberty*.

LIBERTY

Our desire for liberty

Casting your mind back – a shorter or longer time as the case may be – did you enjoy your school days? 'Yes' or 'No', you will surely remember the happy moment of relief when the final bell of the day rang and you were free. Unless everyone's working flexitime, you can notice the same feeling outside offices, factories and suchlike when employees rush to their cars to regain their freedom. But the desire for liberty runs much deeper. Though we may hardly be aware of it in our mercifully free society, people in dictatorial or totalitarian regimes hunger for it. Moses's plea, 'Let my people go!' has reverberated down the centuries and may still be heard today – in Myanmar, North Korea, southern Sudan and wherever human rights and freedoms are trashed. The desire for liberty is instinctive.

Naturally, the first freedom people the world over want is the freedom to survive – to have sufficient food and fresh water, to be released from debilitating disease. They also want the freedom proper education brings and the freedom a job provides. They want freedom of belief, speech, assembly and travel. They want to choose what work they do and where they live. In short, they want a culture of liberty that allows them to plan and live their own lives. Sadly, for a range of reasons, many of these aspirations will remain dreams for great numbers of our fellow humans – although, thanks to a series of campaigns (like Drop the Debt and Make Poverty History), many millions *are* already beginning to enjoy a better material standard of living, with its accompanying freedoms.

The liberties I listed are extremely important and, in many instances, must take precedence. Without them, people cannot possibly achieve their physical or intellectual potential. At the same time, isn't there another – and in the long-term – absolutely crucial kind of liberty?

Spiritual liberty

I have in mind 'spiritual' liberty, the type of liberty the Bible extols. With the benefit of hindsight, we might even see it as the dominant theme and purpose of the Bible. How often Old Testament priests, prophets and proverbs urge leaders and citizens alike to cold-shoulder evil and embrace goodness! How often they warn people to throw off the shackles of religiosity and its excessive ritualism: "What does the Lord require of us but to do what is just, to show constant love, and to live in humble fellowship with our God?" (Micah 6:8)

The New Testament takes up the theme of spiritual liberty, supremely in its presentation of the example and message of Jesus. All three authors of the Synoptic Gospels tell of Jesus teaching in the synagogue at Nazareth. But Luke elaborates the story explaining that Jesus claimed the passage he read from Isaiah could apply to his own mission. Now it may well be that it was Luke who added the quotation from the prophet in order to summarise Jesus's world-changing agenda. Whatever the story behind the text, it is surely indisputable that both the teaching and the ministry of Jesus as a whole show he *did* wish to liberate people – from poverty, false imprisonment, physical disability and political oppression.

At the same time, the Gospels also show us Jesus recognised that such liberation depended hugely on a more fundamental liberation: more than anything, people needed release from their self-absorption and its character-stunting effects. How Jesus rejoiced when taxman Zacchaeus chose to throw off his greedy, cheating ways and grasp the freedom he offered, the freedom to be his true self: "Salvation has come to this house today!" Then, summarising Jesus's entire mission, Luke adds: "The Son of Man came to liberate the lost" (Luke 19:9-10)

So civilised living certainly requires law – for law defines what is socially beneficial, law restrains anti-social conduct, law protects the vulnerable. But law, we all know, has its serious limitations. Civilised living also needs liberty, especially spiritual liberty, the kind Christians believe is available supremely through faith in Jesus Christ.

If Law and Liberty *are* both vital to the wellbeing of society, are they sufficient? No, for both can be abused. For Law to serve its purpose well and for Liberty to be truly beneficial, something else is needed. But what?

Self-regulation?

There are those who claim the 'something else' is 'self-regulation'. They advocate the notion for areas of public life like advertising, the press and the drinks industry. While acknowledging the need for a framework of law to constrain the most seriously harmful practices, they believe liberty is vital in such areas and that self-regulation will ensure a responsible and socially beneficial attitude. So we get bodies, like the Advertising Standards Authority, the Press Complaints Commission and the drinks industry's Portman Group, advising here, ticking-off there and providing a measure of moral constraint but lacking legal teeth, thereby all too often allowing advertisers, newspapers and alcohol businesses to get away with socially corrosive behaviour.

Of course, there's bound to be a big element of honourable self-regulation in a free society if Law and Liberty are to be kept in equilibrium. But, it seems to me, 'self-regulation' can all too easily become a respectable-looking cover-up for what are actually self-serving and community-damaging practices. Is the *primary* motive behind the drinks' industry's passion for self-regulation really a noble love of freedom? Or do its barons simply wish to keep the law at bay and allow profits to rocket, whatever the resulting mayhem?

A healthy society *does* need *honourable* self-regulation in conjunction with Law and Liberty. But it needs something far more important still – something which may certainly enoble self-regulation – but something which can, and ideally should, pervade law, liberty and *every* facet of life. And you know well what it is! It is imaginative, other-people-centred *love*, *Christlike love*.

LOVE

Phones, sex, and trade

I now draw together all three concepts – Law, Liberty and Love – with a few concrete examples …

Starting with mobile phones … For the most part, as we know only *too* well, people are free to use them where and when they wish. True, most people realise it's socially unacceptable to leave them on, let alone deliberately use them, in a concert or play or service; you are not supposed to use them in designated quiet carriages in trains; and the law prohibits drivers using hand-held phones. However, whether or not mobile phone owners – now virtually all of us – consider people nearby, let alone keep to the law, or selfishly flout the law and abuse their liberty, depends on their innermost attitude. So what is needed if mobile phones are to be a blessing and not a curse? Nothing less than the empathetic, considerate and self-disciplined quality of love Jesus highlighted.

Consider sexual behaviour... While there are laws designed to protect younger people, non-consenting adults and, to some extent, the public at large, people are otherwise free to behave as they wish and it would be absurdly unrealistic to try to determine conduct comprehensively through legislation, even if society could agree on such legislation. So what is needed if sexual behaviour is to be a blessing and not a curse? A healthy, innermost attitude. When this is truly empathetic, considerate and self-disciplined – when it bears the marks of Christlike love – then sexual (indeed all) relationships and conduct can become wholesome and beneficial.

Take international trade... Laws can provide a vital framework for efficient commerce. Liberty is highly desirable, too, enabling producers and nations to sell their goods wherever there's a market: in principle, free trade is a worthy ideal. But we well know that some nations and some corporations abuse their liberty, keeping far too much profit for themselves, allowing but a pittance to hard-working producers. We know the laws governing trade are made by nations which can afford teams of lawyers to draft self-serving rules. So what is needed if global trade is to be fair as well as free? Wealthy nations must change their attitude, becoming genuinely empathetic, considerate and self-disciplined in their attitude to those now exploited; they must show a real measure of, yes, Christlike love.

Civilised living

Finally, back to those cameras! While legal limits do persuade many drivers to travel at sensible speeds, law in this area is notoriously difficult to enforce and so most road-users, most of the time, are free to behave as they wish. You'll only get people to drive at consistently safe speeds – whether they are in restricted zones or not, whether there are cameras around or not – when they develop an empathetic, considerate and self-disciplined attitude, when true love rules mind, heart and right foot!

In a sentence: civilised living requires *wise laws*, *responsible liberty*, and *Christlike love*.

9   LORDS OR SERVANTS?

The animal kingdom and the Kingdom of God

What have the animal kingdom and the Kingdom of God to do with each other? How might our understanding of God influence our attitude to our fellow animate creatures? Should humans be 'lords' or 'servants' of the animal kingdom?

I wonder what image the phrase 'the animal kingdom' brought to your mind. Snowy, hoping for a cuddle on your lap? Blue tits pecking at the fat on the bird table? Tranquil cows cooling themselves in the river on a hot summer's day? A school of porpoises leaping out of the water off a Cornish beach? A gigantic bull elephant you encountered in an African park? Or the spider trapped in your bath?

Astoundingly extensive and stunningly varied
Whatever creature you envisaged, it was one of an astoundingly extensive and stunningly varied form of life we call 'the animal kingdom'. It was one of a mighty 'army', 'air force', 'navy' and subterranean legion of animals, many, if not most of them, vital to our own and other species' existence.

The second phrase in my opening question was 'the Kingdom of God', a familiar metaphor for any facet of creation believed to be fulfilling God's intentions.

So, the question before us is this: how might God, the Creator of ALL-THAT-IS, wish the human species to relate to the countless other animate species which share the planet? Putting the question another way, when we submit to the ubiquitous Spirit of God, how do we treat our fellow creatures?

Guidance from Christian Theology

In my most recent search for an answer, I first investigated the world of Christian theology, hoping to gain enlightenment from the reflections of past and present theologians. As my guide, I used a book called 'Animal Theology', published in 1993. It was written by the first ever Fellow in Theology and Animal Welfare at Oxford, Andrew Linzey.

A sparsely stocked cupboard

From the outset, Professor Linzey makes it clear that the cupboard of Christian theology on animals is sparsely stocked. For the most part, Christian theologians have regarded this whole area of life as a distraction, liable to deflect theology from its main foci. Certainly in my time at college, we spent years studying every manner of doctrine and heresy but barely hours on 'animal theology'. How many sermons have you heard on the subject, in comparison with the number you have heard on, say, 'praying more diligently' or 'growing in discipleship'?

The cupboard of Christian theology about the animal kingdom and the Kingdom of God is sparsely stocked but it's not empty.

Dominion Theology

One packet the cupboard contains is sometimes labelled 'Dominion Theology'. The idea behind it goes back maybe 3000 years. For we find it in the opening chapter of Genesis, verse 26, where (as the King James version has it) God is understood to say:

> "Let us make man in our image, after our likeness; and let them have dominion over the fish of the sea, and over the fowl of the air, and over the cattle, and over all the earth, and over every creeping thing that creepeth upon the earth".

From this one, overworked verse – I remember studying an entire book devoted to the phrase 'the image of God' – from this single verse, a whole theology emerged, surviving to the present day.

One of the most influential theologians, Thomas Aquinas of the 13th century, clearly sympathised with the essential idea of 'Dominion Theology' – the belief that humans have been commissioned to act as 'lords' over the rest of creation. He made three assertions. One, that animals are irrational, possessing neither mind nor reason; two, that they exist to serve human ends by virtue of their nature and divine providence; three, that they therefore have no moral status in themselves, but only

70

when human interest is involved. In his *Summa contra Gentiles,* he goes so far as to argue;

> "By divine providence animals are intended for man's use in the natural order. Hence it is not wrong for man to make use of them, either by killing them or *in any other way whatever".*

When I took the Dominion Theology packet from the cupboard, my immediate reaction was to exclaim: 'Pooh, this stinks!' Then I thought about all those animals someone has killed for my nourishment and, indeed, pleasure, because I really do enjoy my bacon. And I recalled all the other ways I have benefited from man's dominating exploitation of the animal kingdom!

Incarnation Theology

In the 20th Century, the Protestant theologian Karl Barth added his own package to the cupboard, one we could label 'Incarnation Theology'. The ingredients overlap with those of the Dominion concoction. For Barth draws a very thick line between human and animal life, contending that people are intrinsically superior to other creatures. Why? Because, according to traditional theology, God became *man*, not animal. Barth didn't suggest this gave humans carte blanche permission to do what they liked with animals. But he did assert the animal kingdom was of a lower and less important order.

Again, I didn't like the smell of Barth's packet. Then I paused and realized I do, in practice, treat non-human creatures as subordinate. I will, for instance, readily squeeze between my thumb and forefinger those newly born greenfly festooning the stems of my roses.

'Compassionate' Theology

The third packet I took from the cupboard could be labelled 'Compassionate Theology' and its smell immediately appealed to me. Various theologians and serious-thinking Christians have intermittently refilled this packet. St Francis of Assisi comes to mind. Even if some paintings of him surrounded by birds and little furry creatures are unrealistically twee, his celebrity status has been a positive influence in the field of animal welfare. Interestingly, in 1980 he was designated patron saint of ecology.

Another minor theologian Linzey's book introduced me to, was Humphry Primatt. In 1776, he published his 'Dissertation on the Duty of Mercy and the Sin of Cruelty to Brute Animals'. Whereas he agrees with Aquinas about the inherent superiority of humans, he makes a passionate plea on the subject of pain.

> "Pain is pain, whether it be inflicted on man or beast; and the creature that suffers it... suffers evil; and the sufferance of evil, unmeritedly, unprovokedly, where no offence has been given... but merely to exhibit power, or gratify malice, is Cruelty and Injustice [by] him that occasions it".

Which suggests that even if we are superior in status to the non-human animal kingdom, this doesn't allow us to do what we wish, and certainly doesn't permit careless or gratuitous cruelty.

'Life as such is sacred'
Albert Schweitzer, the later 19th and early 20th century intellectual, based his theology on the belief that all creation owes its existence to the same Creator. Therefore, all life forms, human, animal, insect and vegetable, are sacred. So, Schweitzer argued, the ethical person who "comes across an insect which has fallen into a puddle, stops for a moment in order to hold a leaf or a stalk on which it can save itself".

Later recognizing that no one could consistently be so scrupulous, he modified his stance, saying that "Wherever I injure life of any sort, I must be quite clear whether it is *necessary*" to rescue it. That qualification begs many questions, but his overall plea for compassion does have a pleasant odour and, to some extent, can be practised. When teaching and children tried to swat an insect buzzing round the classroom, I insisted they open the window and let it escape. But I confess I am not so tolerant when I'm trying to get to sleep and hear the whine of a mosquito!

So, the cupboard of historic Christian theology on animals contains three big packets: 'Dominion Theology' (we're boss, animals exist for our benefit, so don't let's worry too much about their welfare); 'Incarnation Theology' (since God became *Man*, we are intrinsically superior, so animal interests are decidedly subservient); and 'Compassionate Theology' (animals are as much a part of creation as we are and therefore warrant our consideration). On balance, then, both Christian theology and the Christian Church have sided more with the view that humans are 'lords' of creation rather than its 'servants'.

Although all three packets claim biblical support, I decided to explore the Bible for myself.

Guidance from the Bible

My immediate impression was that the Bible doesn't offer very much illumination on the relationship between the kingdom of God and the animal kingdom. Domesticated animals were important economically in Biblical times, but the ethics of how you treated them seem to have been less important than such matters as hygiene, sexual conduct, food purity, business dealings, treatment of foreigners and property rights. Wild animals could be a nuisance, even a danger, but they were so numerous that there was no need to worry about their management or survival.

When I dug deeper, however, I found there is quite a bit of relevant material, even if much of it is implicit.

Creation precious, beneficial and interdependent
The very threshold of the Bible is a poetically expressed statement of faith about the origin, nature and interdependence of creation. Here we find a cosmogony declaring that creation: owes its existence to an Almighty Being; is essentially good; and is a coherent entity.

We may, I believe, legitimately infer from this opening chapter that creation is intrinsically precious, basically beneficial, and its creatures interdependent. If true, it means all creatures really do matter, both in principle and in practice. Furthermore, and very significantly, I suggest, these claims exquisitely concur with modern notions like the Gaia hypothesis and biodiversity principles.

Dipping into the rest of the Bible, we find animals are referred to in all sorts of ways. Leviticus chapter 11, for example, lists animals you may and may not eat. Elsewhere, we find advice about the ritual use of animals. Such as the melancholy custom whereby a priest confessed the sins of the people over the head of a chosen goat before driving the doomed creature off into the desert, supposedly taking away people's transgressions. For centuries, the Hebrew scriptures endorsed animal sacrifice, maintaining that the smell of a burning carcass 'delighted the Lord', a practice slammed only when prophets like Amos and Micah complained that it deflected people from their moral obligations.

'A good man takes care of his animals'

Yes, animals do feature in the Old Testament, even if there's very little about their welfare. True, there's the verse in Deuteronomy 22 which forbids your taking a mother bird from her nestlings – even if the prohibition is not so much for the creature's sake but so the finder will 'live a long and prosperous life'. Out of about a thousand proverbs in the Book of Proverbs, I found just two specifically on animal husbandry: "A good man takes care of his animals, but wicked men are cruel to theirs' (12:10) and "Look after your sheep and cattle as carefully as you can" (27:23).

The Wisdom Literature as a whole – Proverbs, Job, Ecclesiastes, two books in the Apocrypha, arguably the Song of Solomon and Psalms – is full of references to animals. Again, there's virtually nothing explicitly about animal welfare. Yet there are long sections showing profound veneration for the animal kingdom. The barrage of questions which came to Job's mind as he pondered the greatness of God's Creation persuaded him even his grim suffering must have some worthy purpose, in such an amazingly diverse and integrated habitat.

New Testament insights

In New Testament times, animals were still regarded as existing largely to satisfy human needs. Yet, there are certain passages which, we may surely infer, show that Jesus was concerned about the good of the animal kingdom. He spoke with approval about oxen yokes fitting smoothly, about rescuing and watering animals even on the holy day. He illustrated God's love for the sinner with the picture of the good shepherd searching for the lost sheep and protecting his flock against hungry wolves. He talked about God's care for the humble sparrow as well as the birds of the air in general.

In his letter to the Christians at Colossae, theologian Paul looks forward to the time when the whole cosmos would be truly under God's rule. He offers no precise guidance on how people should treat the animal kingdom, yet he does present a vision of a harmonious and flourishing creation – an aspiration surely only realizable through an attitude of care and compassion.

So it seems the Bible, as a whole, tends towards the view that, under God, humans are 'lords' rather than 'servants' of Creation. At the same time, there are passages favouring a humbler, more compassionate attitude.

Lordship a matter of serving

For me, however, it is Jesus's personal interpretation of lordship which convinces me he would have preferred the servant model. I am thinking of how he used his status and power not to dominate but to serve. As when, John 13 tells us, he washes his disciples' feet. Reflecting Christian belief as it had developed some seventy years after Jesus's ministry, the writer explains: "Jesus knew that the Father had given him complete power" – he was Lord, all right. And yet, John continues, "Jesus … poured water into a basin and began to wash the disciples' feet" (John 13:3,5). For Jesus, lordship (or leadership) was not a matter of dominating but serving.

And in that incident, and the entire Servant-Messiah notion, might we not have a sound basis for our attitude to both the human world and the animal kingdom?

So, both Bible and historic Christian theology *do* affirm that we are, under God, 'lords' of Creation. But there is also sufficient in both sources to let us infer that we should exercise our lordship in a compassionate, serving way.

Regrettably, for most of its history the Christian Church has so elevated the 'lordly' aspect that, especially where its authority has been strongest, it has permitted a cavalier attitude to animals to prevail. To this day, that attitude is still widespread in certain southern European countries: the R.S.P.B., for instance, has fought an uphill battle to curb the slaughter of songbirds in the region.

Challenges for Today and Tomorrow

Reconciling ideal and reality

It's the present and future that matter, however. And the big question is: just how do we reconcile the *reality* that we *are* lords of creation (to an unprecedented extent, thanks to modern science and technology) with the *ideal* that we exercise our lordship in a serving manner?

But what a colossal range of issues this question touches on! Such as: the permissibility of animal experimentation; the use of animals in sport and leisure; the genetic manipulation of animals and the patenting of the outcome; the stewardship of wild creatures in an ever more populous human world; the captivity of animals in zoos and circuses; the care of domestic animals; the place and treatment of pets; the way we design and manage our gardens; what we believe it is ethical to eat; what principles we follow when shopping for food – how do we resolve the cheap food/healthy eating/animal welfare trilemma?

A guiding principle and a worthy aim

I cannot take any more of your time by attempting to comment on such issues. In any case, they are far too complex for any preacher alone to acquire the knowledge and information needed to offer adequate answers.

So I end by offering you a principle and an aim. The *principle* is this: that, as agents of the Kingdom of God, disciples of Jesus should always *take into account the welfare of animals as well as humans.* The *aim* is: that we should persuade the world at large *to move from dominating and exploitative attitudes and practices to those which are realistically compassionate.* Over to you!

10   BELIEVING AND BEHAVING

How should religion and ethics interrelate?

What have religion and ethics – or faith and morality – or believing and behaving – got to do with each other? The question is probably as old as humanity. It was certainly raised, implicitly and explicitly, in Biblical times. Ordinary people as well as philosophers have asked it ever since. And it's a question every generation needs to address, for the answer may profoundly affect an individual's or a community's quality of life.

A burning issue
It is also a burning issue today judging from the escalating attacks against anything in any sense 'religious'. You don't have to open many issues of a newspaper or listen to very much radio or watch a lot of television, to pick up that a range of secularist academics take every opportunity to savage religion, not least its claims about its role in illuminating ethical issues. One such person, a lecturer in philosophy, has written that "it can easily be shown that the churches are either largely irrelevant to genuine questions of morality, or are positively anti-moral". If that isn't a jugular attack on religion, what is!

So our question 'What have religion and ethics – or faith and morality – or believing and behaving – got to do with each other?' is not purely academic. Nor is it at the margins of our personal and shared discipleship. It is one of massive importance and one we must face for there are those who would shut us up. There are those who would exclude us from helping our hugely diverse society work out a widely agreed moral foundation. There are those who dismiss the very idea that religious faith may offer something valuable for personal interaction let alone the complex ethical dilemmas rapidly changing technology throws up. So, the old question 'How should religion and ethics interrelate?' is more pressing than ever.

Religion and ethics defined
To some extent, the answer depends on how you understand each term.

For some people, religion and ethics could each be boiled down to 'doing good' and are therefore two ways of describing essentially the same thing. But that understanding is a superficial one.

We shall get further, I believe, if we think of the terms like this: religion is primarily to do with *what people believe about life's meaning* and ethics is primarily to do with *how people should live their lives.*

Understood in these ways, religion and ethics are clearly distinguishable entities, whatever their relationship might be. Moreover, as observation and experience affirm, they are entities that most certainly *can* be kept apart. We all know people with a strong sense of right and wrong who do not profess any religious faith and certainly don't belong to a faith community like a Christian church. We also know religious adherents for whom doctrines and rituals are central while questions of behaviour are subsidiary. *In practice*, there appears to be no absolutely essential link between religion and ethics, between faith and morality, between believing and behaving.

A close relationship?
So the vital question is: *should* there be a close relationship between the two entities?

No, the arch-secularists reply! As the one I quoted earlier asserts: "The churches' obsessions with pre-marital sex and whether divorced couples can remarry in church appears contemptible" in the light of truly "great moral questions of the present age" such as "human rights, war, poverty, the vast disparities between rich and poor, the fact that somewhere in the third world a child dies every two-and-a-half seconds because of starvation or remediable disease".

"Religion", he adds, "can often be immoral, too. Elsewhere in the world, religious fundamentalists and fanatics incarcerate women, mutilate genitals, amputate hands, murder, bomb and terrorise in the name of their faith." And, just to leave us in no doubt as to his contempt, he warns: "It is a mistake to think that our own milk-and-water clerics would never conceive of doing likewise: it

78

is not long in historical terms since Christian priests were burning people at the stake if they did not believe that wine turns to blood when a priest prays over it or – more to the present point – since they were whipping people and slitting their noses and ears for having sex outside marriage..."

Ouch! Truth hurts, doesn't it? Even if it's nowhere near the *whole* truth!

Wrong priorities
Who would deny that, throughout its history, not least in recent years, a hefty slice of the Christian Church's time and energy has been spent on sorting out how people should or should not behave sexually? Rightly so, it could be argued, for working out how to manage sexual aspects of life in the interests of both individual and society, is extremely important. Yet, when you trace the history of the Church's ethical values, a case could be made out that its concern with sexual conduct, contraception, reproduction, abortion and homosexuality – not to mention its endless debates about the role of women in its leadership – has, at times, been at the expense of other vital concerns. The Church has not always taken heed of Jesus's scale of values where virtues like sincerity, empathy, compassion, justice and peace-making are far more important.

Who, in the light of 21st Century events, never mind earlier eras, would deny the appalling damage religious fundamentalism has inflicted in terms of violence against individuals and communities? In recent years, Islamic extremism has been in the spotlight but, historically, Christian extremism is no less guilty. And still, religious fanaticism stirs up prejudice, hatred and division in families, local communities and international relations.

Is it any wonder secularists and fellow travellers strive to keep 'religionists' (as they call people with religious faith) out of the ethics 'kitchen'? Is it surprising that many educators argue that ethics should be one hundred per cent autonomous, based solely on 'pure reason' and personal judgement? Sadly, the case against religious involvement in ethics is all too understandable.

The Christian response

Of course, we could simply retort: talk about the pot calling the kettle black! For secularists are just as likely to do unethical things, as the atrocities perpetrated by atheist regimes last century grimly exemplify. But a mature Christian response would be, I suggest, first, for individual believers and religious communities to admit their historic and current failings; then, to point out that, in their crusade to demonise religion, our adversaries actually select their evidence and distort the picture. They may tell the truth but nothing like the whole truth.

The benefits of religion

For a start, they ignore the hugely beneficial impact of religious faith both historically and today. They close their eyes to the care and hospitality the Christian Church, for example, has offered the stranger. They belittle the reforming passion and achievements of faith communities. While rightly reminding us that many so-called Christians espoused the slave trade, they play down the role of other Christians in its demise. While rightly reminding us of the racial arrogance of those Christians who violently perpetuated the 'colour bar' in the States and apartheid in South Africa, they overlook the role of other Christians in the elimination of those evils. While rightly attacking contemporary Christianity where it *is* obsessed with sexual matters, they give little credit to the hugely influential role of the Church in changing public attitudes through such campaigns as Drop the Debt, Make Poverty History, Trade Justice and a chain of other movements before them.

More profoundly, those who shout down religious faith generally fail to distinguish between the way fallible adherents may apply their religion and their faith's core ideals. For, at the heart of the major world religions, you find strong justice and compassion ethics, and supremely so in the Christian faith.

In the teaching and way of Jesus, there is a pattern for living that was revolutionary at the time and remains revolutionary. Even when it is taken with only limited seriousness, the Jesus model generates personal contentment, considerate conduct and good relationships – all vital attributes of happy and flourishing communities. The essence of Jesus's vision, contained in the Sermon on the Mount anthology, has made an incalculable contribution to ethical thinking and standards. And, because it gets to the heart of what it means to be truly human, Jesus's glorious vision will go on challenging and inspiring thought and conduct, long after today's noisy secularists have tried to debunk it.

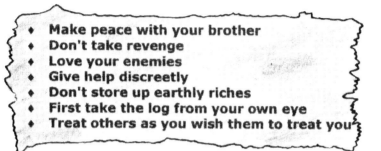

- **Make peace with your brother**
- **Don't take revenge**
- **Love your enemies**
- **Give help discreetly**
- **Don't store up earthly riches**
- **First take the log from your own eye**
- **Treat others as you wish them to treat you**

Reason, desire and the Spirit

What's more, aren't those who demand that moral decisions should be based on 'pure reason' unrealistic? For *is* there such a thing as 'pure reason' – reason totally untainted by presupposition, prejudice, subconscious feeling, and all the other factors which influence human thinking, conduct and judgement? Moreover, *is* it the case that when you have worked out what you think is the right thing to do, that you will inevitably (a) *want* to do it and (b) *actually do* it?

Every analysis of the human condition I have come across suggests that we are extremely complex and perverse creatures, instincts and conscience often being at war with each other. We don't always behave logically. We don't necessarily do what our rational self instructs! As Paul so neatly put it in his letter to the Galatians: "What our human nature wants is opposed to what the Spirit wants, and what the spirit wants is opposed to what our human nature desires." No one could accuse the apostle of ignoring the role of reason in guiding ethical conduct but he knew it was not the only vital piece of equipment people needed in their moral journey. The values, insights and conscience-rousing dynamic of honourable religious faith were, and are, important, too.

'Pure reason' is highly unlikely to trigger the quality of forgiveness Michael Henderson describes in his moving book 'The Forgiveness Factor'. Citing examples from all over the world, he shows how religiously motivated reconciliation has helped change people's perception of each other, causing conflict to give way to peace and former enemies to become allies, even friends.

That has happened many times over in the recent history of South Africa. A striking example of forgiveness and reconciliation took place in August, 2008. A former cabinet minister performed an extraordinary act of contrition. He washed the feet of an anti-apartheid activist he had conspired to murder. In imitation of Jesus, he chose to perform his act of atonement on the Rev. Frank Chikane, a senior official in the South African presidency. It wasn't 'pure reason' that inspired an attitude and an action unimaginable not many years ago. It was religious faith, as it has been in the case of hundreds of other such gestures.

Ethics based solely on 'pure reason' is as elusive as a soap bubble. Experience shows that ethics needs a realistic understanding of the human condition, an understanding which religion – at its best – can provide.

True religion demands an ethical outcome
But if ethics needs the best and wisest religion can offer, true religion demands an ethical outcome! Just as Jewish prophets, and later Jesus, fearlessly contended.

'Third' Isaiah slammed his people for their religious shallowness: "You worship the Lord every day, claiming that you are eager to know his ways and obey his laws... The truth is that at the same time as you fast, you pursue your own interests, you oppress your workers, you quarrel and fight... But the worship God wants is for you to remove the chains of oppression and the yoke of injustice... to share your food with the hungry and open your homes to the poor..." (Isaiah 58:2-7)

Prophet Amos was equally angry over people's selfish religiosity: "The Lord says: 'I hate your religious festivals. I cannot stand them! When you bring me burnt-offerings and grain-offerings, I will not accept them... Stop your noisy songs; I do not want to listen to your harps. Instead, let justice flow like a stream, and righteousness like a river that never goes dry.'" (Amos 5:21-24)

Jesus despised the hollow piety of many religious leaders. For them, religious teachings and rituals had become ends in themselves, failing to transform their values, attitudes and conduct. "How terrible for you, teachers of the Law and Pharisees! You hypocrites! You give to God a tenth even of the seasoning herbs, such as mint, dill and cumin, but you neglect to obey the really important teachings of the Law, such as justice and mercy and honesty. These you should practise, without neglecting the others." (Matthew 23:23)

But isn't *any* religion where creeds and rituals swamp moral principles and conduct a perversion of true faith? Aren't ethics a vital aspect of *every* genuine religion?

Both need each other
So, to sum-up...

Religion is surely only genuine and mature when it generates ethical conduct. As the down-to-earth Letter of James timelessly puts it: "Suppose there are brothers or sisters who need clothes and don't have enough to eat. What good is there in your saying to them, 'God bless you! Keep warm and eat well!' – if you don't give them the necessities of life? So it is with faith: if it is alone and includes no actions, then it is dead". (James 2:15-17)

At the same time, while it is possible to live a morally responsible life without conscious or formal commitment to a religion, history suggests that ethical thinking and practice *can* be hugely enriched by the insights, experience and dynamic of wholesome religion.

11   *WHY* DO YOU FORSAKE US?

An attempt to make sense of undeserved suffering

The biggest obstacle

What do you reckon is the biggest obstacle to belief in God, apart from the very concept of God? If you share the traditional notion of God as a Being that is all-powerful and all-loving and, in some sense, 'personal', the chances are your answer will be 'undeserved suffering'. It's therefore right for preachers to give the question an airing and this is what I'm going to do now.

But I won't be offended if you groan! Over the years you may well have heard quite enough sermons on the subject already. Or you might feel it's a futile quest, liable to produce pious platitudes, and inevitably inconclusive. What's more, it's an intrinsically gloomy topic and you already have enough woes to cope with!

On the other hand, it may be a very long time since you heard a sermon on the theme. This wouldn't surprise me because, speaking as a preacher, the question of 'undeserved suffering' is not only a depressing one but it is inherently difficult and demanding. So you opt for an easier, preferably cheerful, theme! Which is entirely understandable, if you are a full-time minister responsible for a big church or several smaller ones, with all the mentally-, physically-, emotionally-, and spiritually-draining tasks that face you.

So, from the perspectives of both pew and pulpit, a service on the problem of 'undeserved suffering' is both unattractive and unpromising! That said, our better selves know that it is a critically real obstacle to faith and one that therefore should not be ducked. So, as a retired 'gentleman of leisure', I offer you my reflections which I hope will be at least a little helpful.

Reading: Job 9:1-18 G.N.B.

Disasters great and small

Natural disasters struck in Job's time as they always have done. Every year, typhoons and hurricanes, thunderstorms and cyclones, earthquakes and volcanic eruptions, mudslides and floods, maim or kill men, women and children in their tens if not hundreds of thousands, usually destroying their homes and livelihoods, too. From time to time, mega catastrophes strike, as the opening years of the 21st Century have amply shown, with the great tsunami of Boxing Day 2004, the hurricane in New Orleans, earthquakes in Kashmir, Turkey and China, and in 2008 a devastating cyclone in Myanmar and catastrophic flooding in India. Periodically, horrific pandemics strike down vast numbers causing pain, fear and death in the process. Globally, all sorts of nasty diseases threaten rich and poor alike.

Each disaster causes: *shock* at its enormity; *pity* for the multitudes suddenly bereaved, injured, homeless, jobless and destitute; sometimes, *anger* that the consequences could have been less tragic had warning systems been in place or the authorities been quicker to respond; *guilt*, felt by survivors who escape and by distant observers who, in stark contrast to the afflicted, carry on their secure and comfortable lives. Yes, natural disasters and terrible diseases evoke a huge range of emotions.

Why do they happen?
Tragedies of every kind also spark off profound puzzlement, summed up in the cry: '*Why* do they happen?'
Now the word 'why' is ambiguous, something some otherwise intelligent people don't always realise. 'Why' may refer either to the *cause* or the *purpose* of something and the two uses should be distinguished.

If our 'why' is concerned with the *cause* of devastating natural events, we must turn to *science* for the answer. Admittedly, many answers it offers are necessarily provisional but to deny the contribution of science altogether, as some ultra-conservative Christians do, is to close the stopcock of a vital pipeline of Truth. If our 'why' is concerned with the *purpose* of destructive natural events and their grim effect on human and wild life – if we are really asking: "What possible justification in the grand scheme of things might there be for these cataclysms, afflicting as they do rich as well as poor, young as well as old, people of all or no faiths", then we are asking a *philosophical* question. Whilst theists – people who believe in a God that exists independently of the human mind – are asking the *theological* question: "How can a God who, according to historic definitions, is supposed to be all-powerful as well as wholly good, and the source of pure love (even identified with it in the Fourth Gospel), how can such a God allow so much seemingly undeserved suffering?"

That question, you know well, is age-old. It's raised in the Old Testament, supremely by the Wisdom writers and in particular the Book of Job. It is posed in the Gospels, for instance, by those disciples wanting a theological explanation why anyone should be born blind. It is acknowledged by Paul in his cameo about "all creation groaning like a mother in labour". It has been tackled by theologians and philosophers of religion down the ages. Isn't it, indeed, a question anyone is bound to ask who, being told that "God is almighty, God is good, God is love", comes face to face with the pain of the innocent?

Pruning the problem
So much for the question! Now for the sweat – offering an answer that sheds at least a pinhole of light on the problem.

Let's start with a little pruning, always a tricky business, especially when the rose bush or apple tree in front of you bears little resemblance to the diagram in the gardening book. If your observation of human suffering in all its wretched diversity is like mine, you will have concluded that a huge proportion of human suffering is indisputably attributable to human ignorance, folly or selfishness, sometimes going back a generation or more.

We may rightly blame so-called *Homo sapiens* for the great bulk of human misery, as place-names like the Somme, Auschwitz, Dresden, Hiroshima, My Lai, Srebrenica and Darfur, sombrely testify. Added together, the number of those deliberately slaughtered and those killed by human folly and greed probably totalled somewhere around 100 million in the 20th Century alone! Vastly more people perish because of 'man's inhumanity to man' than because of what insurance companies call Acts of God. Human misconduct is massively more blameworthy than the Creator's natural systems.

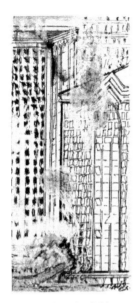

What's more, if our species is increasingly affecting Earth's climate – as is now almost universally agreed – people (and especially those in affluent, developed countries with their high CO_2 emissions) are at least partly to blame for severe weather phenomena and the damage they cause. Maybe, we need to take the logs out of our own eyes before considering what might be in 'God's eyes'!

God ultimately responsible

That said, there remains a proportion of suffering for which, in all fairness, our species cannot be held responsible. However much human foresight and technology might have lessened the impact of the Great Wave or subsequent natural disasters, it would be absurd to hold humanity as responsible for their actual occurrence. Earthquakes happen and volcanoes erupt because the Earth is still forming; Creation, here and throughout the cosmos, is still going on and the process necessarily involves movements of Earth and Water of sometimes awesome power, power which, sadly, is sometimes unleashed on human communities. And if God is the Creator of All-That-Is (as theologians put it) or the 'Cosmic Intelligence' responsible for the astoundingly 'finely tuned' laws and forces that hold the universe together (as certain cosmologists posit), then isn't God ultimately responsible?

If so, isn't it perfectly understandable to question either God's almightiness or God's all-lovingness or both? When natural disasters strike and the innocent suffer – and particularly when you or your loved ones are directly affected – might it not be wholly reasonable to cry out, like the psalmists, the prophets and even Jesus, "Why, God, have you forsaken us?" Isn't that part of our brain responsible for moral awareness bound to wonder whether an Almighty Being who, by definition, has the power to halt something about to cause horrific suffering, like a tsunami, yet chooses not to, is, frankly, immoral?

It's not surprising that militant atheists (conveniently taking very seriously the God they normally claim doesn't even exist) gleefully pounce on these so-called 'Acts of God' as evidence of God's impotence and callousness. However much we might put the blame on human selfishness and folly, however much we might prune the problem, there remains a core of suffering that seems wholly undeserved and unfair. It seems God does have at least a hefty *splinter* in his eye! So believers find themselves still significantly on the defensive.

Reading: Romans 8:18-27

"These things are sent to try us"?
Just as Paul grappled with the problem of suffering, so people have ever since. And they have proposed possible explanations.

A widely held view is that natural catastrophes, however severe, are examples of the 'trials and tribulations of life' God habitually promotes in order to test our mettle, a view encompassed by the saying: "These things are sent to try us". That's certainly a phrase which can easily trip off the tongue and, some people find, provides a measure of at least cold comfort. It's not a phrase I use myself, however, because, I believe, it's simplistic, certainly at its face value.

For one thing, the phrase doesn't differentiate between human and divine responsibility. What is all too easily attributed to God's intention may, on closer analysis, be the result of human action – human ignorance, folly, carelessness, greed, or downright selfishness.

The phrase "These things are sent to try us" may also reflect a certain fatalism implying that *whatever* happens is necessarily the deliberate will of God, a stance which surely denies humans not only the dignity of free will but also their very physicality. As Chief Rabbi Jonathan Sacks has put it: "Without genuine physicality, we would not know freedom, pleasure, desire, achievement, virtue, creativity, vulnerability and love. We would be God's computers, angels programmed to sing his praises".

What's more, the phrase "These things are sent to try us" could suggest God deliberately does all sorts of *really nasty, cruel things* to us to toughen our spiritual fibre. Rightly, people are appalled when parents batter and bruise their children in order 'to teach them a lesson'. Yet there are those who seem to think it's 'OK' for *God* to manage the human family in that sort of way. Surely, life throws up more than enough demands and challenges in its normal course, without God intentionally piling on the agony!

If God really *does* deliberately send trials and tribulations to test us, we are bound to ask: why is God so arbitrary, inflicting incessant suffering on *this* widely regarded good and kind person yet letting off scot-free *that* notorious rogue? If God deliberately triggers horrific natural disasters in order to teach wayward humanity a lesson, if these catastrophes really are the 'judgement of God' (as many Fundamentalists and their like assert), why does God almost invariably choose to take it out on poorer rather than better off people, people whose defiance of God's intentions and greedy abuse of the Earth may be far more blameworthy? (Of course, if humans knowingly and persistently trifle with the physical and moral laws God has provided for the planet's survival and well-being, people and pretty well everything else suffer, sooner or later – it's the way things are and there's a measure of at least rough justice in it).

To be fair to *many* of those who say "These things are sent to try us", what they probably mean is: whereas God *has* made the world such that trials and tribulations are an inevitable part of life, such troubles may be faced with an attitude that generates desirable qualities like courage, patience, empathy and love. On balance, therefore, trials and tribulations are beneficial. Now that may make sense for humanity as a *whole*, but it's still mighty tough on *individuals* relentlessly and disproportionately hammered by life's misfortunes.

Is God all-powerful and wholly good?
The unwelcome truth remains, *natural disasters do challenge the traditional idea of God being consistently both all-powerful and all-good*. Surely, if God were omnipotent, then God *could* intervene and stop them in their tracks; and if God were wholly good, let alone wholly loving, God *would* intervene to prevent the slaughter and destruction! That's a perfectly logical reaction.

So, what's the jury's verdict so far? For the great bulk of undeserved suffering – such as the euphemistically dubbed 'collateral damage' caused by war or that resulting from anti-social behaviour like alcohol-induced crime, careless driving, mindless pollution, and promiscuity – so-called *Homo sapiens* must be declared guilty; and, for often making the results of natural disasters worse, guilty of 'aiding and abetting'.

But those verdicts haven't dealt with the accusations completely. As was the case millennia ago, when Job challenged the Almighty over his own relentless suffering or when Jesus uttered his despairing cry 'Why have you forsaken me?' God, dare I suggest, is still in the dock. So where do we go from here?

An inevitable possibility?
We could simply accept that suffering is an inevitable possibility in a still developing universe. God – whether perceived as Creator or Cosmic Intelligence – appears to have given Creation a degree of freedom to develop and evolve. Which means, on planet Earth, that nature is often unpredictable and humans abuse their freedom, realities which can both trigger undeserved suffering. But this notion of a largely 'detached' God isn't much comfort if you or your loved ones are 'in the thick of it'!

A radical challenge
Some theologians offer a radically different way forward, one which may be anathema to dyed-in-the-wool traditionalists. So if that's you, please be assured I never say anything from the pulpit simply to 'stir it up'; my sole goal is always to catch a glimpse of Truth.

These theologians question the whole idea of an interventionist God, of a God 'out' or 'up there' who comes to our aid when we pray for it. For one thing, such a God seems to be very arbitrary when responding, wonderfully delivering *this* worthy person from their affliction but ignoring *that* equally worthy person, in spite of both praying, or being prayed for, with equal fervour! Who of us has never thought of God as at least a trifle, if not culpably, capricious?

These theologians argue that we should abandon the idea of an interventionist God – with all the conceptual and moral problems it throws up. Instead, we should think of God more as a universal Presence, an ever-available spiritual resource to which we can open our innermost selves, or souls, to gain the spiritual wisdom and strength we need to face life's challenges – not least the suffering that feels and seems so unjust. Might not such a concept of God release us from a humanoid image of God, with all its confining, puzzling and disturbing implications?

Our practical response

But whatever our concept of God, however much of the blame for undeserved suffering we transfer to ourselves and our fellow humans, however convincingly we argue (with the 17th Century philosopher Gottfried Leibniz) that innocent pain is a necessary concomitant of freewill – however much we prune, probe and philosophize – we are still left with the wretched, age-old, worldwide reality of suffering – be it self-inflicted, the result of human wickedness, or apparently totally undeserved.

Such was the reality Jesus experienced as he regretfully yet lovingly endured the excruciating agony of crucifixion. Such was the reality he faced daily, throughout his ministry – as in the incident, described in John chapter 9, concerning the man born blind. Even if John doesn't record the exact words of Jesus, he leaves us in no doubt that Jesus himself was intellectually and theologically baffled by the problem of suffering. "This man's blindness", he explained, "has nothing to do with his sins or his parents' sins".

Then Jesus adds: "He is blind so that God's power might be seen at work in him". If that is somewhat ambiguous, at least in translation, the punch line is crystal clear: "As long as it is day, we must keep on doing the work of him who sent me" (John 9: 3-4). So, whatever the philosophical answer, the practical one is that suffering is a fact of life and always provides a chance to express God's love. Certainly, whenever and wherever Jesus met it, he responded with indiscriminate compassion. You and I can do no better than that!

12   RELAX!

The grace of the present moment

Psalm 46:10: Relax… and know that I am God.

Have you ever said to someone "For heaven's sake, keep still"? Of course you have, and you've probably thought about saying it countless times. You're trying to change a particularly messy nappy but the baby won't stop kicking! The child you are looking after is a bundle of energy and doesn't give you a moment's peace. Your friend or partner has no sooner sat in their favourite chair than they get up to see to yet another 'pressing' matter. I'm sure we have all had our patience tested by someone who is irritatingly restless. (I'm not referring to children or adults with a serious mental or physical illness which makes them hyperactive; I have in mind the person who is healthy but habitually 'on the go'.)

We don't have to be advanced students of personality to realize that some people, either by temperament or genetic composition, are more active while others are more reflective; some mainly 'doers', others primarily 'thinkers'. Yet others, possibly the majority, are a mixture – busy people who nevertheless spend a decent portion of their time reflecting and trying to make sense of life.

Now some people may well not be as active as they should be and, in recent years, if they spend a lot of time glued to 'the box', are likely to be called 'couch potatoes'. Not that there's anything new about laziness. Indeed, it's an ageless foible. Judging from the number of Biblical proverbs censuring the idle, slothfulness was just as common in those days – but it was a hot climate, and who doesn't slow down when its sweltering?

More pressure, less time

However, isn't the greater temptation for most people nowadays to be *too* active, to be so busy that time for reflection is elbowed out? It's certainly a temptation that can be extremely hard to resist. Talk to people in just about any walk of life and what do you find? Teachers, nurses, social workers, council employees, shop-keepers, people in industry, commerce and pretty well every occupation – not least ministers of religion – tell you the same story: they are under ever-increasing pressure to produce more goods or better service in less time and with fewer personnel. Maybe, it's the price we pay for allowing a culture of competition to prevail over a culture of co-operation, but it undoubtedly leaves people less time and energy to pause and take stock.

Perhaps the prevalence of 'soundbites' is a symptom of our corporate rush. Those in power, or who aspire to it, argue with slogans rather than with carefully constructed discourse, largely because they are under great pressure themselves but also because they know their audience is unlikely to give the time or energy to listen to in-depth reasoning. The case for people to slow down and pause for calm and serious thought has never been stronger!

Insights from the Bible
Not surprisingly, the writers of the Bible were aware of both the underlying problem and the fundamental answer.

Consider, for example, Psalm 46.

Now the commentators differ about what prompted its composition. Some suggest it was uttered in gratitude for a specific deliverance. Others believe it was a more general affirmation of faith in God's continual protective care. Whatever the psalm's origin, its message is that God will always be a refuge in time of trouble. Whatever the tumult, however terrifying the circumstances or great the pressures, God has been and will be faithful. As the psalmist himself puts it:

> God is our shelter and strength,
> always ready to help in times of trouble,
> So we will not be afraid, even if the earth is shaken
> and mountains fall into the ocean depths;
> even if the seas roar and rage,
> and the hills are shaken by violence.

Whenever I read those words now, I recall my visit, a few years ago, to the remarkably well preserved ruined cities of Pompeii and Herculaneum. As you well know, when Vesuvius erupted, over 1900 years ago, the earth shook and spewed deadly ash and mud over the hapless citizens. But it still broods, now threatening the lives of hundreds of thousands.

After his words of reassurance, the psalmist beckons:

> Come and see what the Lord has done.
> See what amazing things he has done on earth.
> He stops wars all over the world;
> he breaks bows, destroys spears
> and sets shields on fire.

In short, however gloomy the prospects, God is utterly reliable. So, he implies, there's no need to let the fears and pressures of life overwhelm you. Therefore, RAPHAR!

Raphar!

I've used the Hebrew simply because there's no precise or adequate equivalent in English. You've only to compare a few versions to appreciate what a tricky task translators face. Depending on its precise form and context, RAPHAR can mean "desist, sink, loosen, let down, let go, be slack, be dejected, withdraw militarily". No wonder you find so wide a range of words and phrases in different Biblical versions, including "Be still" in the King James translation, through "Let be then" in the New English Bible, and "Stop fighting!" in the Good News edition. You and I may prefer to stick to the familiar "be still" whereas people in turbulent areas of the world might go for "stop fighting". But I'm going to offer a possibility I've not come across elsewhere but which I think is a perfectly legitimate translation of RAPHAR – "relax!" or, as younger people may well put it, "chill!"

"Relax" is certainly a fashionable word, judging from the spate of books and the popularity of classes on relaxation techniques (not to mention the tediously frequent exhortations to relax on Classic FM!). Increasingly aware of the damage excessive stress causes – and therefore extra costs – more and more businesses send employees on stress management courses where participants learn to relax therapeutically. There's now a legal obligation on employers to monitor their staff's stress levels. Not surprisingly, at least one NHS Trust has been threatened with legal action if it doesn't ease the pressures it puts on staff.

Now the language used, the physical environment involved and the techniques adopted may be light years from the world of the psalmist and from the practice of Jesus, who regularly withdrew from the hurly-burly to the quiet place, but the problem and need are essentially the same – how to cope with stress and the importance of regular relaxation.

The grace of the Present Moment
A key feature of effective relaxation is the ability to be truly aware both of oneself – including one's breathing – and of the present moment. One of my favourite concepts, indeed, is "The grace of the present moment". In fact, it's not just a concept I like but an experience I cherish.

How easy it is to be so wrapped up with the demands of life that we fail to notice the present moment! We find ourselves 'buzzing', either going over some incident in the past again and again or worrying over this, that and the other hurdle ahead. Even when we've paid handsomely to enjoy the present moment and are meant to be revelling in the concert or dinner, yesterday's gaffe or tomorrow's problem gets mixed up with the pianist's arpeggios or stares up at us from the steak! If only, we could discipline ourselves to be still, to *relax*, and appreciate the present moment!

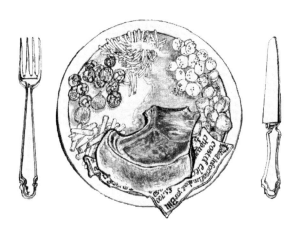

Of course, it's not always easy to do so. Especially if you've had a traumatic experience which persistently haunts you. Similarly, you may sometimes find it's virtually impossible to stop focusing on the future – such as when an exacting interview is imminent or you await the results of an important exam or medical test. If you're suffering from clinical depression, part of the illness may be that you simply cannot extricate yourself from a nasty memory or fearsome prospect. Focusing on the present moment can be extremely difficult.

Giving space

Enjoying the grace of the present moment is often, if not usually, enhanced by companionship. But, if we are honest, can it not also be spoilt by the presence of other people? You're appreciating a stunning view, imbibing the sounds and smells of sea or land, captivated by the joy of the moment, when someone makes what may be a perfectly reasonable and well-intentioned comment but in so doing sets off a chain reaction of thoughts and worries, and the therapeutic experience is wrecked!

When I led school trips to Israel, in one of the briefing sessions I would say: "I don't think I'm generally a prickly sort of person but I *shall* bristle, if you start talking about tomorrow's programme when we are meant to be appreciating today's possibly once-in-a-lifetime experience. There's a half-hour slot each evening to prepare for the next day's programme". There are times, would you not agree, when we need to give our companions space – space for them to receive the grace of the present moment, space to relax their souls.

Of course, there are times when it's right to dwell on the past and there are times when we need to prepare for the future. There's ample Biblical support for so doing, for the people of both Old and New Covenants were pilgrims, profoundly aware that God had been their shelter and strength and confident God would remain so.

Yet, as the Bible also reminds us – and indeed as Eastern religions affirm, with their emphasis on meditation and spiritual relaxation exercises – a positive, receptive awareness of the present is so important. There are times when we need to delight in the evening song of the blackbird, the butterfly on the buddleia, the sunshine between the showers, the beauty of the picture on the wall, the precision of the cricketer, the laughter of friends, the embrace of a loved one, or whatever joy the present moment offers us.

Know that I am God
You may well have visited the little church at Godshill on the Isle of Wight. I remember climbing the hillock on which it's perched one January when the sun was trying to break through the enveloping mist and the rooks were calling from the nearby trees. On entering the porch, my eyes lighted on a notice which read:

> 'SILENCE! Be still and know that I am God.
> Please talk to God before Mass
> and to each other after Mass.'

The notice contained the vital, second part of our text, 'know that I am God', thereby pointing us to the other, essential part of the antidote to stress which goes that crucial step further than many relaxation therapies. The psalmist knew that being still, letting go, ending strife, relaxing – however you like to translate his Hebrew – was not enough. Total spiritual renewal required a personal awareness of God, a deliberate offering of oneself to the divine source of beauty, truth and goodness – a deliberate exposure of one's innermost self, or soul, to the forgiving, cleansing, renewing power of God.

Isn't it ironic that church life can be so busy – so full of business and social functions – that its supreme role of providing spiritual renewal can be all but squeezed out? I wonder how many church secretaries go to bed on the 31st July thinking "Thank God, it's August tomorrow!" Does the treadmill have to turn quite so fast? Couldn't our church diaries be trimmed here and there? Apart from Sunday worship, mightn't it be wiser to organize our church life into, say, eight-week terms? Would it be so remiss to have at least one other 'August' built into the church calendar?

Slow down!
Certainly the first part of the psalmist's exhortation appears to be getting across in some quarters. You may have come across the leaflet which advocates 'tourism with insight and understanding'. One of the pledges supporters are invited to make is this:

"I want to take my time and avoid hectic travelling. I want to have more time to observe, to meet other people, and more time for my companions: more time to experience new things and take them back home".

You'll be aware that an increasing number of people are now 'downshifting' – turning their backs on the high-tech, high-stress demands of their jobs and trading income for the precious commodity of time. As one 'downshifter' explained:

"Technology was driving life faster and faster, and it became manic. In the end something had to give and I decided it wasn't going to be me... I wanted to reclaim those lost evenings and weekends... and have the time to engage in a better quality of life..."

If those two examples indicate the beginning of a shift in values, I say "rejoice!" At the same time, let's never lose sight of the second part of the remedy. Yes, the psalmist did urge his people to "raphar". But he added "and know that I am God". Relaxing in the presence of God (and there's no need to worry if our definition of God is vague – by definition, God's nature is beyond our comprehension, 'hid from our eyes' as the hymn puts it), relaxing in the presence of God is vital. But we should do so not to escape reality; but to help us manage better the business, and *busyness*, of contemporary life.

13   SOMETIMES OR ALWAYS?

A Christian response to relativism and absolutism

Which are you?
Are you a 'relativist' or an 'absolutist'? That's hardly a question you would put to the stranger sitting next to you in the bus. If you did, you'd probably be given a funny look! Yet the question actually refers to two very significant historic and contemporary options.

In case you are not quite sure what I'm asking, I'll put it in the form of a concrete choice.

A concrete example
Here is a young, female teacher. She falls in love with one of her students, a physically mature fifteen-year-old boy. They go out together, develop a mutually agreed intimate relationship and within two or three years get married.

Here is another teacher, this time a man working in a primary school. He's not been there very long before he starts subtly favouring certain pupils, wins their affection and confidence, and then starts sexually abusing them. He gets away with his misconduct for a time but is eventually caught out.

Now, according to the most recent government policy, irrespective of what the criminal courts decide, in terms of their careers both teachers are treated exactly the same: *both* are *banned from teaching for life.*

Putting aside what the courts might do, *career-wise* do you think the two teachers should be treated *differently* or *the same*? If you answer 'differently', in this particular instance at least, you are a 'relativist'; if you reply 'the same', in this particular case at least, you are an 'absolutist'.

All-pervading attitudes
Well, I hope that that scenario shows that my opening question refers to two attitudes which are anything but airy-fairy, two attitudes that actually shape very many features of contemporary life. Indeed, when articulated as 'relativ*ism*' and 'absolut*ism*', the

attitudes are all-pervading. They are a major element of the context in which the Christian faith (and indeed all faiths) is set and if we are going to respond sensibly to the world 'out there', we need to understand them.

Though not always *called* such – indeed the terms 'relativism' and 'absolutism' were applied only in the 20th Century – they have both been around a very long time. You can detect them in both biblical and classical literature. Protagoras, the Greek sophist of two-and-a-half millennia ago, is often regarded as the father of Relativism thanks to his dictum "Man is the measure (or judge) of all things". You can trace the existence, influence and fluctuations of both 'isms' throughout history. For the last forty years or so, however, the two attitudes have tended to polarize (with Christians in each camp), which makes it even more important that we are aware of what they stand for and how to respond.

Relativism explained

Relativism has burgeoned in the last fifteen years with over 140 of the 200 books published on the subject being written in this period. In essence, relativism is the philosophical idea that what is true or false, right or wrong, good or bad, *varies* from time to time, place to place, and person to person. So what people do in *one* setting is true, right and good for *them* but may well not be so for *everyone*. Nothing is inherently, permanently or universally true, right or good. The situation is arbiter. So truth, moral principles and personal behaviour are all relative – relative to particular circumstances, such as the culture, religion, customs or even inclination of the people immediately involved.

So, if one group believes Creation is ultimately the product of a Cosmic Intelligence but another group believes the existence and nature of the universe is purely accidental, the difference doesn't really matter. Both views are 'right' because truth is not objective but subjective, what people *say* it is.

According to the same line of argument, smoking could be viewed as 'OK' as long as most people believed it was physically harmless and socially desirable. Since the 1960s, however, and the gradual revelation that smoking is seriously harmful to both smokers and those close by, relativists would say the habit may now be wrong for the majority but is still not necessarily so for everyone.

So, in the realms of both belief and conduct, relativism claims truth and morality are not permanently and universally applicable but depend on the relevant situation.

Relativism's value

Now this attitude appears to have its merits, not least for our now pluralistic society. With our great diversity of ethnic groups, beliefs, values and practices – diversity spectacularly demonstrated in any London tube train compartment – with such human variety, we clearly have to come to terms with all sorts of ideas and customs. Surely, relativism implies, other people have just as much a right to their beliefs and practices as I have; *their* perception of truth and goodness may be just as valid as *mine*. *Moderate* relativism, it could be argued, encourages empathy and tolerance.

TRUTH

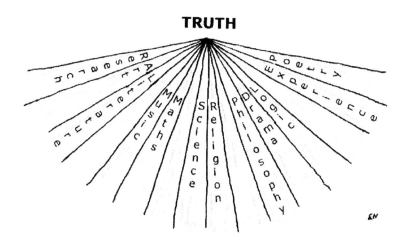

At a deeper level, too, relativism may well be of value. For one thing, it supports the assertion, which the philosopher Wittgenstein made so cogently, that there are different routes to our understanding of our world and our role within it. Vital to the process though science is, there are also other tenable routes to illumination – like philosophy or religion or art or poetry or music. In the 2006 series of BBC Reith lectures, Daniel Barenboim

103

argued powerfully that 'through music you can understand not only yourself but *the world*!' The relativist outlook acknowledges there are different routes to truth.

Relativism's weaknesses
Yet, for all its pluses, relativism has its serious weaknesses.

At a fundamental level, it threatens science. By claiming you can only make culturally determined observations about anything, relativism implies science is not *really* making objective, universally applicable statements about the physical world.

Philosophically, relativism is flawed. For, in its love affair with diversity, it belittles the whole notion of unity. It fails to recognize the fact that you and I, and our six billion or so neighbours, may differ hugely but we are all human beings with the same basic characteristics and needs, all sharing the one planet. It plays down our need of some concept of truth and morality that we can all recognize and live by! Relativism may be strong on human diversity but it is dismally weak on human unity.

Relativism can also be socially damaging. I live in Bath and I walk into the centre several times a week. The distant views are splendid and make me glad to live in such a city. But when I look down – to the bank by the hedge, to the gutters, at the pavements, into various nooks and crannies, and eventually reach the pedestrianized areas – I see discarded fag packets, plastic bottles, crisp bags, paper of every description, rotting food, all sorts of unmentionables and then, on the slabs and streets in the centre, blobs of spit and countless splodges of gum. Why is there such filth? The obvious answer is because people put it there. A partial answer is that there are not enough cleaning teams, an answer which raises questions about the council's priorities and citizens' willingness to pay for the job. But isn't the *underlying* reason for such filth people's inconsiderate carelessness? Such selfishness is as old as the human species but its current status is, in no small measure, due to unbridled relativism – the attitude that thinks, if not says, "I spit, I chew, I drop litter, I swig alcohol, I pee, I drive at speed, when I wish and where I like"; the attitude that claims 'anything goes'; the attitude that goes back to the Sixties' slogan 'do your own thing'; the attitude that denies civilized living demands at least a core of common values and mutual moral obligations.

Moderate Relativism may have its merits but in its extreme form, in theory and practice, it is socially divisive and corrosive. As the present pope has observed: "Recognizing nothing is definitive, [relativism] leaves as the ultimate criterion only the self with its desires… Under the semblance of freedom, it separates people from one another, locking each person into his or her ego".

Absolutism explained
Now let's focus on the second term, 'absolutism'. It's a word that's nothing like as widely used as relativism and is generally used very specifically. In the philosophy of religion, when it's spelt with a capital 'A', it refers to that which is ultimate and uncaused, so is used of God. In political theory it refers to the claim that a leader should rule without restriction. In ethics, it refers to values and principles deemed valid under any and every circumstance.

For my purposes, I am using it to refer to the attitude which underpins the three applications just mentioned – namely, the attitude that asserts there are beliefs and values, principles and practices, which are permanently and universally true and valid. In short, I am using the term absolutism to describe the attitude that is diametrically opposite to relativism.

Absolutism's merits and dangers
Like relativism, absolutism seems to have its merits. In theory, it does offer beliefs and values, principles and practices, by which all the diverse elements of humanity can live in harmony. At its best, absolutism offers the cement that can bind together fragmented humanity.

The snag is, people don't necessarily agree on what the absolutely crucial beliefs and values, principles and practices are. What's more, when one group insists *it* really *does* know the truth, another and another and another group *also* claims *it alone* is right. Worse still, such confident groups can be dogmatic and intolerant, prepared to defend and promote their perception by undemocratic or even violent means. From at least Old Testament times, there have been national, cultural, political, religious and moral absolutists who – albeit sincerely – have stopped at nothing in the quest to assert *their* view and *their* will. Hence many of the bloody battles of the Old Testament. Hence the Crusades. Hence one religious, or secular, war after another. Hence, recent religiously motivated terrorism whose perpetrators claim is their only way of challenging what they perceive to be the moral bankruptcy of Western secularism. In practice, absolutism can so easily degenerate into ruthless bigotry or callous violence.

Less dramatically, but no less undesirably, absolutism feeds authoritarianism – the attitude that says "I know best: it's not for you to question"; "Do this because *I* say so"; "'You do what I tell you or you'll be looking for another job". Of course there may be occasions when loving parents, wise teachers, responsible managers and all sorts of leaders have to make decisions without explaining them at the time, but good leaders will generally try to carry their charges with them. They will avoid the absolutism which rides roughshod over people's personal opinions, feelings and needs.

So moderate absolutism may also have its role but in its extreme forms is likely to be cruel and inhuman.

How might a Christian respond?
What, as Christians, are we to make of these two 'isms'?

I have already suggested it's important to understand the attitudes they represent and to be aware of their huge historical and contemporary influence. I have suggested we need to recognize that in their moderate forms they may well have a positive function whereas in their extreme forms be destructive. And I believe what I have said has been coloured by Christian values. But now, let's consider the teaching and example of Jesus more explicitly.

Jesus's attitude
Was *Jesus* a relativist or an absolutist? You could argue there was something of both in what he said and did. In comparison with the religious purists of the day, not least the Pharisees, he was a relativist. When it came to Sabbath conduct, for example, it's starkly clear he was no absolutist. For Jesus, the rules could be modified when human – or animal – need demanded. He respected the holy day, regularly attending worship in the local

synagogue, but he didn't allow scriptural regulations to interfere with compassion. "The Sabbath was made for Man, not Man for the Sabbath!"

When it comes to marriage, sex and divorce, one's first impression is that Jesus was an absolutist. The marriage bond was sacred so wedding vows had to be kept: "People must not separate what God has joined together". Yet we find him taking two different attitudes to divorce, one rigorous (where he sides with the Rabbi Shammai school) the other more liberal (where he favours the Rabbi Hillel view). In Matthew 19, Jesus goes so far as to say that Moses' teaching on the desirability of marriage "does not apply to everyone". And if John's story, about the Pharisees and lawyers throwing an adulteress at Jesus's feet, is any guide, Jesus certainly wasn't an absolutist. While not condoning her conduct, he stopped her being stoned to death and effectively forgave her!

On the question of taking revenge, Jesus took neither the traditional, absolutist, line – whereby you retaliated commensurately ('an eye for an eye and a tooth for a tooth') – nor a relativist line whereby circumstances determine your response ('it all depends...'). He took a totally different, *radical* line: overcome animosity with generosity – restore the relationship by 'going the second mile!'

His winning way
The more you explore Jesus' response to human problems and moral dilemmas, the more you realize that you simply cannot put Jesus into *any* camp! Jesus took a totally distinct approach, one that was in principle (though not usually in practice) simple and straightforward.

His winning way? The 'threefold love' formula. Asked which was the greatest of the ancient commandments, you know well that Jesus replied: "Love the Lord your God with all your heart, with all your soul, and with all your mind". The second most important, he said, was "Love your neighbour as you love yourself". In a nutshell, show respectful love for *God*, for *others*, and for *yourself*! This is Jesus' one absolute 'absolute'! As long as you keep solidly to this simple formula, you can be as flexible – as 'relative' – as circumstances require.

Our response

How, though, do you *apply* this world-saving formula? Usually with extreme difficulty. Often – not surprisingly, bearing in mind its application eventually took Jesus to Calvary – at great cost, intellectually, emotionally, spiritually, sometimes physically. Taking the way of Jesus seriously never has been, and never will be, easy.

But you know that already! So let me conclude by offering a few concrete suggestions.

I believe the Christ-follower should resist, by word and deed, *relativist* extremism. The 'it doesn't matter what you believe' outlook and the 'anything goes morality' are fragile, sandy foundations for any society.

I believe the Christ-follower should resist, by word and deed, *absolutist* extremism. Its dogmatism, authoritarianism, militancy and even violence cannot unite and sustain our confused and multicultural world.

Above all, I believe the Christ-follower should constantly try to apply the 'three-fold love' formula – loving God, others, and oneself. This will always need the sustenance of worship and prayer. It is often likely to require deep thought, serious research, honest discussion, time, toil and courage. But these costs are inevitable, for we live in socially diverse, technologically revolutionary, and culturally colourful times. There are no quick fixes when it comes to formulating principled but practical legislation on issues like abortion, assisted voluntary euthanasia, drug and alcohol use and abuse. There are no magic wands to wave when it comes to protecting people's religious sensibilities while allowing freedom of speech, or preventing terrorism while preserving liberty. Maintaining a free but caring and just society is intrinsically complex and difficult.

In a sentence, those who take the teaching and way of Jesus seriously, sanely and sensitively, have a special – maybe unique – role: this is to *try* to pilot our nation, indeed our world, between the dangerous sandbanks of relativism and the treacherous rocks of absolutism; and to do so aboard the good ship Threefold Love.

14   THE FIVE JESUSES

Unwrapping Jesus for the 21st century

Do you like looking in the mirror? Whatever your answer, when you look in a mirror, you see just *one* 'you'. Yet each of us is really a *series* of 'you's.' There was the 'you' conjured up in your parents' minds before you were born, a 'you' loaded with dreams and hopes. There's the present 'you' loved, liked (or otherwise!) by family, friends and contacts. One day, there'll be the 'you' of memory. But there is also the 'you' not even your nearest and dearest fully perceive, the 'you' only God knows, the *actual* 'you'.

What's true of you and me is also true of Jesus, though on a much grander scale. He, too, has been perceived in consecutive phases. And there's also an elusive Jesus. Let's now focus on each of them, in turn.

The Old Testament Jesus
The first Jesus could be called '*The Old Testament Jesus*'. You will be aware that, for centuries, the Jews looked forward to a 'Jesus figure', to a promised Anointed One of God (called 'Messiah' in Hebrew, 'Christos' in Greek). A vulnerable people, the Israelites yearned for a deliverer to free them from oppression and usher in the Day of the Lord. Mostly, they envisaged a politico-military saviour, only the odd prophet foreseeing a merciful servant.

So, when Jesus started his ministry, people's hopes were readily raised and they looked for signs that he really was the promised Messiah who would liberate them from their Roman masters. Such hopes, however, Jesus refused to foster because he knew he must disappoint them. At the same time, his understanding of God's intentions for humanity most definitely was coloured by his reading of the Hebrew scriptures, and the writers of the New Testament consistently put the Jesus Event in the context of the Jewish faith tradition. In short, the Old Testament makes a major contribution to the long build-up of Christian belief about Jesus. In a very real sense, there is an 'Old Testament Jesus'.

The New Testament Jesus

The second Jesus I call *'The New Testament Jesus'*. According to these scriptures, it isn't long after his baptism before Jesus becomes 'the talk of the town', at least around Galilee, and wins a following. Within three years, leaders of 'The Way', as the Jesus Movement is first dubbed, are jotting down notes about their experiences and zealously broadcasting their faith. Such is their impact that a scholarly Jewish activist switches sides becoming the Church's most articulate advocate, taking the Gospel overseas and founding clusters of churches.

Yet soon, these distant converts find themselves floundering, intellectually and socially. Who *exactly* is this Jesus and what does his life and death *really* mean? Just *how* should they live as disciples in alien cultures?

Vexed by such questions himself, Paul shares his thoughts in his pastoral letters, written between 20 and 30 years after the crucifixion. They contain plenty of robust reflection about Jesus's life and death as well as bold attempts (as in the one to Colossae) to put the Jesus Event into a cosmic context. But all Paul says about the physical origin of Jesus is that he was 'a descendant of David' and 'the son of a human mother'. There's no mention of a miraculous birth nor any hint that his mother was a virgin. Neither are there any miracle stories in his writings.

Now Jesus's resurrection is so 'real' for Paul that he argues 'one's faith is in vain' without it. Yet nowhere does he talk about an empty tomb and there's no indication that he's talking about *physical resuscitation* – though he does talk about the radically new 'resurrection body'. His focus is Christ's spiritual triumph and continuing presence. Certainly his about-turn on the Damascus Road ignites a blazing conviction that the crucified Jesus lives on.

Turning to Mark, chronologically the next New Testament author, we now find miracle stories abound, some where Jesus heals, others which suggest he overcomes the forces of nature. But there's still no story of a miraculous birth and Jesus's mother is portrayed in all-too-human terms. Furthermore, in the *original* version of Mark's Gospel, which ends at chapter 16, verse 8, the raised Jesus doesn't appear.

112

When, however, Matthew and Luke put pen to paper, respectively 50 and 60 years after the crucifixion, we find Birth stories, Baptism, Transfiguration, a string of Resurrection experiences and quite a number of other narratives, all painting an *increasingly theistic* picture of Jesus.

But it's the Gospel according to John, written between 95 and 100, which provides a thoroughgoing theistic interpretation. As the opening prologue so dramatically illustrates, Jesus is presented not just as the Son of God, sent at a particular time to a particular people: he is the divine Logos or Word, present with God from the dawn of creation! Jesus and God, indeed, are inseparably identified: "The Father and I are one", as the Fourth Evangelist puts it.

So, as we race through the evolution of the Christian scriptures, we find Jesus steadily elevated. To begin with, he is portrayed more as a very remarkable man in whom God is uniquely active, but by the time the Fourth Gospel is completed, some 70 years after his death, he is predominantly presented as God incarnate, a deity who visits planet Earth by means of a miraculous birth and who departs by the miracle of ascension.

The 'Unofficial' Jesus
The third Jesus, I suggest, is one who could be given the clumsy label '*The Non-canonical Jesus*' but I am calling *the 'unofficial' Jesus*. I have in mind the Jesus described in the documents produced around the same time as the New Testament but excluded from the 'canon' or selection the Church officially accepted.

The documents portraying the 'unofficial' Jesus add up to quite a weighty body of literature, a fragment of it popularised by the novel 'The Da Vinci Code'. To a considerable extent, this literature reinforces the witness of the New Testament. But it also adds some intriguing and, for the conservative Christian, rather disconcerting material, not least about the humanity of Jesus and his personal relationships. The honest student of Christian doctrine should not overlook the 'unofficial' Jesus. That said, this one is nothing like as significant in the grand sweep of history as the next Jesus.

The Credal Jesus

This fourth Jesus could be called *'the Credal Jesus'*. He emerges more than a hundred years after the death of Jesus when theology as we find it in the historic creeds begins to take root. Now, the Apostolic Fathers – such as Clement of Rome, Ignatius of Antioch, Hermas, and Polycarp of Smyrna – spark off a lengthy debate about the nature of Jesus and his relationship to God.

Eventually, the influential Bishop Irenaeus realises the debate could rapidly degenerate and cause a split in the Church – even deeper than that threatening the Anglican Communion today over the appointment of homosexual or women bishops. To halt the galloping threat of schism, Irenaeus takes a strong line, making his historic assertion: 'There is truth that is essential and necessary to the very being of the Church. This truth was given by Christ to the Apostles and is to be had from them alone'. Henceforth, no Christian is to question the original, earlier, current or future teaching of the Church, for its leaders, from the apostles onwards, have *infallibly understood and transmitted the truth!* Irenaeus's motives were honourable but his claim made the present ever after prisoner of the past, thereby hanging a millstone round Christendom's neck not even the Reformation could dislodge entirely.

What's more, Irenaeus acted as if the truth handed down by the apostles was crystal clear. But it manifestly wasn't for the debate simply hotted up, pausing only when the historic creeds were eventually 'cobbled together'. I use that phrase deliberately because the all-too-human bishops were only too ready, in their special assemblies (like that at Nicaea in 325), to use their fists as well as their minds in working out God's intentions!

Human frailty notwithstanding, the Creeds materialised and Jesus was proclaimed the incarnation of the holy God and the second person of the eternal Trinity of three persons in one God (though we should note that the word 'persons' *then* meant something more like 'facet' or 'mask'). These doctrines, along with everything else the Creeds declared, were binding and ever more strictly imposed so that those who challenged them were punished, excommunicated, or burnt at the stake, though in flames gentle enough to allow time for last minute repentance (an attitude to opposition no less ruthless than that practised today in states like Zimbabwe or Myanmar). The Church – the so-called Bride of Christ – has too often claimed a certitude that has triggered periodic eruptions of atrocious violence, not least in those diabolic ventures known as the Crusades. Some bride!

So mighty – and, paradoxically, insecure, one might observe – did the Church become that it could add what it wished to the Credal Jesus. In fact, in what became the Roman Catholic Church, the official pronouncements of Christ's earthly representative, the pope, were, in the 19th Century, declared infallible. Next, the position of Jesus's mother was further elevated: she was pronounced a permanent virgin (demanding tricky explanations about Jesus's siblings' conception), a postpartum virgin, and herself the result of an immaculate conception (a *normally* conceived Mary would have passed on Adam's sinful nature to Jesus). Finally, as late as 1950, it was decreed that Mary – again like Jesus – had been bodily assumed into heaven: the belief she was 'Mother of God' required *her* 'divinisation' to be completed. True, most Protestants don't accept these recent claims and the Free Churches evolved partly as a reaction against the excessive promotion of doctrine, but a complex Credal Jesus survives, a still solid bedrock of faith for many, a crumbling foundation for an increasing number.

So far, then, we have focused on four Jesuses – the 'Old Testament', the 'New Testament', the 'unofficial', and the 'Credal' – a Jesus built up over two millennia, in a process a little like the creation of an oil painting where the artist adds layer upon layer of pigment to complete the picture.

The Actual Jesus
Now for the Jesus who is *not* the product of a culture's dreams, *nor* one portrayed by disciples writing between 20 and 70 years after his death, nor one envisaged by unacknowledged observers, *nor* one enshrined in creeds and traditions... but the most elusive Jesus of all, 'the actual Jesus'.

Obviously, we cannot now, two thousand years later, expect to discover an image of this Jesus comparable to a sharply focused photo. Even if First Century copies, let alone the *original* Gospels and Letters, were unearthed, we should be little wiser because the New Testament writers were not primarily biographers. Their paramount purpose was to proclaim the significance of Jesus. Indeed, all four evangelists refer to no more than forty days of Jesus's ministry. Over the years, scholars have tried to rediscover

the actual Jesus. In the 19th Century, Albert Schweitzer made a valiant attempt in his tome 'The Quest of the Historical Jesus'. Since the 1990s, Biblical theologians belonging to the Jesus Seminar have been trying to reach a consensus on what words and actions in the Gospels they believe really *are* those of Jesus. But the actual Jesus remains tantalisingly hard to pin down.

Not that his elusiveness should surprise us. For it seems the Actual Jesus did not particularly wish to be clearly defined. The Synoptic Gospels of Matthew, Mark and Luke show us a Jesus who, true to his own teaching on humility, was consistently self-effacing, reluctant to make any claims about who he was. (Yes, there are the great 'I am' sayings in the Fourth Gospel, but these, Biblical scholars assert, almost certainly reflect Christian belief 70 years after the Crucifixion, rather than the words of Jesus). And, the Gospels tell us, that when people sought his help, Jesus didn't ask for any statement of belief but just a gesture of personal trust.

Yet, if my personal observations are anything to go by, many people among the 90% of the population who have no serious contact with a church, have the impression that to be a Christian you have to accept a clearly defined bundle of beliefs. Some of these they may accept while others just don't seem to 'click' – and so they reject the whole package.

There are people 'out there' who would dearly like to take Jesus seriously but whose intellectual integrity deters them from accepting some of those beliefs about him that traditional Christianity deems essential. Sometimes, I feel the Church's complex doctrines *dis*courage the life-transforming 'Jesus experience'. Sometimes, I ask myself: in its zeal to *mother its faith* might not the Church inadvertently *smother the Christ*?

What do we *really* believe about Jesus?

If we are ever to persuade a significant proportion of the population 'out there' that faith in Jesus Christ is vital to their and all the human family's well-being, I am convinced one vital thing we must do, is to think through – radically and rigorously – what we *really believe about Jesus*. We must ask ourselves: which of our inherited beliefs are crucial, which questionable, which revisable, and which untenable? Which wrappings should we keep and which discard?

We already do select what, and what not, to believe. Even those who claim every word of the Bible must be taken at its face value, do not do so in practice: they use their personal judgement over, for example which ancient Jewish laws to keep (if any such person protests they *do* heed every instruction of the Bible, show them Leviticus, chapter 15!) and they choose which instructions of Paul's to observe (like what to wear in church). Protestants don't accept certain Catholic doctrines. And Free Churches give doctrines and creeds a low priority, allowing members freedom to make up their own minds.

Profoundly grateful though we may be for the prophets of the Old Testament, the authors of the New, the bishops and scholars who devised creeds and doctrines, hasn't the time come to follow their example – and distil the truth about Jesus for *our* times?

But whatever Christ of Faith we do present must, I believe: be rooted in the Jesus of History; cohere with such God-inspired paths to truth as science, logic and philosophy; and engage people's real spiritual needs and experiences.

A Christology for today
Let me close by briefly offering an understanding of Jesus I believe just might appeal to people for whom traditional doctrines and language don't 'gel' – a personal 'Christology for today', if you like.

I believe the '*actual Jesus*' was:
fully human
but a truly remarkable and unique person who:

had a profoundly perceptive understanding
of the human condition;

was a highly skilled exponent of moral wisdom;

and a spiritual leader with:

the *courage* to challenge unjust and restrictive
religious conventions;

the *compassion* to smash through ethnic, social and
cultural barriers;

the *love* to satisfy people's deepest needs, whatever the
personal cost.

He possessed wisdom, goodness,
and love of such sublime quality

- and was so totally open to their Ultimate Source -

that we can wholeheartedly endorse the Biblical assertion:

'God was in Christ'

I believe:

this same Jesus also lives on as a spiritual presence,
able to help us overcome our persistently selfish inclinations
and become the kind of people we are meant to be;
and, if taken seriously by the world at large,
would transform the human scene...

I believe Jesus is:
truly worthy of our lifelong commitment

What are *your* innermost beliefs about Jesus?

15 WHAT'S *YOUR* IDOL?

The Christian antidote to idolatry

Exodus 20:5 *(The Second Commandment):*
'Do not bow down to any idol or worship it, because I am the Lord your God and I tolerate no rivals'

Luke 12, first part of v.31*:*
'Instead, be concerned with the Kingdom of God...'

When did you last break the Second Commandment? You can't remember? Of course not, because you have *never* broken it! How could you, as you don't believe in idols!

Images and artefacts

Certainly, when we skim through the mass of Biblical references to idols and idolatry, we might conclude that the idols they describe really do belong to a bygone era. Idolatry of that kind may still be practised in certain tribal societies where animism persists but it's quite alien to life as you and I live it. *We* don't behave like the carpenter described in Isaiah 44:13 who "takes and measures a piece of wood, outlines a figure on it with a piece of chalk, and carves out a handsome human figure" which he then treats as his personal god to help him escape life's trials. No, the idolatry of around three millennia ago is a world apart from secular, scientifically-orientated 21st Century Britain! So here's one Commandment about which we may feel quite relaxed, if not smug!

Or is it?

Think for a moment about the rising popularity of that huge range of beliefs and practices in Britain which bears the umbrella title 'occultism'. Judging from the expanding space in bookshops and libraries given to astrology, witchcraft and allied practices, not to mention burgeoning web sites and dedicated magazines, veneration of human artefacts allegedly invested with superhuman powers – idolatry of the obvious kind – thrives. What's more, its cousin superstition is equally alive and kicking, and not just among fisherfolk and footballers. So the ancient prohibition against idolatry continues to challenge a flourishing feature of human conduct.

But the Second Commandment doesn't *really* impinge on *you and me*! We might avoid walking under a ladder, or touch wood when we make an optimistic comment, or have a sneaky look at our horoscope when we're waiting to see our dentist or doctor, but otherwise our conscience is blissfully clear... At which point I think it would be nice of me to finish!

Everyday idols
The trouble is, the Bible doesn't let us off the hook so easily. For its writers don't, in fact, confine idolatry to the superstitious worship-of-objects variety. Great chunks of what especially the prophets and wisdom writers asserted focus on the broader type of idolatry, on those everyday things and activities which can so readily take us over, distorting our values and priorities, maybe spoiling relationships and promoting damaging conduct – in other words, things and activities which have the potential to become idols.

Now both the First Commandment, "Worship no god but me" and the Second, "Do not make for yourselves images of anything in heaven or earth... Do not bow down to any idol or worship it", refer most obviously to idolatry of the narrower 'rival-gods' type. But I think we may justifiably infer that they also apply to any conduct or life style which effectively dishonours God.

'Second' Isaiah – called such, you'll remember, not because of the relative height of his eyes, but because he was someone different from the writer of chapters 1 to 39 – 'Second' Isaiah is equally firm. In chapter 44, he advises that idolaters will be let down and humiliated by their manmade idols and, worse still, their idolatry will lead them to "close their eyes and minds to the truth".

Prophet Amos repeatedly denounced citizens' ceaseless clamour for luxury goods because it encouraged traders to cheat and the rich to ignore the poor, both of which were contrary to divine law.

Large numbers of Biblical proverbs expose the dreadful personal and social consequences of excessive indulgence, especially of sex and alcohol.

What people craved and did, prophets and sages of the Old Testament warned, could so easily take the place of God and all that God represents.

The apostle Paul takes up the theme in one of his pastoral letters to the church at Corinth. Here, he urges members not to 'worship idols' in the narrow sense nor to make an idol of such things as food, drink or sex. They should not behave like their distant ancestors who, as his own Hebrew scriptures recorded (Exodus 32:6) 'sat down to a (religious) feast which turned into an orgy of drinking and sex'.

Significantly, some five hundred years later, one, if not the, spark that ignited the religion of Islam was Muhammad's shock on seeing the hundreds of idols openly worshipped in Mecca.

'The sin of idolatry'
So the scriptures of the three Abrahamic faiths – Judaism, Christianity and Islam – all agree that idolatry, whether of the 'graven image' or the 'indulgent behaviour' type, is taboo. Both deflect us from our true purpose and fulfilment as human beings.

The author Susan Howatch includes an illuminating incident on idolatry in her contemporary novel, 'A Question of Integrity'. In a conversation between a priest associated with a community centre and one of his clients who has lost her way in life, the writer has the cleric explain: "Human beings need *some* kind of God in order to feel whole, and if they lose touch with THE God, the right God, they can't rest until they've put something else in his place and elevated it into a false god. The spiritual vacuum always has to be filled. It's the way of the world. It's another part of the human condition and in religious language is called 'the sin of idolatry'".

Idols today

Let's now move on to the present and ask just what are the idols 21st Century society worships? What are the things, attitudes and practices that can all too easily deflect you, me and people generally, away from the things, attitudes and practices in life that really matter? Precisely what might discourage, or even stop, people from growing spiritually and socially, from becoming all that they might otherwise be? What features of life *now* have the potential to become idols?

You had better forget your Sunday roast! On the other hand, I, too, am looking forward to my lunch. So I'll focus on just five potential idols in a little depth before merely touching on a few others. You'll think of plenty more. Mind you, many of today's idols have been around centuries, if not thousands of years.

Food

Having mentioned lunch, isn't *food* one potential idol? To state the blindingly obvious, none of us would be here without it, and we should certainly be profoundly thankful for its nurture and variety. And yet, judging from the explosion of interest in its preparation – evident in the surfeit of TV programmes (with their godlike experts), magazine articles, and cookery books on the subject, for many people food is an obsession, an idol. Some 'foodies' pay vast sums to satisfy their craving for new and way-out tastes, oblivious to the air miles or even animal cruelty that may be involved. In 2007, a group of super rich gourmands (defined as 'gluttons' in my dictionary) met in Bangkok paying £15,000 each for just one meal! (That said, shouldn't we all remember the sobering reality that *every* meal involves the deaths of some plant or creature or several of both?)

Alcohol

Isn't another potential, if not actual, popular idol *alcoholic drink*? Now history shows that alcohol has always been a 'hazardous chemical' and certainly was two and half thousand years ago in the Israel-Judah region. The Book of Proverbs paints a string of colourful word-pictures of what happens when people have a free and easy attitude to alcohol. Then, as now, large numbers of people didn't seem to care how they behaved or what harm they did to others, as long as they had their endless supply of booze. Read about those depraved scenes in a modern translation and

124

you find they could be describing scenes common in contemporary Britain, with its adulation of intoxicating – literally, 'poisoning' – liquor.

One thing that disturbs me, however, about the present situation is how many church people who did not drink twenty, thirty of forty years ago and were perfectly content to live alcohol-free lives, have subsequently joined the band-wagon. Now most of them, I assume, generally manage to discipline their alcohol intake but by using the drug at all, isn't one effectively supporting our booze-sodden culture? Church-going Christians should surely be countering it, exposing the immense damage alcohol does, in terms of disease, casual or forced sex, marriage and family break down, work absenteeism, street pollution, crime of all sorts, road injuries and deaths.

'Stuff'

Food and drink, however, are just two examples of a bigger idol whose name is *Consumerism*. Granted, we all need goods like clothes and fuel to survive. I doubt if any of us would fancy walking or driving to church naked on a cold winter's day, or, I hasten to add, even on a hot summer's day! But do we *really* need 'stuff' in such massive quantities and in such extravagant variety, as the constant bombardment of adverts implies? Do children? Because marketing gurus increasingly aim their fire at younger boys and girls, putting pressure on them to keep up with images of how they should look and what they should own, pressure, according to the think-tank Compass, that results in stress, depression and low self-esteem. Children, the Compass study claims, are being forced to grow up too soon, with lacy underwear targeted at pre-teens and toys such as the 'Bratz secret date collection' promoting champagne glasses and 'date night accessories' to *six-year old girls*. According to a Mintel report, "Britain has become a nation of unashamed big spenders… Glitz and glamour, jet-setting around the world and splashing out on champagne and designer clothes are no longer the reserve of the rich and famous".

Do we *really* need such luxury goods, let alone the gadgets or even downright junk commercials and junk mail urge us to buy? The simple answer is we don't, and if you have ever visited a society where people have enough to live on but not the grotesque surplus many modern Britons possess – excess that commonly banishes the car from the garage – you soon learn that affluence is emphatically not vital to happiness. Resisting the idol of consumerism, however, is not easy for so many goods undoubtedly are useful, wholesome and attractive. Just *where* do you draw the lines between need, desire and extravagance? And what would happen to the jobs market if we cut down too drastically on buying? Yet the Second Commandment's solemn prohibition, echoed in Jesus's sober warning 'beware of greed of every kind', surely still holds.

Celebrities

Isn't a fourth major, contemporary idol – and one readily used to foster consumerism – *the cult of 'celebrity'*? The trouble is, celebrities influence others, not necessarily for the good of society. Often treated as experts and authorities on matters way outside their specialism, fans uncritically heed every word that falls from their lips. This has become so serious a problem that a charity called Sense About Science has been set up to advise and correct celebrities whose misguided support for special foods and diets, or medicines and treatments, is based on false science and therefore misleading if not dangerous. In the Radio Times, Nicholas Lyndhurst of 'Only Fools and Horses' fame told the interviewer why only fools fall for the cult of celebrity, and it's time it stopped. Beware! Even the best of celebrities are human and therefore fallible.

Even religion!

A fifth potential – or actual – idol is, yes, *religion*! The prophets habitually slammed the communities of their times for abusing it. Claiming to speak for God, Amos protested: "I hate your religious festivals. I cannot stand... your burnt-offerings and grain-offerings... Stop your noisy songs! ... Instead, let justice flow like a stream and righteousness like a river that never goes dry". Rituals had become more important than moral integrity and compassion. Years later, during Jesus's ministry, it seems the Pharisees (as a group) took more interest in religious regulations than in the religious priorities of justice, mercy and walking the way of God.

But who are we to criticize? Cannot such subsidiary features as dogma, rituals, institutions, buildings and organization, *still* boot out God's priorities? Sadly, even religion can become an idol!

Everything from science to sex!

Now I can but flick through a few final but important potential, if not actual, idols. For all its obvious benefits, *science*, can be one, in the form of scientism. It can so easily be treated as if it were guaranteed to answer humanity's needs and woes, instead of something that will only serve our true interests when subjected to strict moral values and principles. *Gambling* is another very real idol and, thanks to the rash of new casinos, promises to be so for many more, in spite of its often terrible social impact. For all their positive value, *sports and hobbies* can become idols, all-consuming passions for those involved. For several centuries, *economic growth* has been an idol of capitalist societies: only in very recent years have we begun to grasp the fact that our finite planet simply cannot survive on *un*sustainable development. Oh, I nearly forgot: *sex*! In a loving, committed relationship, this strong, natural instinct can be an enriching feature; but well we know it can so easily become an obsession, a volatile idol that threatens health, relationships and personal well-being.

Put God's ways first

Yes, idols abound *today* as in Biblical times. Now as then, they can be alluring and potent. We may not notice when a wholesome object or desire or interest is becoming an idol. We certainly need to help each other in detecting and tackling our potential or actual idols.

But isn't the only reliable and long-term antidote to all idolatry to keep our eyes on Jesus – on the vision and values his life and teaching offer humanity?

In chapter 12 of his account, Luke tells of a – presumably agitated – man in the crowd saying to Jesus: "Teacher, tell my (if he added an expletive the author has edited it out), tell my brother to divide with me the property our father left us". Refusing to arbitrate in a family dispute, Jesus chose to home in on the root cause of their argument and offer a timely word. "Watch out and guard yourselves from every kind of greed; because a person's true life is not made up of the things he owns, no matter how rich he may be" (Luke 12:13,15). The point is reinforced with the parable of the rich retiree who, looking forward to an indulgent life style, is suddenly struck down with a fatal illness.

After the parable, Luke, logically and eloquently, continues with material that Matthew includes in his Sermon on the Mount anthology. It is, of course, the eloquent passage about the futility of getting in a tizzy about food and clothes, and taking a tip from God's care for birds and flowers. "So", Jesus concludes, "don't be all upset, always concerned about what you will eat and drink" – that's what 'pagans' worry about, that's what those who shut out the God dimension obsessively hanker after. There's no need to panic because "Your Father knows that you need these things" – cherish the Earth and it will meet your needs. (Luke 12:29-31)

"Instead, be concerned with God's kingdom", with whatever really matters, with doing what God requires – like being merciful, having a pure heart, working for peace, controlling your anger, forgiving those who wrong you, loving even your enemies. *Put God's ways first,* isn't Jesus saying? *For that's the way to resist life's idols.*

16   DOES IT ALL ADD UP?

Three secular views on the purpose of life and a Christian alternative

Have you ever wondered what the purpose of your life – at the very deepest level – might be? Of course, you have!

Whether procreated by design or accident, you and I have completed a shorter or a longer portion of the one journey that every human, along with every other living thing, must tread. The going may have been mainly smooth or mainly rough or some of each. No matter, whatever the trek has been like so far, we know it will sooner or later end. *But does it all add up?*

You will also have extended the question asking whether what we call 'life' – all living things and what they need for their survival – are part of a meaningful whole. Does our planet... our galaxy... the Universe... the 'Multiverse', maybe... all make some kind of sense?

A colossus of a question

You may well have asked this colossus of a question as quite a young child and caused your parents some intense head-scratching. You may have discussed it at various stages in your school career. As a secondary school teacher, I found pupils were profoundly interested, even if their answers were sometimes cynical and dismissive. You may have found circumstances thrust the question to the forefront of your mind – perhaps when you were finding your daily work seemingly pointless or someone close to you was suffering intensely.

The composer Gustav Mahler was deeply affected by the misery that confronted him as a child. In the space of a year or so, several of his young brothers and sisters died. He remembered how their little bodies would be taken gloomily through the back door. Yet, at the selfsame time, in the front of the pub where he lived, there would be laughter and jollity. Such bitter contrast confused him, confusion reflected in his music on which one commentator has remarked: "Mahler was both a 'major' and a 'minor' person, constantly swinging between optimism and pessimism in his understanding of life".

You and I may not personally have had so many close encounters with tragedy, but we may well be deeply affected by what we read, hear and see in the media – perplexed by the ubiquity of human wickedness and the seeming futility of countless people's daily lives. In total contrast, we may well have wondered about the mystery of life in some moment of quietness, in the middle of the night or amid uplifting scenery.

For most of the time, however, we are too busy to think about life's over-all significance: there's the 7.47 train to catch; we have to meet the boss's impossible deadline; family or neighbours need to be looked after; a hundred-and-one duties clamour for our attention. Yet sometimes we *do* wonder what our own life and life in general are all about.

All we can attempt to do
As with every metaphysical question – questions beyond the scope of total comprehension – all we can attempt to do is search for possible answers, ones that make a measure of theoretical and practical sense, ones made in faith.

You will be well aware that all sorts of 'big' answers have been put forward in response to the question "Does it all add up?" Some of them are passionately promoted and have been extremely influential. Some of them, many people would say, are socially or morally subversive. There are certainly far too many to consider in one sermon! So all I shall do now is to consider *three major secular answers* before offering *a radically different standpoint based on Christian belief.*

The 'negationist' view
One, fairly common secular response to the question "Does it all add up?" is what I have chosen to call the *'negationist'* view. I have in mind those attitudes which deny that human life, along with the entire cosmos, has *any* deep purpose.

Now some 'negationists' are arrogantly dogmatic. I remember a so-called academic declaring over the radio: "There simply is *no* purpose either to the universe or to human life". Not only did he fail to support his assertion, but he made an elementary logical error in treating opinion as fact.

Others of this persuasion, however, are sincere and reasonable people. The great mathematician, philosopher and political radical of the first half of the 20th century, Bertrand Russell, once remarked "I think the universe is all spots and jumps, without unity, continuity, coherence or orderliness". Would he nowadays have made such a rash statement, following the surge of knowledge about the universe cosmologists have provided in the last fifty years? I hope not! For in this period, theoretical physicists have shown us that the cosmos is held together by laws and forces which are constant and universal, making the whole an awesomely coherent unity. This being the case, isn't it reasonable to infer all the constituent parts of the universe have at least physical significance? And if the resources and potential of planet Earth require Homo sapiens to unlock them, haven't humans therefore at least a measure of significance?

Theoretically, yes... And yet, when I think of the those hundreds of Ethiopian women I saw, some years ago, bent double by the heavy bundle of eucalyptus branches they had gleaned for fuel from the mountain forests surrounding Addis Ababa – a gruelling journey they spend several hours making day after day, year in and year out – when I reflect on the squalor and ill-health hundreds of millions of my fellow humans suffer for their entire lives, I find myself wondering whether life *does* have the meaning philosophical reflection might suggest it should. I find myself sympathizing with the gloomy observations of the philosopher recorded in the Book of Ecclesiastes:

> "Life is useless, all useless... You spend your life working, labouring, and what do you have to show for it? Generations come and generations go, but the world stays just the same... The sun still rises, and it still goes down, returning wearily to where it must start all over again... God has laid a miserable fate upon us. I have seen everything done in this world, and I tell you, it is all useless... It's like chasing the wind!" (Ecclesiastes 1: 2-5,13-14)

So don't let's be too harsh on the dejected 'negationist'. For aren't there times when we, too, feel life is, as one cynic put it, no more than "birth, copulation and death"? Maybe we can recall at least moments when we could truly sympathize with those who suicidally retort "life for me b. well *doesn't* add up"? And yet,

131

apart from those lowest of low moments, isn't there always a remnant of our being that feels life *is* worth clinging to and must make *some* sort of sense?

The reproductionist view

A second secular view about life's purpose could be labelled the *'reproductionist'*. Now there is a mild version of this view in the Bible where the childless woman is frequently scorned and even blamed for her failure to bring children into the world. But the truly 'reproductionist' view is much more recent and describes the conviction that humans, along with every other form of life, exist solely to reproduce themselves. It's an idea which stems from a particular interpretation of the theory of evolution and one that enjoys widespread popular support, ironically among many who openly renounce having children themselves!

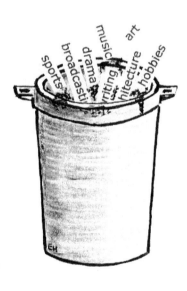

But if (and it's a huge 'if') evolutionary theory really does imply life's purpose is to reproduce, then huge facets of life become redundant and meaningless. In fact, everything not directly or indirectly related to reproduction of the species becomes valueless. If, for any reason, you don't have children you are a parasite, using up resources which the reproducers and their offspring need. Once you have passed on your genes and have nurtured your progeny long enough for them to repeat the process, you, too, are redundant. If our only significant function is to reproduce, a gigantic swathe of human endeavour (like art and elegant architecture, music and drama, writing and broadcasting, sports and hobbies) are superfluous.

What's more, any evolutionary theory that ignores the contribution to human survival of the spiritual factor is, I suggest, fundamentally deficient. History, not least that of modern times, shows that when the 'soul' of a people is spiritually sick, they indulge in self-destructive behaviour. Where there is prejudice, fear and hatred, such evils as persecution, conflict and even genocide are likely to follow. Whereas, when the 'soul' of a people is healthy, reconciliation, peace and co-operation are more likely to happen. In other words, important though genetic superiority might be to survival, even more important is spiritual fitness, and any evolutionary theory that neglects this factor is, surely, flawed.

When it is appropriate and possible, human reproduction is obviously important, as the theological poem of Genesis chapter 1 implies:

> "God created people male and female, blessed them and said 'Have many children, so that your descendants will live all over the earth'". (Genesis 1:27-28)

But to say reproduction is the sole, ultimately significant purpose of life is a repugnant notion, grossly devaluing all sorts of human activity and belittling the very existence of a huge number of people.

The materialist view

My third major and extremely popular secular view about life's meaning could be called *'the materialist'*. This view embraces several ideologies and attitudes.

One of these is Marxism-Leninism. Karl Marx, you will remember, believed that history is shaped by 'material need', which means that wealth holds the key to power. If oppressed people are to have wealth and power, however, they will only get them by force. Some fifty years later, Lenin and his fellow Bolsheviks took Marx at his word. But in their quest for wealth and power, expressed through massive industrialization and agricultural collectivization, they brutally debunked religion and the vital spiritual nurture it offers.

Not surprisingly, when Marxism-Leninism collapsed in the USSR, there was a mass return to religion and the dimension of life it represents, a return celebrated by the glorious restoration of the great Moscow Metropolitan Cathedral. In very recent years, however, it seems Russia has been increasingly suffering the downside of another form of materialism: capitalism. Unbridled, this ideology, too, is blatantly materialist, fostering the notion that the more people buy and possess, the happier they will be.

As we well know though, the buzz 'retail therapy' and consumerism generally might give you, soon vanishes. For all its material affluence, our technologically developed part of the world is shot through with social problems and personal emptiness. Material things can be good and wonderful but their acquisition is a totally inadequate basis for life. "Watch out", Jesus warns our materialistic culture, "and guard yourselves from every kind of greed; because a person's true life is not made up of the things he owns". (Luke 12:15)

Religious views

So much, then, for secular ideas about life's purpose. Whatever their merits, however, the three I selected are, I believe, defective and inadequate. We need a more substantial understanding of our human role.

So, *can* religion can help us? Perhaps. I say 'perhaps' because when it comes to religion we are still trapped by uncertainty. "What we see now", as Paul so eloquently put it, "is like a dim image in a mirror... What I know now is only partial" (1 Corinthians 13:12). Bound by the limitations of our five senses and our brain's powers of imagination, we can do no more than make speculative statements of faith. So the question really is: can religion give us the best 'working hypothesis' about our mortal life's purpose within the universe and, more relevantly, on our planet?

Their broad agreement

Time prevents any serious exploration of what the world's major religions say about life's purpose. But my own studies suggest they broadly agree that you and I are here to discern and do whatever we believe accords with the nature of the Ultimate Reality commonly called 'God'.

A Hindu teacher expresses this conviction with these delightful words:

> "O the beauty of the universe!
> How did you, my Lord, come to create it?
> In what outburst of joy
> Did you allow your being to be revealed?
> But I know you need *me*
> In your play of creation".

The same underlying belief is found in the familiar Jewish text I quoted earlier where God, it was believed, commissioned humanity to manage the planet.

You have only to skim through the Holy Qur'an to learn that Islam claims the supreme human duty is to submit to God. Surah 2, clause 112, declares:

> "Whoever submits his whole self to Allah and is a doer of good – He will get his reward with his Lord."

The Christian claim

But what does the faith based on the teaching, life and self-giving of Jesus claim is life's main purpose?

The writer of the Letter to the church at Ephesus asserts in chapter 2, v.10:

> "God has made us what we are, and in our union with Christ Jesus he has created us for a life of good deeds".

And doesn't that text echo so much of what we find in the New Testament? True, the letters are packed with theology, especially in their earlier chapters, but there's always a moral sequence. Being in touch with God carries with it a moral imperative.

This crucial connection we find sublimely demonstrated in the life style of Jesus. Keeping in regular touch with God through his synagogue worship and times of personal reflection, he also immersed himself in the world around him – caring, loving, healing, forgiving, doing all manner of good deeds.

It may seem unsophisticated, if not naïve, but the Christian answer to the question 'Does it all add up? Has life any ultimate meaning?' is, I believe, extraordinarily straightforward. Granted, we cannot possibly *know* what is the ultimate purpose of ALL-THAT-IS. Yet, taking our cue from Jesus, we can very reasonably *believe* what is life's here-and-now purpose. We

135

may affirm it is to expose our soul (our innermost self) to the all-pervading, life-transforming presence of God, and, thereby, be empowered to make the world a tiny bit better.

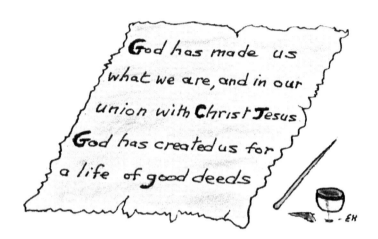

God has made us what we are, and in our union with Christ Jesus God has created us for a life of good deeds

17   AS WHOLESOME AS HONEY

Proverbs from the Bible – mainly about speech

"Never get lazy people to do something for you; they will be as irritating as vinegar on your teeth or smoke in your eyes" (11:26).

"Beauty in a woman without good judgment is like a gold ring in a pig's snout" (11:22).

"Stupid people always think they are right but wise people listen to advice" (12:15).

"When hope is crushed, the heart is crushed, but a wish come true fills you with joy" (13:12).

"Laughter may hide sadness for when happiness is gone, sorrow is still there" (14:13).

"Righteousness makes a country great; sin is a disgrace to a nation" (14:34).

"Better to eat vegetables with people you love than to eat the finest meat where there is hatred" (15:17).

"Go to the ant, you slob [my translation], and learn from her ways!" (6:6).

More than a mini-dictionary of quotations!

As you will have spotted, those pithy and perceptive sayings all come from the Biblical Book of Proverbs. This collection of wise thoughts, put into writing around two and a half thousand years ago and forming part of the so-called Wisdom Literature, is a rich source for speakers and writers searching for the choice phrase or concluding punch line. But, as those of you familiar with it will probably agree, the Book of Proverbs is very much more than a mini-dictionary of quotations. It is, in truth, a collection of profound and penetrating observations, which well deserve a place in a sacred text whose theme is God and God's concern for human life, in its richness and diversity. When read with an open mind and receptive heart, there is much within its pages which stabs the conscience and nourishes the spirit.

Viewed in the light and wisdom of Jesus, some of the ideas and values of the book are questionable, if not false. But the more you reflect on its contents, the more you appreciate its overall percipience and relevance. When read in a modern version, it is often uncannily appropriate to life today, addressing *our* personal and social problems, *our* hopes and aspirations, *our* foibles and failures, *our* innermost thoughts and attitudes.

Anyhow, it's this section of the Bible I should like to dip into now. Although the compilation is not very tidily arranged and large chunks of it consist of separate and unrelated sayings, there are some long passages dealing with particular subjects and certain themes recur.

A fountain of life
One favourite theme is the matter of speech – what we say, when and how we say it, and its effects. Indeed, when preparing this sermon, I read Proverbs right through and discovered over seventy verses dealing with this subject, seventy observations and reflections that "hit the nail on the head" today as much as they presumably have done over the last two-and-a-half millennia.

Here are a few sample verses, samples which are indeed fascinating and even entertaining but which, being preserved in the Bible, are likely to offer spiritual nurture.

> "Sensible people accept good advice. People who talk foolishly come to ruin" (10:8).

> "A good person's words are a fountain of life, but a wicked person's words hide a violent nature" (10:11).

> "The more you talk, the more likely you are to sin. If you are wise, you will keep your trap shut" [my translation] (10:19).

The author of that one clearly knew how easy it is to "open your mouth only to put one foot, or even both feet, into it"!

> "A good person's words are like pure silver; a wicked person's ideas are worthless" (10:20).

> "Righteous people know the kind thing to say, but the wicked are always saying things that hurt" (10:32).

The second part of that one is unquestionably true but I'm not so sure about the first bit for there are times when even the best of people are tongue-tied. On balance though, wouldn't you agree that a decent person is far more likely to say the kind and fitting thing?

Dealers from Hell?

There's a candid passage in the sixth chapter which claims:

> "Worthless, wicked people go around telling lies. They wink and make gestures to deceive you, all the while planning evil in their perverted minds" (6:12,13).

The writer may well have had in mind unscrupulous 'dealers from hell', of whom there were plenty, according to the prophets of the time. As if to underline the point, the writer continues:

> "There are seven things that the Lord hates and cannot tolerate: 'A proud look, a lying tongue, hands that kill innocent people, a mind that thinks up wicked plans, feet that hurry off to do evil, a witness who tells one lie after another, and a man who stirs up trouble among friends'" (6:16-19).

Note how closely thought, word and deed are bound up with each other, the evil thought so easily prompting the mean word and the mean word so readily provoking the nasty deed.

Gangs and prostitutes

Repeatedly showing us that human behaviour in those days was pretty well the same as it is today, one contributor warns those who might be tempted, to beware the persuasive chatter of the gang-leader:

> "Don't give in when someone says to you: 'Come on… Let's attack some innocent people for the fun of it! They may be alive and well when we find them, but they'll be dead when we're through with them! We'll find all kinds of riches and fill our houses with loot! Come and join us and we'll all share what we steal'" (1:11-14).

You and I are hardly likely to be tempted in that sort of way, but some of our fellow citizens find themselves under intense pressure – sometimes in the form of a knife at their throat – to join the criminal community. And, as our newspapers keep reminding us, too many of them find themselves yielding to the bully boys' or girls' promises and threats.

There are also long sections where the Book of Proverbs warns against the prostitute trying to seduce men with 'her smooth talk'. Sex, paid for or free, is another major area of life where speech can have a powerful, and sometimes devastating, impact on people's conduct.

Assuming we have managed to resist gang pressure and sexual temptations, who of us has not been seduced into *some* sort of sin through clever argument or persuasive charm? Who of us has *never* used the power of speech in the service of evil rather than good?

'Gossip is so tasty!'

Or who of us never engages in negative and destructive idle gossip? Again, the writers of Proverbs display an embarrassing familiarity with human nature.

> "Gossip is so tasty – how we love to swallow it!" (18:8 and 26:22)

they observe but, with equal candour add pertinently,

> "Anyone who spreads gossip is a fool" (10:18).

> "Whereas the wisdom of the righteous can save you",

they continue,

> "you can be ruined by the talk of godless people" (11:9).

How many people, whose reputation and life has been wrecked by malicious and false media reporting, would add a wry 'amen' to that!

> "It is foolish to speak scornfully of others. If you are sensible, you will keep quiet" (11:12).

'The Lord hates liars!'

There is much in Proverbs about telling the truth and lying.

> "When you tell the truth, justice is done, but lies lead to injustice" (12:17).

> "A reliable witness always tells the truth, but an unreliable one tells nothing but lies" (14:5).

Just think of the number of people who have been falsely convicted and imprisoned in recent years, many of them because witnesses or even police officers have lied. When I was little, I was often told that if I lied, sooner or later my lies would find me out – little did I know then, that someone else had made the same point, more than a couple of thousand years earlier, in the proverb:

> "A lie has a short life, but truth lives on for ever" (12:19).

Indeed, the Book of Proverbs effectively declares that telling the truth is fundamental to the fabric of civilised human life; it is nothing less than God's intention for his people:

> "The Lord hates liars, but is pleased with those who keep their word" (12:22).

In the light of Jesus's example and teaching, we might prefer to say 'The Lord hates *lies*'. But we would surely not dispute the evil, corrosive nature of lying except, of course, for the *white* lie told in the interests of love – love, according to Jesus's scale of values, being the over-riding imperative of God's rule. We well know that kindness sometimes demands we pretend to like someone's garish new dress they're proudly showing us, or pretend to enjoy the yukkish cake someone has made 'specially for our visit'!

Hot tempers and kind words

There's quite a lot of food for thought in Proverbs for people with a hasty temper. In fact, it's extremely harsh towards them:

> "People with a hot temper do foolish things; wiser people remain calm... If you have a hot temper, you only show how stupid you are" (14:17,29).

Apt words for every age since, including ours, with its road rage, cycle rage, plane rage, soccer rage, shopping trolley-rage and all the other circumstances where people tend to 'lose their cool'.

As so often, however, the compilers balance their words of condemnation with those of commendation, spotlighting an evil attitude but also focusing on its opposing good attitude:

> "A gentle answer quietens anger... Kind words bring life... Patience brings peace... Intelligent people think before they speak..." (15:1,4,18 and 16:23).

> "Kind words are like honey – sweet to the taste and good for your health" (16:24).

There are many other timeless observations and warnings about the use and dangers of the spoken word but I'll round off with just three:

> "The customer always complains that the price is too high, but then he goes off and brags about the bargain he got" (20:14).

> "If you know what you are talking about, you have something more valuable than gold or jewels" (20:15).

> "An honest answer is a sign of true friendship" (24:26).

The power of the tongue

Yes, the Book of Proverbs is a priceless collection of wise sayings – many of them entertaining, many of them perceptive, most of them as true and applicable as when first spoken and written down. The sayings cover just about every facet of life you care to mention, not least the precious but perilous gift of speech. The book shows how, in its own words:

"death and life are in the power of the tongue" (18:21).

And this time-honoured collection surely asks the reader: how do *you* handle this gift?

Whether our speaking is a power for evil or for good, causing sadness or generating happiness, destroying or building God's rule, depends – like every other feature of human conduct – on the state of our soul. But, we can rest assured that when we welcome the Spirit of Jesus into our innermost selves, our words *will* be as good and wholesome as honey!

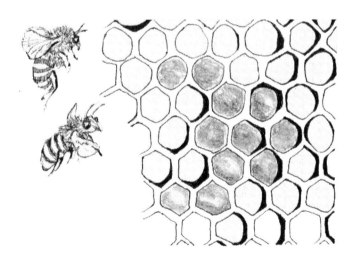

18   POLES AND AXES!

A Christian perspective on the Human Situation

You will discover the text of the sermon at the end! Meanwhile, its title is 'Poles and Axes', yes 'poles and axes'! And what could be clearer? There's really no need to pull a "What-on-earth's-he-on-about-face?" Even as I speak, you realize I am constructing an analogy (fully aware, I hasten to add, that analogies are risky tools for any communicator because they can so easily distort and mislead).

The sermon's framework
The picture I would like you to visualize, as the framework of this sermon, is actually four poles with two axes, which, at their halfway point, cross each other at right angles. One further feature of my analogy is that the four poles have a magnetic quality, able either to attract or repel. Picture, if you like, a big plus sign with a magnetic pole at each of its four extremities.

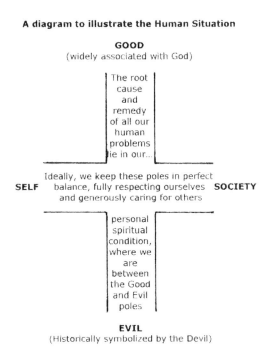

A diagram to illustrate the Human Situation

GOOD
(widely associated with God)

The root cause and remedy of all our human problems lie in our...

SELF   Ideally, we keep these poles in perfect balance, fully respecting ourselves   **SOCIETY**
and generously caring for others

personal spiritual condition, where we are between the Good and Evil poles

EVIL
(Historically symbolized by the Devil)

So much for the analogy. What, more importantly, is the truth I hope the analogy will help to illumine? It's the nature of the 'human situation'. The two axes represent two fundamental *aspects of the human situation* and the poles represent *the major factors that influence each aspect.*

Clearly, the very term 'human situation' suggests we are dealing with a matter that concerns everyone, everywhere.

The vertical axis

Now, I will try to unpack my analogy, beginning with the vertical axis. Its upper pole I label 'Good', its lower pole, 'Evil'. This axis represents the spiritual conflict between the two constantly waged in everyone's 'soul' or innermost self, the battle being human involves. It is a model portraying what personal experience, observation and Bible all tell us about one major feature of the human situation.

What experience and observation tell us

Personal experience and observation show us that both poles may certainly *attract* us. In the course of a day, we may sincerely wish to do what is right and good yet also find ourselves tempted to do what is wrong and evil. But life also teaches us that both poles may also *repel* us. Regrettably, we all too often find we are unwilling to pay the price of doing what is good. Mercifully, we generally find the likely consequences of doing what is evil not worth the candle. But whichever pole is attracting or repelling us at a given moment, we are always at *one* point on the Good-Evil axis.

What's true of ourselves, it would seem is also true of our six billion neighbours. They, too, are perpetually torn between good and evil. The media leave us in no doubt about the universality and power of the Evil pole. Unfortunately, the power of the Good pole doesn't usually get a fraction of the news space – such as the cheering fact that, in Britain, every month 300,000 people freely give blood for the sake of total strangers.

The Bible's testimony

The great collection of literature we call the Bible, and embracing over a thousand years of experience and observation, also amply testifies to the conflicting pulls of Good and Evil.

144

Take the chronologically earlier creation story found in Genesis 2. After the Lord God is said to have made the universe, he formed a man. At first the man was surrounded by a beautiful garden situated in Eden and everything was good. But before long, the man was tempted to disobey God's instructions and chose to do evil. Now you and I may not go along with the idea of original sin to which the story gave rise, but the parable nevertheless conveys the fundamental truth that humans are born with a capacity for both good and evil.

To which the Law books that follow, also testify. While they show the early Jews acknowledged their spiritual fragility and need of rules to live by, the very fact they spent time and energy devising them shows they were confident that people would, to some extent, heed them. Judging from the range and realism of their laws, those lawmakers were profoundly aware of the bipolarity of the human condition.

As were the writers of the Wisdom literature. In both homely and public contexts, goodness is extolled and evil censured, as these two proverbs show:

> "Good people will be remembered as a blessing, but the wicked will soon be forgotten". ((Proverbs 10:7)

> "Righteous people know the kind thing to say, but the wicked are always saying things that hurt". (Proverbs 10:32)

Like the prophets in general, Isaiah was in no doubt about people's spiritual vulnerability: "Every word that passes my lips is sinful and I live among a people whose every word is sinful". (Isaiah 6:5) Yet he also perceived people's immense potential for good: "On Zion, my sacred hill, there will be nothing harmful or evil". (Isaiah 11:9)

No one has ever been more conscious of the human capacity for wickedness than Jesus, from the moment the crowd threatened to throw him over the cliff to his torturous death on a cross. Yet he consistently spotted the image of God in people, even in the most unpromising of characters.

145

The apostle Paul knew first-hand the volatility of the human situation. In his letter to the Roman Christians, he describes his own 'soul battle' between conscience and instinct. "I don't do the good I want to do", he cries, "instead, I do the evil I do not want to do'". (Romans 7:9)

So personal experience, our observation of life, and a diversity of Biblical writings all agree about the human condition: we are neither essentially good nor essentially evil but torn between the two poles and day by day a mixture of both.

The horizontal axis
Now, let's think about the horizontal axis. The left pole I label 'Self', the right, 'Others'.

Once again, these poles can both attract and repel. We can love but we can loathe ourselves. We can like but we can hate others.

Unlike the 'Good' and 'Evil' poles, however, I suggest that there's no intrinsic value, or moral, difference between 'Self' and 'Others'. Judging from his endorsement of the precept to "love your neighbour *as you love yourself*", Jesus appeared to give them equal weight.

Before and after his ministry though, certain people have sincerely believed they were being extra holy, by not merely denying themselves normal pleasures and comforts but actually hurting, or even mutilating, themselves. In fact, a wide range of individuals and communities has practised such asceticism.

If you have been to Israel, you may well have visited the site of one such community, at Qumran. It's a blisteringly hot, lonely spot (at least it was when I was there) situated in the Judaean desert close to the Dead Sea. The modern tourist can readily imagine how austere was the life of the group that chose to live there, away from the hustle and bustle of town life. Judging from his rough clothes, basic food and stark message, John the Baptizer was one of ascetic outlook.

Later, there were the 'stylites' whose extreme self-denial led them to spend their lives perched on pillars in the desert, enduring all sorts of miserable discomforts. As writer Karen Armstrong

146

has graphically disclosed, harsh asceticism – including self-mortification in which you whipped yourself until your back bled – lived on in the British Roman Catholic monastic tradition well into the second half of the 20th Century. And asceticism still continues in some parts of the world. I remember meeting a hermit in Lalibela, Ethiopia. He lived in a tiny cave next to those famous churches carved out of the solid rock, day in and day out denying himself even an arm chair in his quest for spiritual excellence.

Now all this extreme, self-inflicted deprivation may show an admirable measure of 'mind over matter' and offer a salutary contrast to our self-indulgent materialism. But, we are bound to ask, is it *really* spiritually enriching, let alone socially beneficial? While Jesus did deny himself in many ways during his ministry and withdrew from mainstream life for brief interludes, the purpose of such denial and withdrawal was to enhance his mission, not to gain merit, let alone a kind of heroism.

No; faithful to his own scriptures, Jesus said we are actually to *love* ourselves. For we are each wonderfully made, each infinitely precious, each, as the apostle Paul put it, "a temple of the Holy Spirit". The 'Self' pole is an important and worthy one and a wholesome pride in our unique selfhood is basic to our human fulfilment.

Am I my brother's keeper?
At the same time, being truly human is also to care profoundly about others, as the Bible again makes plain.

Whether fact, yarn or some of each, the well-known story of Cain and Abel raises the critical question: "*Am* I my brother's keeper?" (Genesis 4:9) The blunt response, and Cain's subsequent punishment, reflect the Hebrew conviction that self-serving individualism is totally unacceptable, for we are all members of a community with solemn obligations to it.

We find the same principle underpinning the mission of the prophets. Appalled at the dishonesty, fraudulence and self-serving greed of his compatriots, Amos protests: "You are doomed ('doomed, doomed' as Frazer in Dad's Army so memorably pronounced it), you that twist justice and cheat people of their rights!" (Amos 5:7) Their only hope, he warns them, is to take God and his moral demands seriously, to change their mean ways and care for each other.

Returning to Jesus, while he persistently acclaimed the infinite value of the individual per se, he also spelt out that the individual's duty extended not just to Jews but outcasts, gentiles, enemies, even Samaritans – in other words, the whole world!

New Testament Letters endorse the same 'golden message'. James repeatedly advises church members of their social obligations. "My brothers... Suppose there are brothers or sisters who need clothes and don't have enough to eat. What good is it your saying to them, 'God bless you! Keep warm and eat well!' – if you don't give them the necessities of life?" (James 2:14-16)

Our personal experience, our observation of life, and the Bible, all show we are only truly human when we allow *both poles* of the horizontal axis to shape our lives, when we fully respect ourselves and generously care for others.

The model's implications
But what does our understanding of the human situation, represented by our model, imply for our Christian witness?

I believe the Jewish-Christian perspective on the human condition has two vital messages for the world at large.

The first message
Firstly, that *both the root cause and the remedy of our personal, local, national and global problems lie in the spiritual state of every member of the human species.* It is this aspect of a person's humanity that determines attitudes and conduct and, because we all have some kind of effect on those around us, determines the quality of our shared life. So, where you, I, anyone, is located on the vertical axis is of critical importance to our own and society's well being.

But how on earth do we communicate this vital message? Having generally dismissed religion, the great majority of people seem oblivious to the good it might offer for the benefit of all. For all its intellectual questionability, its organizational quaintness and its advocates' fallibility, religion remains the one and only global

148

institution whose supreme purpose is to nurture the human spirit – to help people resist evil and reach for the good, with all the priceless personal and social dividends this yields.

Yet so many, highly intelligent and knowledgeable people – in government, law, the media, the healing and social services, even in education – appear blind to the pivotal role of spiritual health and nurture!

Yes, a few do 'see the light' offering convincing diagnoses and prescriptions for humanity's malaise. According to its mission statement, the National Curriculum is at least supposed to put children's spiritual development first. When interviewed on Radio Four's Today programme, former army chief Sir Mike Jackson said that "if you really wish to understand why wars happen and why victors torture captives, you have to start with the human condition". Rounding off his superb series on 'The Power of the Planet', Iain Stewart concluded: "It's not planet Earth we should worry about – it will survive and eventually recover as it has done before – what we need to worry about is *us*!'

Such sane analysis is all too rare, so many 'experts' coming up with every sort of explanation and cure for our corporate ills *except* the one that underlies them all, the human condition, the state of people's soul, or innermost self. Tackle that and we might begin to get somewhere!

The second message
With the horizontal axis in mind, the second message I believe our Jewish-Christian understanding of the human situation should offer, is that *both individuality and society are equally important.* For we are only truly human when we cherish our selfhood and our social nature equally.

Regrettably, there are those who promote a one-sided understanding of what we are. Certain biologists have so pushed the 'selfish gene' notion that huge swathes of the population now assume we are biologically programmed to be predominantly self-serving, and to live accordingly. Apart from the fact certain other biologists point out that there is also much in the evolutionary story that indicates a *propensity for co-operation,* should one simply snap one's fingers at the three thousand years of spiritual experience, reflection and insight embodied in the Jewish-Christian story, not to mention that of other belief systems?

The Jewish-Christian tradition asserts that the 'self' pole and the 'others' pole are equally important so that any individual, party or government which excessively elevates one at the expense of the other has got things seriously wrong and will fail. The human situation demands that, at every level, governments strive to *balance* the interests of individual and community.

MESSAGE 1: cause and remedy of all human problems: spiritual

MESSAGE 2: individual and society: equally important

A concrete application

I close by offering just one concrete example of how our two-fold understanding of the human situation might work out in practice. You'll be able to think of other examples.

We may not all pay income tax yet, one way or another, all of us pay some tax. But I wonder in what spirit we do so! Now we may not like the actual form filling and may not like the way a portion of our tax is spent. But if our whole attitude is resentful and grumpy, are we not being selfish, giving way to the Evil pole rather than reaching for the Good pole? Aren't we also thinking too much about the Self pole at the expense of the Others pole?

Yes, we should 'love ourselves' sufficiently to try and generate enough wealth to be financially independent (health and personal circumstances permitting), but we are also 'members one of another' and therefore have an obligation to our 'neighbour' – which means paying taxes for their benefit! So, if self and neighbour really are equally important, it suggests to me that, on average, the rate of total tax we pay should be 50% of income. Spent judiciously, that extra sum in the public kitty could markedly improve many, now neglected, features of our communal life.

A text that says it all!

The Jewish-Christian understanding of the human situation – that to be fully human we are involved in a continual struggle between good and evil, and between the interests of our self and that of others – is a vital key to the happiness of every individual and the harmony of the world at large. So, one way or another, we must go on helping people to live by the commandments:

"*Love the Lord your God*" – the source of Goodness –

"*with all your heart and soul and strength and mind*" and

"*Love your neighbour as you love yourself*".

(Deuteronomy 6:5 and Mark 12:30; Leviticus 19:18 and Mark 12:31)

19   FOES OR FRIENDS?

The roles and interaction of science and religion

Who was right: the second century Greek astronomer Ptolemy or the 15th century Polish astronomer Copernicus? You and I know the answer immediately. Many comparably educated people of the 16th century, however, would have given the wrong answer. They just could not accept the word of the Italian scientist Galileo, who, in his book, "Dialogue on the two Principal Systems of the World", declared that what he saw through his giant telescope proved, beyond any reasonable shadow of doubt, that Copernicus was right! Indeed, as we well know, Galileo's conviction that the Sun, and not the Earth, is the centre of the solar system, got him into dire trouble with the Church authorities. In fact, in 1632 the Inquisition ordered him, under threat of torture, to deny his claim. What's more, it wasn't until 1989, some three-and-a-half centuries later, that the branch of the Christian Church involved, officially caught up with what was widely known for a very long time, that Galileo was correct all along!

That story provides a telling introduction to the subject I invite you to think about now, namely, the relationship between science and religion. For much of the 20th Century, the two co-existed fairly peacefully. But in recent years, at least in popular thinking, they have increasingly become regarded as foes.

To make our exploration manageable, I am posing two specific questions. One: *what are their distinctive roles?* Two: *how should they interact?*

A profoundly significant subject

Before going any further, a disclaimer: whereas I believe I am qualified to speak on religion, I am *not* a qualified scientist- so I'm at a disadvantage. However, I am reasonably well read in the philosophy of science and have long been interested in cosmology. Moreover, I feel the relationship between science and religion is so intrinsically important that I should still explore it.

What's more, isn't their relationship also sociologically important? For the way people perceive science and religion, both separately and together, affects many facets of their personal and communal life. If either discipline is misunderstood or misrepresented, idolized or trivialized, society is impoverished – its education curricula, its legislation, its values, its quality of life and much more are liable to suffer. We are focusing on a subject profoundly significant in both principle and practice.

The roles of science and religion

So now to question one: *what are the distinctive roles of science and religion?*

The role of science

First, science. Those of you with at least a smattering of Latin know the root of the word 'science' is 'scire', meaning 'to know'. So science is about knowledge. It is about knowledge gained by observation and experiment, knowledge that is critically tested and systematized, knowledge that has passed the tests of verification or falsification. Yet it is also knowledge open to question and modification or repudiation: it is always provisional.

Because of the characteristics I have just described, science is not *directly* concerned with *every* kind of knowledge.

You might make a case that emotional knowledge (that you 'know' you love someone and he or she loves you, for instance) is partially verifiable by an observer but can you ever truly know how two other people feel about each other? You may offer a scientific description of the physical symptoms of love (such as the blush and the racing pulse) but you cannot dissect the feeling itself.

The Biblical claim, movingly expressed in Handel's Messiah, that "I know that my redeemer liveth", is a statement about a perceived experience the detached observer can neither verify nor deny, and therefore not the concern of science. When someone makes such a claim, they are making a *meta*physical statement and therefore (whatever an individual scientist may personally believe) one that is outside the scope of science per se.

"They don't know right from wrong these days!" Individual scientists may personally be extremely concerned about moral principles and contemporary values, but these are not the subject matter of science itself.

154

"I can't explain why, but I just *know* that painting is stunningly beautiful!" Our sense of beauty, and our aesthetic opinions generally, may sometimes be widely shared, but that doesn't make them objective and open to scientific investigation. Science may contribute indirectly to aesthetic satisfaction through, for example, the synthesis of new chemicals for painting or picture restoration, but aesthetics itself lies outside the scope of science.

If I understand it correctly, the aim of science is to deepen our knowledge about the observable, measurable and testable physical or material world rather than the predominantly subjective worlds of love, belief, morality and beauty. And, ideally, scientists achieve their aim with absolute integrity, allowing neither prejudice nor personal gain, let alone private or public pressure, to deflect them in their quest for truth. That said, like the rest of us, scientists are intellectually and spiritually fallible and conditioned by a range of cultural, economic and perhaps even genetic factors.

The role of religion
Now, let's think about the role of religion. As you have heard often enough, the Latin root of the word could well be 'religare' meaning 'to bind'. True or not, the concept is surely apt, for every religion does demand commitment. The religious adherent 'binds' him- or herself to a particular community and set of beliefs and way of life in order to nourish the spirit or innermost self.

Like science, religion has its own method of achieving its goals. In its services, worshippers are confronted with what, or who, is *worth* their binding commitment. Through their personal prayers or reflections disciples galvanize their moral resolve. By studying their sacred writings, adherents gain insights into truly good, or 'holy', living. Through its long tradition of encouraging art, music and literature, religion deepens people's understanding of the human condition and offers them a vision of a better world. Together, these activities aim to deepen believers' respect for creation, to sharpen their conscience, to intensify their empathy, to extend their compassion, to fortify their will – in short, to develop their spiritual awareness and performance.

Science and religion, then, each have a distinctive and vital role.

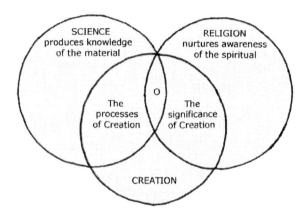

A Venn diagram suggesting how Science, Religion, Creation and its origin (O) interrelate

Thank God for honest science!

So I, for one, thank God – and I hope I am not so arrogant, or foolish, to prescribe exactly what the designation 'God' should mean to you or anyone else, though notions of ultimate truth, goodness and love will probably be part of our thinking – I, for one, thank God for honest science and its countless beneficial outcomes.

Think of all the medical treatment, perhaps life saving, that you and I have received from conception onwards – and even to facilitate conception for some people. Think of the ways we can now access gigabytes of information or communicate instantaneously with people across the globe. Think of the array of everyday gadgets which make life easier or more enjoyable. Let's be truly grateful for the good and rich harvest of science and its partner, technology.

Be grateful for honourable religion!

So, too, I thank God for honorable religion – for me, Christian faith in particular – and its own countless, beneficial outcomes.

Think of the kindness, understanding, forgiveness, and encouragement you have received from people whose spirit (or innermost self) has been imbued with the quality of wisdom and love found in full measure in Jesus. Think of the supportive fellowship of the churches to which you have belonged. Think of the spiritual enlightenment and nurture you have imbibed through services of worship. Think of the inspiration and vision that great religious buildings, beautiful rituals, historic and contemporary music, art, and literature have imparted to you. Be aware of those precious moments when these media of religion have done their job well and, in the words of the apostle Paul, filled:

> "your minds with those things that are good and deserve praise: things that are true, noble, right, pure, lovely, and honourable". (Philippians 4:8)

Let's be truly grateful for the good and rich harvest of religion and its partner, faith.

The interaction of science and religion

Question two: *how should science and religion interact?*

Keep them separate?
One view is that they should be kept totally separate. This is because each has its own definable role and there are no overlapping concerns. This is the so-called NOMA principle, NOMA being the acronym for 'no overlapping magisteria'. Keeping science and religion strictly within their own domains avoids confusion and conflict.

To my mind, this is an attractive and sensible standpoint. However, it may sometimes be tricky to decide whether an area of life belongs to the House of Science or the House of Religion. And when it comes to the ultimate question, 'what set off Creation?' – was it some kind of 'supreme intelligence', or was it a totally autonomous accident, that caused the infinitely tiny 'singularity' to explode and become the still-expanding universe – the two domains inevitably interact. So strong are human curiosity (the motor of science) and human hunger for significance (the motor of religion), that science and religion are both bound to be involved.

Let them fight it out?

Radically different from the NOMA view that science and religion should each keep strictly inside its own 'house', is the view, or attitude, that the two should 'fight it out' for dominance, not least when it comes to understanding the origin and story of life. Claiming the Bible is the literal word of God and, therefore, should be taken, from cover to cover, at its face value, religious fundamentalists dismiss the theory of evolution outright and vigorously oppose scientists who promote it.

In the opposite corner, secular fundamentalists, with equal dogmatism, ridicule any suggestion that the evolutionary process just might ultimately derive from an intelligent source – even though the process functions according to physical laws present from the moment of creation, and has engendered development from single-celled organisms to the staggeringly versatile, and now 'Earth managing', 'you' and 'me'.

Such is his contempt for religious faith, professor of chemistry Peter Atkins said recently (on Radio 4's 'Sunday' programme, 21st September, 2008): "I am willing to enter into dialogue but only so that I can stamp out religion". Egged on by such populist academics, many people today perceive science and religion as implacable foes.

A third way?

So, some say "keep science and religion well apart". Others claim they are foes locked into conflict which only one will win. But you and I feel there *must* be a third type of interaction.

I looked up the word 'science' in my hefty Concordance of the Bible, not really expecting to find any reference to it at all. To my surprise though, there are actually two mentions, both translated as 'knowledge' in modern translations. According to Daniel 1, verse 4, King Nebuchadnezzar expands his royal court by skimming off the cream of his Israelite exiles, in particular young men "of good looks and at home in all branches of knowledge". In his First Letter to Timothy, chapter 6 and verse 20, Paul urges the young minister "to avoid the profane talk and foolish arguments of what some people wrongly call 'knowledge'". So, we might infer from these texts, leaders should choose broadly educated advisers and inexperienced ministers should be careful to whom they listen! Sound advice, but not immediately relevant to our quest.

Then I looked up the word 'religion'. Guess what! There were a mere three mentions, one in Acts, two in the Letter of James where "genuine religion" is defined as taking "care of orphans and widows" and "keeping oneself free from corruption". Good advice, but still not very helpful.

The reason for the dearth of explicit Biblical material on our theme is simply that science and religion were not understood then in the way they are now. Such science as there was, was speculative rather than experimental. Religion was so bound up with everyday life that it just wasn't thought of as a separate entity. So we have to dig deeper.

Timeless values from the Bible

Awe, gratitude and humility
When you take the whole thousand-years-plus sweep of the Bible, you pick up a sense of awe at the size and splendour of Creation. We find such awe: in the theological poem of Genesis 1; in many of the psalms; in the Book of Job when, for instance, the Lord is said to reply to Job in his misery:

> "Who are you to question my wisdom
> with your ignorant, empty words?
> Stand up now like a man
> and answer the questions that I ask you.
> Were you there when I made the world?
> If you know so much, tell me about it..." (38:2-4)

In the Sermon on the Mount anthology, we find Jesus extolling the bounty and reliability of nature. One detects a sense of awe in the first chapter of Paul's letter to the Christians of Colossae when he tries to put the Jesus Event in the context of Creation.

Writing solely as scientists and economists, the authors of the groundbreaking book 'Natural Capitalism' reached a conclusion remarkably similar. It is only with an attitude "of humility and reverence before the world", they claimed, "that our species will be able to remain in it".

Sadly, there are religious extremists who pick out and grossly inflate particular texts for their own purpose: hence 'dominion theology' which justifies Man's right to exploit creation solely for his own indulgence; hence 'prosperity theology' that promotes the simplistic idea that those who prosper necessarily enjoy God's favour. But mainstream Christians take the Bible as an entity, perceiving its dominant response to Creation as one of awe, gratitude and humility.

Love and justice
A further constant value of the Bible is compassion. At first, it was to be confined to the local tribe. Later it was extended to 'the foreigner in your midst'. Only in the teaching and attitudes of Jesus, did it come to mean universal love and justice.

So the vital, timeless values we glean from the Bible are *humble respect for Creation, love and justice for humanity*. And these, surely, are what should shape the interaction between science and religion.

What a prophet today might say

With those two core Biblical attitudes in mind, I wish to finish by imagining what a prophet today might say – first to people of religious faith; then to scientists; and finally, to both.

Implications for people of religious faith
To people of religious faith, might not a prophet today say something along these lines? Take heed of what genuine scientists tell you about the way Creation, especially planet Earth, actually works. Don't take the Bible so literally that you defy an understanding of the physical world built on billions of person-hours of observation, testing and theory refinement. There's a surfeit of things to admire, of 'miracles' in the everyday world ('admire' and 'miracle' coming from the same root) without your needing to believe Jesus really did walk on water or turn water into wine without the presence of grapes. Be thankful for the knowledge and understanding of our astounding habitat that science has given us and must go on supplying, if our species is to survive.

Implications for scientists

To scientists, might not a prophet today say something like this? Use your immense knowledge and skill wisely and respectfully, as servants rather than masters of truth. Don't be seduced into using them in the service of government or commercial schemes that ravage the planet or impoverish its people. Don't allow yourself to be bribed into distorting your evidence. Bear in mind that your knowledge and understanding are always provisional. Take heed of what learned and wise people, not least those of mature religious faith, advise is good and right and wise. In broad terms, while *you* reveal the *'is'* of Creation, remember that *religion*, at its best, reveals the *'should be'*.

Work hand in hand as friends

To both scientist and religious believers, might not a prophet today say something like this? Pool your knowledge and understanding, your values and wisdom, and do your utmost to apply them generously and fairly for the benefit of *all* your six billion brothers and sisters. As never before, the world needs you both... Where you must, agree to differ. Otherwise, work hand in hand, as friends.

Honest science reveals the 'IS' of creation

Honourable religion reveals the 'SHOULD BE' of creation

20 BLESSING OR CURSE?

A candid consideration of the use, non-use and abuse of alcohol

Is it a blessing, a curse, or something of both? I refer to alcohol. Whatever the answer, what should our attitude be as Christians, people commissioned to be the 'yeast in the dough', the leading good influence in society?

Useful stuff

If you have been a patient or visited a hospital in recent times, you will be aware of the gel dispensers stationed in every corridor and ward that staff, patients and visitors alike are expected to use to curb the spread of harmful, perhaps lethal, bacteria. You will also know that the vital ingredient in the gel is a form of alcohol. As a bactericide, alcohol is indisputably a blessing.

A huge range of other products – including medicines, anaesthetics, dyes, paints and perfumes – contain some form of alcohol. True, it's used in explosives that can mutilate and kill, though even that application can also be used positively, as in quarrying. So, as a manufacturing agent, far more often than not, alcohol is useful stuff, a blessing. So it's silly to rubbish alcohol itself.

Changing views

The tricky and urgent question, however, is whether the 'leisure' use of alcohol in food, but supremely in drink is a blessing, a curse, or something of both.

Over the years, the opinion of Christians has fluctuated, shaped in large measure by prevailing circumstances. In response to widespread drunkenness around a hundred years ago, the temperance movement, led by Free Church ministers and members, made a vigorous counter-attack against what they dubbed the 'demon drink'. As a result, not only did alcohol abuse decline but a generation of Free Church Christians grew up avowed teetotallers, their influence dominating up to the 1950s. Then, in the 'swinging sixties', the 'do your own thing' mindset took over. You were 'stuffy' if you didn't drink and intolerant if you objected to those who did. Steadily, Free Church Christians abandoned abstinence until, today, non-drinkers are a tiny minority in our churches. For the great majority of ministers and congregations, the old 'alcohol question' is a dead duck. So any preacher trying to resuscitate it is unlikely to get a very sympathetic hearing.

The facts shout 'No!'

But should we, both as individual Christians and as churches, any longer brush this issue under the carpet? The facts shout "No!" For the evidence that alcohol abuse is increasing at an alarming rate in Britain, seriously damaging great numbers of men, women and children personally as well as society as a whole, is indisputable.

Consider the devastating impact of excessive drinking on millions of marriages, partnerships and families – on loving and loyal spouses, on confused teenagers, on younger children and even babies.

"Dad gets drunk every day, he hits me and mum," cries one wretched girl, "he broke my arm once. If I have bruises he… stops me going to school. He says if we ever tell anyone he will kill us… I'm scared… It's getting worse".

"Please don't stop my mother smoking… I would rather she smoked than drank", pleads a boy suffering from foetal alcohol syndrome.

"He is prepared to lose his family rather than stop drinking. He mustn't love us and I find myself wondering if he ever did or if all our life together was a lie. I feel sad and frightened and angry", reports an anguished wife.

Those are just three quotations from a report to the European Union called 'Alcohol Problems in the Family'. In Britain alone, it is estimated there are at least a million children trying to cope with alcohol-abusing parents.

Illness, accidents, crime

Consider the surge of alcohol related illnesses – and when I use that phrase, I'm not thinking of a sick head in the morning that goes by the afternoon. I am thinking of the havoc excessive alcohol inflicts on liver, pancreas, heart and bowel; of the ever-increasing number of men, women and young people who find blood in their urine, or their skin turning yellow, or their body immobilized by a stroke, or their leg amputated, or their brain failing – thanks to the great god Booze. In the Lancet medical journal, experts

164

have claimed that alcohol is as destructive to health as smoking, causing or aggravating over 60 medical conditions!

Consider the number of working days lost because of hangovers. Or the toll of motor, industrial and other accidents and deaths caused by the same seductive idol – currently, 8 out of 10 people attending NHS emergency units have alcohol related injuries. Alcohol misuse in England alone costs the NHS £1.7 billion a year. Tim Straughan, chief executive of the NHS Information Centre said, in May 2008, "Alcohol is placing an increasing burden right across the service, from the GP surgery to the hospital bed. These rises paint a worrying picture about the relationship between the population and the bottle".

Consider the high proportion of crime committed under the influence of alcohol.
1.2 million, or half, of all violent crimes each year are linked to alcohol misuse.
But if statistics leave us cold, who of us isn't moved by the personal effects of such conduct? It is an odd feature of the British psyche that, ten years on, the nation at large still grieves the gruesome death of Princess Diana – caused largely by her chauffeur's drunken driving – yet blandly accepts similar family tragedies occurring daily somewhere in the U.K.

Consider the explosion of binge drinking whereby, every Thursday, Friday and Saturday evening, in villages, towns and cities across the UK, millions of young people go out, girls scantily clad, boys with cans in hand, with the prime purpose of 'getting sloshed' but seemingly unconcerned about the consequences of their 'night on the town' – such as litter, urine, vomit, on pavements and in doorways, vandalized property, noise, intimidation, and may be – in due time – the frightening discovery of a sexual disease or pregnancy.

Add to these nationwide features of our so-called 'alcohol culture' the human and financial costs of dealing with the repercussions – £7 billion for dealing with the crime factor alone – and you have a national crisis. Can any faithful disciple of the Lord of Love ignore such evil?

To recognize the gravity of an issue is important but what matters far more is what we do about it.

Thoughts from the Bible

So, first, let's turn to the Bible to see if it offers relevant guidance. In my view, it most certainly does. For even though our urbanized society is outwardly poles apart from the mainly small rural communities of Biblical times, the underlying problems and solutions are essentially the same. Being careful, as always, to avoid 'text plucking' – by which you can find ammunition for virtually anything you want to believe – there is actually plenty of relevant material scattered throughout the Bible's pages.

A few verses openly extol alcoholic drink, verse 15 of Psalm 104 as memorably as any, where the psalmist exults in man's capacity to produce "wine to gladden his heart". Whatever your and my view of alcohol might be, it is patently obvious that, down the centuries and throughout the world, vast numbers of people would add a resounding 'Amen' to the psalmist's assertion. They do find that drinking wine and other forms of alcoholic liquor gives them pleasure, and, for some, a brief escape from whatever 'hell' they are suffering. Clearly, worldwide, the great majority of people regard alcoholic drink primarily as a blessing.

'Out on the ocean'

Other Biblical observers of life, however, see it more as a curse. Such as the startlingly vivid close of Proverbs chapter 23:

"Show me someone who drinks too much, who has to try out some new drink, and I will show you someone miserable and sorry for himself, always causing trouble and always complaining. His eyes are bloodshot, and he has bruises that could have been avoided. Don't let wine tempt you, even though it is rich red, though it sparkles in the cup, and it goes down smoothly. Weird sights will appear before your eyes, and you will not be able to think or speak clearly. You will feel as if you were out on the ocean, sea-sick, swinging high up in the rigging of a tossing ship. *'I must have been hit'*, you will say: *'I must have been beaten up, but I don't remember it. Why can't I wake up? I need another drink'*". (23:29-35)

Beat that passage for a piece of timeless writing! There are others just as graphic in the same collection of 'shrewd observations'. Two thousand or so years ago, drunkenness most definitely was a familiar part of life and the effects of alcohol were just the same. Then and now, the inebriated person looks awful, sounds off, loses self-control, behaves in all sorts of anti-social ways, often hurts himself or herself – and yet, such is the addictive power of the chemical consumed, that he or she only wants more of the same. Yet so many people think drunken conduct is funny, even admirable – 'cool'!

Another proverb warns: "'Drunkards and gluttons will be reduced to poverty" (23:21). That, too, is bang on target. For excessive indulgence still impoverishes drinkers and families alike. You don't have to talk with many clients at Julian House in Bath or similar night shelters, before you meet someone once comfortably off but now poor, thanks to alcohol.

"Wine is a mocker, strong drink a brawler", another proverb cautions, "whoever is led astray by it is not wise" (20:1), a sentiment echoed by prophets such as Isaiah, Joel and Habakkuk.

'Take a little wine'
The New Testament reinforces the message of the Old. True, the elder pastor Paul does advise the young minister Timothy to "take a little wine to help your digestion, since you are ill so often" (1 Timothy 5:23). Elsewhere though, he urges Christians engulfed by an alcohol 'culture' to "walk becomingly, as in the day, not in revelling and drunkenness" (Romans 13:13).

Turning to Jesus, there's nothing to suggest he frowned at disciplined drinking. He readily attended social functions where wine was served and he used the symbolism of the vine for some of his most profound teaching.

"And didn't our Lord turn water into wine?" I remember one keen drinker ask me, when she noticed me consuming nothing stronger than orange juice at a celebratory meal. I was a young man at the time and made a fumbling reply. Now I would answer: "Actually, almost certainly, no!" And I would justify my opinion with a string of reasons that time prevents me stating now. But, however we understand the story of the marriage at Cana, at most it verifies that to some extent Jesus took alcohol himself and did not condemn the drug as such.

Fundamental questions

If we wish to 'discern the mind of Christ' on this issue, we have to ask fundamental questions. Such as: what does love – true concern for the wellbeing of self and neighbour – demand? How can we best protect the vulnerable whom Jesus so cherished? What sort of example should we set to those Paul described as 'weaker brothers and sisters'? How far might drinking alcohol counter the Holy Spirit's gift of self-control?

'Use your bodies for God's glory'

Personally, I find Paul's discourse in First Corinthians, chapter 6, about the human body profoundly relevant. After considering how Christ-followers should deal with bodily desires – in terms of food and sex – he concludes: "Don't you know that your body is the temple of the Holy Spirit, who lives in you and who was given to you by God? You do not belong to yourselves but to God... So use your bodies for God's glory" (1 Corinthians 6:19-20).

When I think about the effects alcohol has on the body, it makes me wonder how anyone taking that text seriously – viewing their body as the 'holy house' of God's own presence – can take a cavalier attitude to something so liable to damage it. By blocking the inhibitory centres of the brain, alcohol might initially appear to be a stimulant but it's actually a depressant, prolonged drinking often causing clinical depression. In popular thinking, it's 'good for sex' but the truth is it has exactly the opposite effect, prolonged heavy consumption producing all sorts of nasty sexual problems. Being high in calories, alcohol makes the drinker clock up more fat which, in turn, raises blood pressure. As for giving yourself a hangover, with all its unpleasant symptoms, that hardly shows respect for your 'holy house'.

Personal convictions

So, bringing together my survey of today's alcohol scene and my gallop through Biblical observations and principles, just what should our attitude be, as Christians? Let me close by sharing with you my personal convictions. How you respond is your business!

At this point, I'll spell out what you've probably guessed. I follow an alcohol-free life style and always have. And I would commend it to anyone as a very real, relevant and satisfying option – though I sincerely hope I never come across as 'holier-than-thou' in my attitude! Now I know certain medical experts say that taking a little alcohol regularly can help prevent your arteries narrowing and so, maybe, I might have avoided my triple bypass op. And a recent study suggests alcohol can cut the risk of developing arthritis. But, for me, the arguments in favour of total abstinence far outweigh those against.

Total abstinence...
The total abstainer avoids a range of risks, such as the temptation to drink and drive. Without the mind- and body-changing drug in their system, the total abstainer is far less likely to be drawn into anti-social conduct. The total abstainer obviously can never become addicted, a significant risk that any alcohol user does take, for no addict knows when he or she starts to drink that such will be their lot. Abstinence certainly doesn't stop people getting on: there are non-drinkers among leaders in every walk of life. (Mind you, I do wish some hosts at wedding receptions and the like wouldn't treat us as second-class guests, obliging us to ask for an alcohol-free alternative and, when it eventually arrives, having it served in a plastic mug!)

Or strict self-discipline?
But if most Christians choose not to go down the total abstinence road, what should their attitude be? The Bible passages and texts we considered earlier mainly warn against the downside of drinking, about how easy it is to let drinking get out of hand and spark off all sorts of personal and social evils. Which surely implies that those who choose to take alcohol should use it in a disciplined way, bearing in mind that you don't need much in your system to make responsible conduct all the harder!

Undoubtedly, one area of alcohol use that demands far stricter self-discipline and consideration than many people realize, is drinking and driving. In spite of the fact that even a trace of alcohol in the blood impairs judgment, thereby extending stopping distances and possibly making all the difference between injury and death, many people go on imagining its perfectly OK to consume the full legal limit. But it's not! The advice of police, AA, and medical experts is that the only safe amount of alcohol in the blood when driving is *nil*. Of all people, shouldn't the committed Christian take that advice to heart?

Join the wake-up call!

Lastly, if Christians are commissioned to be the 'yeast in the dough', the leading good influence in society, shouldn't we, of all people, be fully engaged in a wake-up call to Britain, and indeed the world? Thank God, judging from the stacks of clips I have from newspapers and journals, there are signs of growing concern and action. While never underestimating the power of the drinks industry – with its ceaseless bombardment of seductive advertising and its seemingly bottomless purse – somehow we must curb the madness before countless more people suffer because of their own, or other people's, worship of the great god Booze.

In practical terms, we can urge our MP to support the World Health Organization's appeal for stricter licensing laws, shorter opening hours and higher tax on alcohol. Or write to drinks companies pressing them to live up to their own code of practice – urging them, among other things, to stop crassly cheap offers or giving cocktails suggestive names like 'Sex on the Beach' or 'Screaming Orgasm'. Or we can contact, or even boycott, irresponsible local stores like McColl's, with its obscene Booze Buster signs. If attitudes to another drug, nicotine, can be dramatically changed, it's not absurd to believe we can bring about a healthier attitude to alcohol.

Is consuming alcohol a blessing, a curse, or something of both? In terms of personal conduct, our verdicts will vary. But communally, there can be no doubt it is again, in many ways, a curse – and, like any evil, needs to be confronted.

21   MANAGING THE EARTH!
(especially climate change)

Old and new wisdom on caring for our planet

"Act now or the world we know will be lost for ever". Those twelve words spell out the stark message of the Stern report published in October 2006. Now I have only read summaries of the 579-page review. But everything I picked up from television, radio and newspaper, underlines its apocalyptic conclusion: climate change is fundamentally altering the planet; the risks of inaction are high; and time is running out.

The report provided a detailed forecast of what will happen if carbon dioxide emissions continue at their present rate. There will be a relentless global rise in average near-surface temperatures which, in turn, will have increasingly dire effects on plant life, creatures, weather and its impact, and human living conditions. With just a 2 to 3 degrees Celsius rise, hundreds of millions more people will be at risk of hunger and disease, especially those in poorer countries.

A wake-up call
If ever there were a wake-up call to Planet Earth and its leaders, Sir Nicholas Stern's Review is it. I doubt if God is mentioned in the report but if we believe that God remains somehow involved in the processes of Creation, it is reasonable to believe God must somehow be involved in the subject of this report. The Review is undoubtedly prophetic both in character and purpose, *fore*telling what will happen if we go on behaving as we are, *forth*-telling what action humanity must take to save its home. It effectively asks the question: possessing awesome and unprecedented power over our entire habitat – its atmosphere, water, crust, fauna and flora – just how should you, I and our fellow world citizens manage the Earth? How, we could add, might God – the Ultimate Source and Sustainer of ALL-THAT-IS, the Ground of All Being, or however else we might think of God – how might God wish us to respond at this critical moment in Earth's story?

Let me, absurdly briefly, put the question into a Biblical, then into a more general historical, context.

'You're in charge!'
The theological poem with which the Bible opens observes what history exponentially shows, that humanity has been invested with the responsibility of managing nothing less than the entire Earth. In the first theological poem about Creation, God is portrayed as commissioning the primordial couple to have many children, so that their descendants would live all over the earth and bring it under their control. "I am putting *you* (human beings) in charge of the fish, the birds, and all the wild animals" (Genesis 1:28)

For people of those and subsequent Old Testament times, the idea of managing the Earth was – both theologically and ethically – relatively straightforward. It was not an issue in the way it is for us. The Earth's beauty was theirs to enjoy and its bounty theirs to harvest. The land teemed with animals, the sky with birds, the sea with fish. Vast tracts of land were green and fertile. Nature could be cruel with rains failing, crops perishing and people starving. But days of plenty would always return.

Tiny by 21st century standards, the human population's impact on the planet was minimal. This or that tribe or nation might suffer famine or disease because of some terrible sin (so it was believed) – but over all, people assumed that "as long as the

Earth existed, seed time and harvest would not cease". Nature's wealth – or capital – appeared to be inexhaustible. As they tilled the land, hunted its creatures, mined its minerals and traded its products, people of the time knew nothing about such dreads as global scarcity, species extinction, climate change, or any other world scale ecological catastrophe. Environmentally, though certainly not socially, the Earth remained a glorious place. People had every reason to rejoice at the Creator's goodness. As psalm 104 exults:

> "You make springs flow in the valleys,
> and rivers run between the hills.
> They provide water for wild animals;
> there the wild donkeys quench their thirst.
> In the trees near by,
> the birds make their nests and sing.
> From the sky you send rain on the hills,
> and the earth is filled with your blessings" (10-13).

The possibility, if not probability, of global catastrophe resulting from defiance of God's intentions and moral demands is acknowledged (and luridly envisaged) in the apocalyptic passages of both Testaments. But the Bible writers could not possibly have had any scientifically validated concept of global climate change. So it's pointless to look to the scriptures for specific guidance on how to respond to the sombre realities we now face.

The changing scene
Apart from intermittent, generally local damage, I believe it's true to say the kind of world the psalmist enjoyed continued up to and through the first Christian millennium and for a large chunk of the second, too. It wasn't that people were notably environmentally aware, let alone morally superior. It was simply that the global population remained relatively small and technology relatively simple, neither big enough to make much impression on the seemingly limitless Earth.

Then things began to change. In Britain, for instance, the navy plundered English oak woods to build their 'men o' war' and mixed-farming crofters were brutally cleared from the Highlands. Coal mining and iron smelting hugely expanded to serve the first industrial revolution. Trees gave way to factories, green fields to mean housing, fresh air to sulphurous smoke, pellucid rivers to stinking drains. This kind of extreme, visible (and often smellable) pollution continued well into the lifetimes of most of us here.

I can vividly remember, back in the late 1950s, sitting in a lecture looking forward to my lunch when the sky turned from light to mid grey, then to charcoal and finally inkjet black. Drivers switched on their car lights and the street lamps flickered into life. That eerie, night at noon lasted for only half-an-hour and the experience, repeated elsewhere, did spur on the Clean Air Act.

Yet, in spite of such alarming signs, industrial nations continued to exploit the world's natural capital, as if it were invulnerable and inexhaustible. In a fiercely competitive world neither private nor state capitalism accepted the stark truth that a finite Earth has finite resources. Out of ignorance, greed or desperation, that attitude has predominated to the present day.

Climate change and our response
The consequences? On a sunny, mild day a week before Christmas, a movement outside my study window attracted my attention. It was the hovering of a humming-bird moth, which, until recent years, was an occasional summer visitor to my part of the world. Hardly a week after Christmas a bumblebee banged against the same window before resuming its tour of the open daisies in the lawn. We know only too well what is happening. Our weather is changing, with all sorts of effects on plants and creatures. Yet, as our papers, the radio, and TV programmes all tell us, humanity continues to ravage the Earth.

Grounds for hope
Well, if you weren't feeling depressed at the beginning of the sermon, you will be by now! So it's time to be positive and, yes, *hopeful!* Not because we can't face reality, but because there *are* very real grounds for hope. The Stern report itself asserts we *can* avert the most catastrophic scenarios IF we act decisively and collectively sooner rather than later. Indeed, a major message of Sir Nicholas – whose *primary* brief was, after all, to consider the *economic* implications of climate change – is that it will be drastically cheaper to take planet-saving action *now* than to *postpone* the crucial economic and technological measures. If we take action now, Lord Stern calculated in June 2008, we will need to invest just 2% of our annual Gross Domestic Product but if we wait, up to 20%.

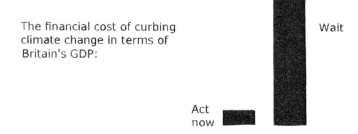

The financial cost of curbing climate change in terms of Britain's GDP:

Wait

Act now

But once financial institutions and big business grasp the economic advantages of early action – as some of them already are doing – the necessary changes and investment are far more likely to happen. So the Stern report itself offers a hopeful way forward.

'Natural Capitalism'
Several years before Stern, however, grounds for hope were mounting. Because necessity, economic advantage and moral conviction have for some time been converging, together sparking off a scarcely acknowledged, but very real, sea change for the better. This change, as you may well know, has been called 'The Next Industrial Revolution'. In fact, this is the subtitle to a book whose main title is 'Natural Capitalism', published in 1999.

The book is packed with well-documented evidence. It is cogently argued. It is totally accessible (you don't need a degree in this, that or anything to grasp its message). It is ethical and compassionate in tone. Questioning what we value and how we should live, it is spiritually challenging.

A new Earth?
Redolent of the Bible, 'Natural Capitalism' opens with a vision. 'Imagine for a moment', the authors invite the reader, 'a world where cities have become peaceful and serene because cars and buses are whisper quiet, vehicle exhaust only water vapour, and parks and green ways have replaced unneeded urban freeways... Living standards for all people have dramatically improved, particularly for the poor and those in developing countries... Houses, even low-income housing units, can pay part of their

mortgage costs by the energy they *produce*; there are few, if any landfills; worldwide forest cover is increasing... ' – which is already happening in China, India, the UK and around 30 other countries – 'atmospheric CO2 levels are decreasing for the first time in two hundred years; and effluent water leaving factories is cleaner than the water coming into them...' – spectacular progress has already been made in Britain in reducing sewage pollution into our rivers and coast – 'industrialized countries have reduced resource use by 80 per cent while improving the quality of life. Among these technological changes, there are [also] important social changes... Is this the vision of a utopia?' the authors ask. 'In fact', they claim, 'these changes could come about in the decades to come as the result of economic and technological trends *already in place.*'

A fourfold strategy

After assessing the nature and weaknesses of *conventional* capitalism, the writers spell out the four central strategies of *Natural* Capitalism.

First, *all resources must be used radically more effectively* – action which can spark off a chain of benefits. (For instance, if you install an efficient toilet flush you not only cut down water usage by three-quarters but you also reduce the chemicals employed to purify the water as well as the energy needed to pump the water to your house; money is freed-up to spend on mending leaky mains which saves yet more water. This, in turn, means the water company does not need to bore for that extra water thereby leaving the water table at a level which won't dry out the land as quickly. That means local farmers don't need as much water for their crops, and even more water is saved ... You get the vital principle!)

Secondly, Natural Capitalism *advocates biomimicry*: find out how spiders make silk tougher than manmade Kevlar or why the abalone's shell is twice as tough as our best ceramics – apply nature's technology!

Thirdly, Natural Capitalism *urges a shift from a goods to a service-based economy:* don't buy but hire, as this encourages firms to produce durable rather than throwaway goods.

Fourthly, Natural Capitalism *involves massive investment in natural capital* – in sustaining, restoring and expanding stocks of trees, fish, creatures, and plants – and promoting biodiversity; massive investment in everything Mother Earth, given a chance, readily facilitates.

Together, these interrelated strategies can reduce environmental harm (including climate change), create economic growth, and increase meaningful employment.

It's happening!
The authors then apply their ideas to every major facet of modern life, never brushing unpleasant facts under the carpet but consistently concentrating on the surge of positive, exciting developments. Such as non-polluting cars powered by hydrogen – a development now likely to be accelerated, thanks to the discovery, at Bath university, of a safe and efficient system of storing the fuel onboard; or superwindows as effective as ten layers of glazing. The book is chock-a-block with ways in which existing know-how can drastically improve our stewardship of natural resources, ways, moreover, which *added together* are extremely attractive economically: where the Earth is wisely managed, there's 'brass'.

The final chapter is full of (soundly-based) hope, not least where the writers declare: "What is remarkable about this period of history [now] is the degree of agreement that is forming globally about the relationship between human and other living systems." Tens of thousands of disparate local, regional, national and international organizations, backed by a series of global agreements, add up to an unprecedented consensus. "This has never happened before", they claim, "in politics, economics or religion, but is happening in the growing movement – increasingly joined now by both religion and science – toward what is known as 'sustainability'."

Our Christian response?
So what, as Christians, do we make of all this? You can make up your own mind. But I personally believe we should be profoundly thankful for the immense effort, skill, information and wisdom embodied in this book. The fundamental ideas of Natural

Capitalism surely accord with those of Jesus who, pointing to the lilies of the field and the birds of the air nearby, urged his hearers to learn from nature's resourcefulness, reliability and integrity. I believe we should be profoundly grateful also for the Stern report with its comparably prophetic challenge.

What matters though, we know so well, is *what we do!*

'Change your missiles into turbines'

Since the Stern report was published, there's been a spate of programmes, articles and books offering concrete ideas. One highly respected journalist has offered a ten-point plan of action. His points include: setting a rigorous target for reducing greenhouse-gas emissions and using that target to set an annual carbon cap; introducing far stricter energy-saving building regulations; banning the sale of wasteful luxuries like patio heaters and garden floodlights; re-deploying money earmarked for new nuclear missiles towards massive investment in energy generation... transferring money allocated to road building to tackling climate change; freezing and then reducing UK airport capacity. Now such measures may be unpopular but don't they represent the kind of radical action needed? What is indisputable, however, is that whatever steps are taken, will involve us all and will most certainly put limits on our commonly profligate life styles.

Jesus's crucial warning

And shouldn't Christians – people who take the words and example of Jesus with absolute seriousness – be in the vanguard of such changes, both in their personal life style and in the way they try to influence society and government? Of all people, shouldn't Christians – Christ-followers – take solemn heed of Jesus's warning that happiness does *not* consist in the multiplicity of things they possess – 'stuff' – and therefore lead the revolt against the prevailing creed that rampant consumerism is the key to human *fulfilment,* even though, as the basic cause of climate changing emissions, it is in truth the key to human *disaster*?

The majesty of Creation

I close by quoting from the authors' preface to 'Natural Capitalism'. *Writing primarily as scientists and economists*, their message is first and foremost a spiritual one:

"We have lived by the assumption that what was good for *us* would be good for the *world*. We have been wrong. We must change our lives, so that it will be possible to live by the contrary assumption that what is good for the *world* will be good for *us*. And that requires that we make the effort to know the world and what is good for it. We must learn to co-operate in its processes, and to yield to its limits. But even more important, we must learn to acknowledge that the creation is full of mystery; we will never clearly understand it. We must abandon arrogance and stand in awe. We must recover the sense of the majesty of creation, and the ability to be worshipful in its presence. For it is only on the condition of humility and reverence before the world that our species will be able to remain in it".

"God looked at everything he had made", the Creation poet concluded, "and he was very pleased..." (Genesis 1:31) God's beautiful and fertile yet wounded planet *can be healed*. Christians claim that Jesus Christ, supremely, offers the spiritual wherewithal. Learned experts offer the vital knowledge and skills. Ultimately however, isn't managing the Earth wisely, up to you, me and every member of the human family?

22   *CONSIDER THE FLOWERS...*

Jesus's antidote to worry

"Worry, worry, worry
there's always something
I'm never (well hardly ever)
totally free...
only in those precious moments
when the air is clear and fresh
but then –
there's always something...
and I long for the day
when it will all be over
and I can walk in the park for days
not having to think about anything...
but the day never comes
because there's always something;
and why not?
it's the way of the world!
Why can't I make peace with it?
peace...
so I can walk in the park for days...
and there will always be something
but I won't care...
yes, there's always something...
someday, may be, I will not worry –
someday... I'll be dead."

Those are the haunting reflections of a student. And they certainly
take me back to my college days, in particular the stressful weeks
leading up to the summer exams. After lectures, I did indeed
walk in the local park eager for fresh air and solace, yet, as that
student knew so well, unwelcome thoughts about the impending
ordeal never completely vanished.

The worries of life
The student's outpouring, however, expresses how probably all
of us feel at least sometimes and perhaps some of us almost
perpetually. We long for respite but 'there's always something'
that worries us, some problem or fear that disturbs our peace of
mind, or our work, or our leisure, or our relationships.

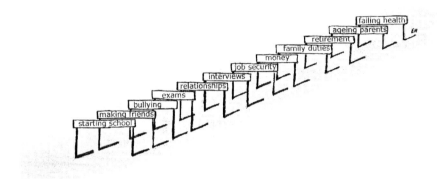

The four-year-old worries about the first day of school. Pupils worry about a new teacher, or a subject they find difficult, or the threats of a bully, or coping with a sport they can't master (how I dreaded cricket afternoons hoping I would be eleventh man in and avoid facing that lethal red missile!).

Young people worry – about what they look like, or what their peers think of them, or their job prospects, or succeeding in an interview, and much else.

People living by themselves, not least single parents, have extra burdens and therefore more to worry about.

Parents – as they always have, and certainly did when the proverbs of the Bible were being compiled – worry about the attitudes, conduct, progress and future of their children. Has there ever been a more worrying time in which to bring up children than now, with so many negative, if not evil, values and pressures bombarding them?

The workplace – whether office, factory floor, shop, common room, farm or hospital – yields its crop of worries, perhaps the worst being insecurity. For there are now few occupations where your job is yours for life: even the most competent and experienced people find they have to re-apply for their own post, with all the hassle and stress the process causes.

Retirement closes the door on career worries. But it may well generate new ones – about coping with a smaller income, or filling in the sudden expansion of free time (though I doubt if many church people have that problem!), or dealing with deteriorating health, or supporting aged parents with *their* ever increasing worries.

'There's always something'

Nowadays, there's one technological wonder that can bring on a 'headache' whatever our age. For all the help and comfort it so regularly provides, 'googling' can also spark off an explosion of worries. You key in a fairly trivial medical symptom, and before you know where you are you've convinced yourself you've got one of half-a-dozen nasty illnesses! Or you visit a travel website to find out more about the destination of your dreams, only to be confronted with all sorts of disconcertingly mixed comments from those who have holidayed there!

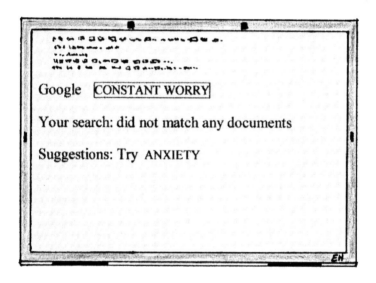

"Worry, worry, worry… there's always something… I'm never (well hardly ever) totally free… ". The anxious student's musings are surely spot on target. Of course, every stage of our mortal journey usually has its compensating joys and 'pluses'. Nevertheless, whether we are royalty, celebrity or ordinary citizen, problems are an inescapable feature of life and where there are problems, worry lurks. In short, worry is a universal and abiding fact of life.

Worry as an illness

However, observation suggests some people are more prone to serious worry than others. For a small minority, worry is a symptom of a mental disorder, perhaps a form of paranoia. Sufferers constantly fear that they have left a light on at work and go back to check. Or they persistently fear a tile has fallen off the roof so repeatedly go and have a look. Constantly worried about what they have omitted to do or what might have happened, they incessantly take remedial action, driving partner or family crazy in the process. People suffering intense anxiety obviously need expert psychiatric treatment, even though healing is inevitably slow and perhaps never complete. They need the support of appropriate organisations and the understanding of acquaintances and friends.

'Born worriers'

But there are plenty more people who, while certainly not mentally ill, appear to worry more than most of us do. You may well know such a person and may have said to him or her on occasion, perhaps with a touch of exasperation, "Oh you're a *born* worrier!" My family used to tease my mother that she was only happy when she had something to worry about!

Now it may simply be that moderate 'worriers' admit and share their worries more readily than others. For some of us do 'keep ourselves to ourselves' and are reluctant to tell others what's on our mind, perhaps hiding our anxiety from even our nearest and dearest. It's often claimed that men, when it comes to personal feelings, tend to be less communicative than women. But might it not sometimes be the case that 'born worriers' are, in fact, very sensitive and caring persons who simply find it all but impossible to put the problems and needs of others to the back of their minds? Certainly we need to beware of making hasty judgements about those we feel are too uptight about life.

That said, isn't it fair to say that worry *can* sometimes get out of hand? So much so, that it destroys our equilibrium, making us tense and irritable, not very nice to live with? Left to fester, worry can distort our sense of perspective, so that we focus more on the negatives of our life than the positives, and behave like the person with the proverbial chip on the shoulder.

Worry in the Gospels

But of course there's nothing new about worry and its ramifications. It's clear from the Gospels, that Jesus met people with all sorts of worry and, after listening empathetically, got to the heart of their need.

You've heard people commend the advice to live life 'a day at a time'. How many of them, however, realise the principle goes back to the New Testament? Both Matthew and Luke report Jesus urging people not to "worry about the morrow" because it would "have enough worries of its own. There's no need to add to the troubles each day brings".

Worry, it could be said, is an attempt to carry the burdens of the future before it actually arrives. Of course, we need to plan and make sensible provision for it, if only so that we don't unnecessarily impose ourselves on the conscience and time of others. It is right to give measured thought to such matters as insurance, pensions and provision for old age. One can be irresponsibly happy-go-lucky. 'Laid back' people may be more relaxing company than 'born worriers' but they may also be ten times more selfish, shifting the unavoidable burdens and hassles of life unfairly on to the shoulders of others.

And yet, there surely *are* circumstances when, whatever our personality, we should cherish the present and put aside thoughts about the future. Poor old Martha learnt this lesson the hard way when Jesus was staying at Mary and Martha's house. She 'got it in the neck', you'll recall, for fussing and fretting – for being excessively worried about practicalities – when the over-riding need at that critical moment was for space and tranquillity. There are times – such as occasions of great joy or sorrow – when we should try our utmost to put life's routine demands on hold, to allow our soul, or innermost self, the respect and calm it needs.

Jesus's remedy

So what is Jesus's remedy for worry? He didn't say, "Don't *care* about tomorrow". He said, "Don't *worry* about it". In other words, without abandoning necessary and responsible concern for the future, we should try to focus more on the demands of the present.

Secondly, Jesus invites us to sort out our sense of values. Instead of 'fussing and fretting' over the relatively unimportant things, we should try to discern and concentrate on what really matters. "Do not start worrying: 'Where will my food come from? or my drink? or my clothes?' These are the things the *heathens* [people who ignore the spiritual dimension] run after' [or "drives to the superstore for", we might add]. "Your Father in heaven knows that you need all these things" – he's provided Sainsburys, M and S, the Co-op, even the corner shop, if you're lucky! "Instead, be concerned above everything else with the Kingdom of God and with what he requires of you" (Matthew 6:31-33). Hanker after love and justice, forgiveness and peace, goodness and joy, and all the other priceless treasures Jesus lived and died to promote. Put God's way first, and you will find many of the things you worry about shrink to their true size and significance.

The supreme antidote
But the supreme antidote to excessive worry is surely found in the sublime poetry of the opening verses of that celebrated passage. There, Jesus points to God's bountiful provision in nature, in the flowers of the field and the birds of the air. You know the passage too well for me to repeat it but a little poem distils its essence:

> "Said the robin to the sparrow:
> 'I should really like to know
> Why these anxious human beings
> Rush about and worry so'.

> Said the sparrow to the robin:
> 'Friend, I think that it must be
> That they have no Heavenly Father
> Such as cares for you and me'"

So often, when we feel overloaded with worries, we lose sight of how amply our genuine needs *are* met; we forget just how many things we once worried about turned out fine in the end; how many things we dreaded proved to be nothing like so grim in reality. Honest reflection assures us we *are* wonderfully provided for and that so much of our worrying really isn't justified. As long as we work faithfully with God's physical and moral laws – an undoubtedly huge proviso – we really can trust God's providential love.

23   IT'S A MIRACLE!

An enquiry into the meaning and significance of 'miracles'

"Sir, do *you* believe in miracles?" The subject always intrigued my (secondary school) students. But the question of miracles – whether of the Biblical era, today or some time in between – is a challenging one for *anyone*. And, for various reasons, the answers Christians give differ widely. So the subject of miracles is a controversial one.

Now, it may well be true, that if we dwell on the question whether the miracle stories describe precisely what happened, we misunderstand the aim of the writers. It seems that they were *less* interested in historical authenticity and *more* interested in showing the significance of the events they were claiming to describe. If that's the case, what matters is the writer's intention. For example, the saga of the parting of the Red Sea was told to show that God was in control. Or, in the case of several Gospel healing miracles, that Jesus put human need before the strictures of the Sabbath laws. Or, in the story of his stilling the storm, to raise the key question 'Who is this man?'

But in my experience, people, both within and outside the church, most definitely *do* want to know whether or not Jesus achieved the apparently 'impossible'. So *this* is the question I am going to address.

A plea for empathy
But I need your help, supremely, your *empathy* – your serious attempt to understand, though not necessarily agree with, those whose views are held with equal sincerity but are very different from your own. In a Free Church like this, such mutual tolerance is, of course, of the essence of its ethos. But whatever our view, we need to keep in mind that matters of faith are, by definition, outside the scope of proof and therefore always provisional.

With that important plea made – probably totally unnecessarily here – I am confident you will bear with me as I examine very different viewpoints, two in particular, before offering some thoughts on the subject that most, if not all, Christians can agree on.

The reason why students asked me about the historicity of miracles, especially those reported in the Bible, was usually because they felt many of them flew in the face of what science says about the workings of the physical world. *How could* a dry path suddenly appear in a stretch of sea? *How could* five loaves and two fish turn into 5000 lunches? *How could* a dead twelve-year-old girl be given back her life?

So what answers might one offer such searchers?

A variety of answers
Christians offer a variety of answers. Fundamentalists take every Biblical miracle story precisely as it stands, as they take every word in the Bible, however historically unlikely or morally repugnant. A few, at the opposite pole dismiss miracle stories outright, in spite of the inherent plausibility of at least elements within them – such as the desperation of the four friends who opened a hole in the roof to get their patient closer to Jesus. From the very earliest days, however, most Christians have belonged to two, broad bands between the extremes – those that basically accept the notion of miracle and those who tend to question it. And today, there are Christians who could be called 'acceptors', others who could be called 'questioners'.

The 'acceptors' answer
Let's focus first on the 'acceptors', dealt with more briefly simply because their attitude is easier to describe.

Some people – and you may be among them – assert that since God (as traditionally understood) is, by definition, all-powerful, God *can* do what might appear impossible. Being 'almighty', God has the power to open up the sea to let through the goodies and close it up again to drown the baddies; God has the power to turn a boy's picnic into any number of meals; God even has the power to resurrect the dead! Whilst we may not *understand* the physical processes involved, 'acceptors' maintain, we need not doubt God *can* do those mind-boggling acts historically described as miracles.

What's more, according to this view, we should accept that some occurrences which might *appear* to defy scientific norms, may not *actually* do so, because there may be some not yet

188

fully understood, or even not yet detected, process involved. As St Augustine put it some 1600 years ago: "Miracles do not defy nature; they challenge what we know about nature." It's a common logical fallacy to assume that because we cannot understand *how* something happens, it therefore *cannot* occur.

So, many Christians, generally more conservative in their theology, take an accepting attitude, content to believe that stories of miracles, especially those in the Bible, can be taken as basically accurate descriptions of what physically happened. And, if one holds to a traditional idea of God, no one can categorically say they are wrong. It's a position, therefore, that should be tolerated, if not respected, by people who, in all honesty, cannot go along with it.

The 'questioners' view

Now the great majority of 'acceptors' *do* recognize that reason should have a significant place in religious faith generally and, in particular, in understanding the Bible and its application to life. But they impose very strict limits on its contribution. Generally, though not invariably, they choose to take the Biblical text very largely at its face value.

Christian 'questioners', however, usually give reason a much bigger place in their faith and their approach to the Bible. I would call myself a 'questioner', by the way, an outlook I have held ever since my junior stage Sunday School teachers memorably introduced it to me. Now this more 'rationalistic' attitude fully acknowledges that there is bound to be an element of incomprehensibility, or mystery, in the realm of faith. At the same time, it maintains that in a *uni*verse all approaches to truth (such as religion, science and logic) must, ultimately, cohere – this is the way the universe functions, this is the way things are. And, therefore, we should always try to reconcile apparent clashes between different approaches to truth.

So when it comes to allegedly miraculous events, 'questioners' are likely to ask searching questions. Did the event really happen in the way described? If not, what did occur? Was the writer's primary intention, in such and such a case, to give a precise, factual account or to convey a spiritual message? Why would God sometimes act physically in ways which appear to defy

God's own system, the 'laws of nature'? Why, in the case of some allegedly miraculous events, does God seem to behave in morally contradictory ways? Questioning Christians just cannot brush aside such thoughts, because they believe the mechanics and the morality of God's world should always concur.

So much for the 'questioner's' rationale. Now let's apply it more specifically.

The healing miracles
Most 'questioners', I suggest, have little difficulty, in principle, with the healing miracles. In certain cases, they might wonder about the speed of recovery but surmise that stories written down decades after they happened lose nothing in the telling. They will bear in mind that the prime intention of the Gospel writers was to express their beliefs about the nature and significance of Jesus rather than provide a Hansard type record.

Or, 'questioners' might argue that whereas *everyone* has a measure of healing ability (empathetic listening, for instance, is therapeutic), and a *minority* of people do seem to have heightened healing faculties, *Jesus* possessed these powers to a unique extent. His body, mind and spirit were so totally integrated; he was so able to perceive and expose people's psychosomatic needs; he was so open to the source of wholeness and healing commonly named 'God'; that he was able to apply his innate healing powers to awesome effect.

In other words, there's no need to believe Jesus's healing actions broke God's own 'laws of nature'. Does this, however, make the outcome any less welcome and wonderful? 'Questioners', too, rejoice that Jesus – who knew full well Jairus's daughter wasn't dead but sleeping, perhaps comatose – restored the girl to the point where all she needed was a little nourishment.

'Questioners', just as much as 'acceptors', similarly rejoiced at the birth of James Sibley. In spite of being given a vaccine at 13 weeks and nine blood transfusions, the medical experts reckoned he still only had a 1% chance of making it. Yet he was born fit and well at 34 weeks. Reflecting on the pioneering treatment, the willing gift of blood from anonymous donors, and the 99% chance of losing the baby, his mother exclaimed: *"It's a miracle!"*

190

We know *how* James's life came to be saved, but does this lessen the *wonder* of his survival?

The nature miracles
So there's a broad measure of agreement between 'acceptors' and 'questioners' over the healing miracles. It's the so-called 'nature miracles' that cause the real problems for people of rationalistic personality or persuasion. This is where I tread on corns, eggshells and burning coals all at the same time!

Conceding that God, by definition, *is able* to suspend the laws of nature, 'questioners' wonder why God should actually do so and, moreover, in such an apparently arbitrary fashion? Why should one individual or group, or even nation, be favoured whilst another is ignored, even treated brutally? For instance, they cannot square the claim, that God parted the sea to let the Hebrews escape before allowing it to drown the pursuing Egyptians, with either their knowledge of the way wind and water really behave, or with Jesus's presentation of God as a loving, forgiving Father.

'Questioners' feel uncomfortable with the story of Jesus walking on water. They claim such a feat would run counter to the Creator's physical laws. Might not the reality be that, because it was 'some time between three and six in the morning', it was dark and the disciples were half asleep – conditions which distorted their perception? Indeed, the earliest version of the story – Mark's – tells us they thought it was a ghost coming to them over the water! The truth might be that Jesus, sensing the disciples' apprehension, walked through some shallows, hauled himself aboard and, by his very presence, wonderfully banished their fears.

The unexpected guest
Before I turn the spotlight on another 'nature' miracle, a personal story. My wife had gone out for the evening so I thought I'd get on with a little service preparation. No sooner had I switched on my computer, than the doorbell rang. On opening the door, I was greeted by a smiling, kind looking, bearded man of about 30. "Hi!" he said, "I saw your light on and thought you might be able to tell me where I could find a B and B – the one on the corner is full". Somehow, I felt he was genuine and, indeed, someone I felt I'd met before. So I replied, "Well, you can spend the night

here – we've got a room made up". "Thanks... if you're sure! As a matter of fact, I'm on a sort of mission tour".

I showed him his room and said, "I'll put the kettle on". "Great!" he answered, "I could murder a cup of tea". And, before the kettle had fully boiled he had found his way to the kitchen. So I reached for the tea caddy, opened it and then, uncharacteristically, exclaimed, "Jesus! It's empty!" To which, my unexpected guest replied, "I wondered how long it would be before you recognised me", before adding, "don't panic about the tea caddy, I'll soon fix it". I was so gob-smacked that I didn't notice him slip out of the room, though I do remember wondering if he just might wave his arms over the tin and fill it with tea bags! But while I was still glued to the spot, he returned. "Here, have this, I bought it barely half an hour ago. I got two packets, so I won't run short". It was an 80 bag Clipper packet of fair trade tea! "So miracles still happen!" we joked in chorus, as I popped the bags in the pot.

The wedding at Cana
That little parable brings us to our last nature miracle, the wedding at Cana, recorded in John, chapter 2.

For me, this story provokes heaps of questions, among them these. Why, if such a story really was a wholly historical incident, should only John appear to have heard of it and not the three earlier, more historically focused evangelists? Why should Jesus so *publicly* use his powers merely to help out an embarrassed hostess when, in his post-baptismal retreat, he had hit right out of court the temptation to use his powers in ways likely to generate celebrity? Most pertinently of all, just how could one compound, water, become another, wine, without the addition of those chemicals (in this case occurring in grapes) without which wine simply would not be wine? If you want to turn water into tea you need the leaves of the tea bush. Similarly, if you wish to turn water into wine, science and logic – two vital pipelines of divine truth – tell us you need the fruits of the vine!

For the serious 'questioner', then, taking this particular miracle at its face value raises some very awkward questions. Personally, I reckon there was probably a simple explanation how kind Jesus came to the rescue and the water jars came to contain wine – just as there was a simple explanation about my fresh supply of tea! That said, many scholars assert that this story is highly symbolic, the phrase about "the best wine being kept to the end" possibly referring to God's climactic gift of Jesus.

What really matters

If my candid questioning has upset you, I'm sorry, but I have reached the stage in my preaching career where I just have to be honest! Perhaps Christians simply have to agree to differ over their interpretation of the nature miracles. What's more, we all know that what matters more than any intellectual question, is the quality of our discipleship.

The root of the word

I should like to close by sharing my own innermost ideas and feelings about miracles and, in the process, offer an approach which, I hope, unites 'acceptors' and 'questioners'.

For me, the most positive and fruitful way to understand and appreciate the notion of miracle is to focus on the etymology of the word. It comes, you may well know, from the Latin 'mirari', meaning 'to wonder at', a meaning evident in the New Testament phrase 'signs and wonders'.

So much to wonder at!

So, a miracle, in my book, is *anything* – physical or spiritual, visible or invisible, historical or contemporary, Biblical or extra-Biblical – you *wonder at* – anything, at the profoundest level, you *admire or puzzle over!* When I think of miracles in this kind of way, my difficulties dramatically shrink for there is *so much* to admire and puzzle over, *so much* to wonder at.

One June, when on holiday in Scotland with my wife, I stopped the car in a place overlooking a magical, lonely loch set amid mountains, sheep, cattle, and birds – the only people there. We admired the view in silence and then tuned in to Radio 3 to hear Evensong, live from Coventry Cathedral. The reception was superb enabling us to hear the service perfectly, including a section of Brahms's hauntingly beautiful German Requiem. Water, rocks, wind, rain, fleeting sunshine, invisible words and music captured from the very air we breathed, all there to be admired or puzzled over, to be wondered at – a truly miraculous occasion!

There's so much to wonder at in the processes and products of Creation ... whether we look, through giant telescopes, at the awesome grandeur of the cosmos ... peer, through powerful microscopes, at the astounding intricacy of the miniature world... or observe, with naked eye, the breath-taking beauty and bounty of the land and sea around us – at the Earth in all its glory... or gaze in love at a newborn baby... there's so much to wonder at in Creation which, thanks to millions of person-hours of scientific study, we can understand and appreciate all the more.

And there's so much to wonder at in the story of spiritual renewal – in the compilation and transmission of the Bible; in the glorious fact that this human cradle of divine truth has survived for two thousand years, speaking to people of every century and every continent; in the truly amazing events and insights reported in its pages; in the astonishing truth that Jesus the Christ *still* meets people's deepest needs, *still* changes lives. Do we *need* to prop up our faith in Jesus by believing what our minds tell us is intrinsically unlikely?

The 19th Century American poet Walt Whitman claimed: "I know nothing else but miracles – to me every hour of night and day is a miracle, every cubic inch of space a miracle". Hyperbole or not, let us thank God for *everything* which *does* make us stop and wonder – whether in the material realm or the spiritual. There are so many miracles of yesterday and today that we *can* be confident about... Let's be truly grateful for them!

24   GOOD *AND* NICE!

Balancing holiness and compassion

Leviticus 19:2: "Be holy, because I, the Lord your God, am holy" (GNB)

Luke 6:36: "Be compassionate just as your Father is compassionate" (NEB)

Have you ever known – or do you now know(!) – someone of apparently sound character yet whose company you do not enjoy; someone whose moral standing you respect but with whom you certainly wouldn't like to go on holiday; someone, though unquestionably a committed Christian, you wouldn't confide in; someone, in short, 'good' but not really 'nice'? Your answer may well be "Yes!" Conversely, you may well have come across likeable rogues: people who are 'nice' but not, in all honesty, 'good'. Whatever our experience, it seems that 'goodness' and 'niceness' each has its particular attraction. What's more, quite often one or the other is more evident.

People of Biblical times were familiar with the gap between aspiration and reality. Stories and prophecies, psalms and proverbs, Gospels and letters, show us they, too, sought to be *both* holy (or 'good') *and* compassionate (or 'nice') but consistently failed in their quest.

Let's look more closely at the Bible, first at the Old Testament then the New.

True Holiness
If one text sums up the spiritual and moral aim of the Hebrew faith which became Judaism, it is that found, at least half a dozen times, in the Book of Leviticus, including chapter 19, verse 2. Here, Moses, believing himself to be God's interpreter or prophet of the moment, urges his followers: "Be holy, because I, the Lord your God, am holy".

As you know from your reading of the Old Testament, the Hebrew-Jewish concept of God developed. So, as time passed, God ceased to be pictured and worshipped as a relatively local deity and came to be envisaged and revered as the one, supreme God of all humanity. From the earliest days, however, the Hebrews believed God was 'holy' – literally, 'set apart', special, distinctive, wholly righteous, utterly good. Indeed, God was so holy that they felt they should use the 'code name' Jehovah, or Yahweh. And, in response to Yahweh's goodness in delivering them from slavery, they believed that they, God's special people, were called to be similarly holy, 'set apart', special, distinctive, righteous, good. Hence the mass of laws in the books of Exodus, Leviticus, Numbers and Deuteronomy spelling out the practical implications of holy living. Hence the Ten Commandments which, depicted as they are outside and inside synagogues all over the world, bear constant witness to God's own holiness and what it implies for God's people.

And what a gigantic debt civilisation owes the Hebrew-Jewish faith community for cherishing and transmitting those ancient moral principles! The two largest faith communities – Christianity and Islam – explicitly revere them. Historically, the wider world has at the very least paid lip service to their wisdom. True, some people clamour for a new set of commandments, including such (ostensibly) conflicting instructions as "Be true to your God" and "Be true to yourself", though the fact there is such clamour could be construed as a *sort* of back-handed compliment to the value of the original Ten. The ancient Ten may not all resonate with our secularised world and do not spell out our now urgent obligations to the natural world. They may even put naughty ideas into our perverse minds. Yet, on balance, they have surely been beneficial. It's impossible to measure their impact, but, over the centuries, probably millions of people would claim these basic rules for living have helped them to develop spiritually, to be 'holier' than they would otherwise be. We may be confident that they genuinely have encouraged 'goodness'.

False holiness
In recent years, cycling has enjoyed quite a comeback and when I retired I took it up again myself. And I have taken part three times in the 100 mile sponsored ride from Bath to London organised by the charity Action Research. However, the first time I hesitated before deciding to join in. This was partly because I wasn't fully confident I would manage the distance in one day, partly because I don't like asking people for money, but also because a part of

me felt uncomfortable at the prospect of missing church – my upbringing and Christian ethos tell me I should, without fail, be in the pew (or pulpit) at least once on a Sunday.

In the end though, I decided to have a go. I felt that, much as I always need the spiritual and moral sustenance of worship, I should nevertheless join in. Fighting disease and relieving suffering, especially in children, are compassionate activities and just what Jesus himself did, not least on the Sabbath, the holy day. Yes, Box and Derry hills were hard slogs; 'Labour-in-vain' hill lived up to its name, as hidden brow after hidden brow mocked me; Savernake hill made the sweat flow. But the thought of lunch at the 65mile mark, refreshments at the end, a hot bath and huge pot of tea when I got home (by coach, our bikes returning by lorry) and, most of all, handing over several hundred pounds to help relieve illness and pain, all kept me going!

I've shared my dilemma at this point because it illustrates, albeit at a humdrum level, the tension between what became the dominant theological and moral thinking of Old Testament times and that of the New. I say 'what *became* the dominant theological and moral thinking' because the original concept of holiness was widely misinterpreted and, by the beginning of the First Century AD, meant something very different. Whereas in the earlier Hebrew period, holiness signified such allegedly divine qualities as moral wholeness, integrity and *inner* purity, as time wore on, many Jews – not least the religious leaders – increasingly identified holiness with external respectability, with ceremonial correctness, with maintaining what is sometimes called 'the purity system' (of which more, later).

What God requires
Thankfully, there *were* people of insight – prophets especially – who noticed what was happening and urged the people to think again and change their ways. Time and again, they urged rulers, priests and citizens to seek and practise true holiness and goodness. Shocked by the evil evident at every level of society, such as blatant cheating and exploitation – the sort of goings-on we read about in our papers or see on our screens every day – the prophet Micah slammed the shallow religiosity of his time, advising that the secret to true holiness lay not in the observation of rituals but through personal encounter with God:

"What shall I bring to the Lord, the God of heaven, when I come to worship him? Shall I bring the best calves to burn as offerings to him? Will the Lord be pleased if I bring him thousands of sheep or endless streams of olive oil? Shall I offer him my first-born child to pay for my sins?" (Human sacrifice was still at least a folk memory and has never gone away entirely) "No, the Lord has told us what is good. What he requires of us is this: to do what is just, to show constant love, and to live in humble fellowship with our God" (Micah 6:6-8).

Two phrases in that familiar quotation – 'to do what is just' and ' to show constant love' – add up to a word as central to the New Testament as the word 'holy' is to the Old, namely, 'compassion'.

To be fair, the concept of compassion definitely is evident in the Old Testament. The great prophets extol it. The Hebrew word for 'compassion' – in the singular meaning 'womb' and implying nurture – is often used of God. So when Jesus taught his followers to "be compassionate as God is compassionate" he was actually recalling Jewish tradition. But that understanding of God and God's wishes for God's people had been largely submerged by the time of Jesus's ministry. Official theology now claimed God's chief concern was with cultural, legal and ceremonial purity and strenuously sought to sustain the elaborate system the belief required.

The purity system

The purity system – shaped by the laws and codes of Leviticus chapters 11 to 26 – established a spectrum of people, ranging from the purest of all (the priests and Levites), through those born as Israelites, then those who had converted to Judaism, next bastards, and, impurest of all, those with damaged genitals (unable to reproduce they were unable to obey God's command to Abraham and his descendants to multiply). But anyone physically or mentally disabled or suffering from a harrowing disease like leprosy was deemed impure. As were people in certain occupations, such as tax collectors (tainted because they worked for a Gentile power) and shepherds (unclean because their job prevented them carrying out certain religious regulations). The abjectly poor, too, were dismissed as impure and Gentiles, by definition, were regarded as unclean.

Inevitably, this purity system created a world with sharp social boundaries between pure and impure, righteous and sinner, male and female, rich and poor, Jew and Gentile. And, by reinforcing the system, temple and priesthood only aggravated the social fragmentation.

Is it any wonder that Jesus (like Micah and other prophets of old) attacked the system? "How terrible for you, teachers of the Law and Pharisees! You hypocrites! You give to God a tenth even of the seasoning herbs, such as mint, dill, and cumin, but you neglect to obey the really important teachings of the Law, such as justice and mercy and honesty. These you should practice, without neglecting the others. Blind guides!" Jesus then went on to call them 'unmarked graves' – which held untouchable corpses – implying they were actually sources of *im*purity!

Jesus's alternative
For the most part, though, Jesus was positive, offering an alternative way of life to the purity system – a way characterised by compassion. Maybe deliberately using parallel phraseology, he urged his hearers to "be compassionate as God is compassionate". In the best known of all parables, the purity system is represented by the Priest and Levite, the way of compassion by the Samaritan. Jesus also challenged the purity ethos through his actions by doing such unthinkable things as healing those with leprosy, welcoming a woman with menorrhagia, restoring a mentally sick Gentile, caring for outcasts on the Sabbath, dining with all kinds of people 'beyond the pale'.

The Jesus movement followed its Lord's example, welcoming women, people with limited abilities, the poor and marginalized, into its fellowship. They even accepted into church membership an Ethiopian eunuch – someone who was not only a Gentile but also mutilated and therefore, according to the Jewish standards of the day, as impure as you could get! For all their inevitable faults, many early Christians sincerely sought to fulfil Paul's memorable assertion "In Christ there is neither Jew nor Gentile, slave nor free, male nor female" (Galatians 3:28). They grasped the vital truth that God wanted his people to be *both* wholesome in character *and* inclusively neighbourly in conduct, both holy and compassionate, both morally upright and empathetic, both pure and kind – good *and* nice!

Holiness and compassion today

And, today, doesn't the living Christ call you and me, as individual disciples and as a church, to be both holy and compassionate, pure and kind, 'good' and 'nice'? Yes, the Gospel record does show us Jesus advocating personal *holiness*, characterised by purity of thought and motive, moral integrity, and unassuming goodness. But it also testifies to the vital place he gave *compassion* and all it implies, in terms of neighbourliness, inclusiveness, empathy and mercy.

This means, doesn't it, that the local church has a dual duty? To nurture members' spirituality, helping them to grow in true holiness *and* to nurture members' compassion, giving them encouragement (and 'space') to be understanding neighbours and caring citizens. To encourage members to be self-disciplined (in, for example, their sexual conduct, driving, and use of alcohol) *and* involved in works of compassion (whether personal, local, national or global).

CHRIST CHURCH
Nourishing the spirit, serving the community
Christian Worship   *Christian Action*

Sundays 10.00am: For all the family   Mondays 7.00pm:World Action Group
Wednesdays 7.15pm: Searchers' Forum   Wednesdays 10.00-12.30: Shoppers' Creche
Fridays 12.30pm: Minister's Surgery   Saturdays 12.0noon: Open Table

There are many other services and activities: full details at www.ChristChurchNow.org...

For the world at large, Christ's Church is called to promote *both* strong, personal moral standards *and* loving, merciful inclusiveness – in family relationships, school life, workplace, political programmes, the formulation and enforcement of law... in *every* facet of society... Because now, as ever, the world needs individuals and communities that are both holy *and* compassionate, pure *and* kind, 'good' *and* 'nice'.

25   CHRISTIAN OR CHRISTLIKE?

The nature of true discipleship

Are you a *Christian?* Your immediate answer may well be "Yes". Given a little time for reflection, however, you might start to wonder. You want to know in what sense the word 'Christian' is being used. For the more you consider the term, the more you recognise it's one with different shades of meaning.

The philosophical meaning of 'Christian'

The term 'Christian' can be interpreted *philosophically*. It can refer to the particular interpretation of the universe, especially planet Earth and humanity's role within it, which is based primarily on the life and teaching of Jesus of Nazareth. When used in its philosophical sense, the term Christian refers to someone who believes that Jesus – as a man, then as a continuing spiritual presence – is the supreme illuminator of Truth: as opposed to the Torah for Jews; The Enlightened One for Buddhists; Muhammad for Muslims; Karl Marx for people (misleadingly) known as Communists; or, say, Socrates for Humanists. Used in its philosophical sense, the label Christian denotes someone who sees commitment to Jesus as the supreme clue to personal fulfilment and communal cohesion – and, indeed, to an understanding of God.

A faith to live by
So, if someone asked you if you were a Christian in *this* sense of the word, I guess your answer, like mine, would be an emphatic "Yes". Though you might well add, as I would, that you find profound wisdom and truth in other faiths, too. The learned sages of Hinduism, the perceptive thoughts of Confucius, the precepts of the Guru Granth Sahib (presented to us for many years by Inderjit Singh on Radio Four's Thought for Today), the timeless insights of the Hebrew-Jewish scriptures – to mention just some of the treasures of our common spiritual heritage – convey much that is inspiring and precious for all humanity. That said, we would nevertheless assert that, for us, Jesus sheds the brightest light on the nature of Absolute Truth, Pure Goodness and Perfect Love; that Jesus Christ offers the surest pointer to the Ultimate Reality widely called 'God'. And so, when the term refers to a worldview or a faith to live by, we are happy to be called 'Christian'.

The doctrinal meaning of 'Christian'

The term 'Christian' may also have a *doctrinal* connotation. Used in this sense, it refers to a person who holds a particular set of beliefs about who Jesus of Nazareth was and what he did of permanent value for humanity, about the 'Person' and 'Work' of Jesus, as theology puts it. Sadly, it is *this* use of the label 'Christian' that causes most of the problems!

From doctrine to dogma

Christians, we know well, hold widely differing beliefs about Jesus and what his life and death signify. Many of these beliefs – generally expressed in formal statements or 'doctrines' – go back to the early centuries of the Church's life, though *not*, it is vital to appreciate, to the time of Jesus's ministry itself. Many of the doctrines became so firmly embedded that they became dogma – teachings both priests and people were obliged to accept – and, eventually, assertions about Christ you questioned at your peril. Indeed, by the Fourth Century, if you were to be deemed a genuine Christian in the eyes of the Church, you had to confess its official creeds – like the one thrashed out by the First Council of Nicaea in 325. As time wore on, Christians were compelled to accept a growing body of doctrines not only about Jesus but also about the status and role of his mother, of the Church, and of its leaders. In the 19th Century, the Roman Catholic Church went so far as to declare that the official pronouncements of Christ's Vicar on Earth, the Pope, were infallible.

Throughout the Church's history, however, there have been Christians who objected to this or that or several of its doctrines and practices, many such 'heretics', as they were habitually labelled, being shut out, punished, or even tortured to death, for their often courageous stand. By the 16th Century though, over much of Europe, the volcano of dissent erupted into the unstoppable campaign for change known as the Reformation. To the Orthodox and Roman interpretations of the faith, there was added the Protestant. But soon, Protestantism itself fragmented with the doctrinally minimalist Society of Friends at one extreme, the doctrinally elaborate Anglo-Catholic Church at the other, and the historic Free Churches somewhere between the two.

In the 20th Century, however, historic denominational differences generally became less significant while differences of another sort intensified and are all too evident today.

Divergent views...

A few years ago, a businesswoman announced her plan to build a huge Biblical theme park somewhere in Yorkshire, her mission being, she claimed, to win youthful converts to the faith. The multimillion complex would offer visitors the chance to slide down the Tower of Babel before climbing aboard Noah's Ark, parting the Red Sea and felling Goliath with a laser-guided slingshot. Before leaving Ark Alive, billed as the place 'where Disney meets the Bible', visitors would also have the experience of expulsion from the Garden of Eden, being swallowed by a whale, and escaping from a lion's den.

...on the Bible

There may be a funny side to the story, but when I first read about the project, I recoiled with horror. Apart from the fact the proposed amusements stem from stories that are either only partially historical or even wholly fictional, or fly in the face of what centuries of science tell us about God's creative systems, or in some cases are morally repugnant, even racist (suggesting God happily protects one ethnic group while readily disposing of another) – apart from those objections – such stories, I suggest, reflect a sincere but immature notion of God's nature and intentions. They may well have *parabolic* value conveying a still valid spiritual truth. But they display – wouldn't you agree? – an understanding of God far inferior to that presented in the inclusive, reconciling love of Jesus.

So, to count as *genuine* Christians, do we *really* have to treat the Bible, from cover to cover, as the 'literal revealed word of God'? Must we *really* take every verse and chapter at its face value? Must we *really* put the Old Testament on a par with the New? That's what Fundamentalists demand. Regrettably, it's also what secular militants eagerly pounce on and portray as the general attitude of those they call 'religionists'. They zoom in on those who are dogmatic, aggressive and anti-intellectual, but overlook those whose faith is tentative, tolerant and intellectually realistic. Mercifully, church people of the latter kind are now responding. Through more confident preaching, and by means of new books, courses and networks, they are telling the world you *don't* have to be a Fundamentalist (or even of conservative evangelical persuasion), to be a genuine disciple of Jesus.

Surely, when we read the Bible, we should apply our God-given intelligence, welcoming the insights offered by centuries of honest study and acknowledging the spiritual development its pages trace! We then find it is indeed a collection of writings produced by fallible people like you and me. But we also discover it is a document that conveys abiding truths about God's nature and intentions. In short, we realize the Bible is a very *human* cradle of, nonetheless, *divine* truth.

...about the death of Jesus

The other contentious area of Christian belief I will touch on concerns the significance of Jesus's death. (Incidentally, I don't enjoy tackling thorny questions because I know I'm likely to upset someone, but preachers who duck them just aren't doing their job). The particular 'thorny question' I have in mind concerns the notion of sacrifice and its application to Jesus.

You will be aware that many Christians believe that God deliberately sent Jesus to our planet to be a sacrifice offered as recompense for the sins of humanity. They base their belief on the imagery of animal, if not human, sacrifice, which Paul uses in his struggle to make sense of Jesus's cruel death. But they hugely overrate his analogy for it is just one of several he adopts and represents only one stage of his theological odyssey.

Now the notion of ritualised sacrifice may well have struck a chord with his Gentile readers since the practice occurred in all sorts of contemporary cults. But I guess his Jewish readers found the apostle's illustration, to say the least, confusing. For their own scriptures (the Christian Old Testament) slammed not only *human* sacrifice (through, for example, the story of Abraham and his first-born son Isaac) but also, through the prophets, even *animal* sacrifice.

For many Christians today, the whole notion of God behaving like an angry tribal chief who could only be placated by a human sacrifice – what's more, the coolly planned brutal sacrifice of *'his only son'* (surely, something no loving, *human* father would contemplate) – for many Christians today, the whole idea of Jesus being a sacrifice offered to 'satisfy God', is pre-Christian both conceptually and ethically. *Whereas,* such Christians *can* buy the idea of Jesus being ready (naturally not eager) to give up, or sacrifice, his life, if the promotion of absolute goodness and limitless love so demanded.

If, *if*, being a Christian *obliged* me to affirm certain of the beliefs Fundamentalists forcefully affirm, in all conscience, I *could* not – nor would I *want* – to say I am a 'Christian'. Thankfully, there is no evidence whatsoever in the Gospels themselves that the would-be Christ-follower should subscribe to such demands. The Gospels show that all Jesus himself required of would-be disciples was faith – trust in his wisdom and power (e.g. Mark 5:34 and 11:52). All the earliest Church required of would-be members was the confession "Jesus is Lord" – an acceptance of Jesus as the predominant influence in their life (e.g. Acts 16:31 and 1 Corinthians 12:3). And this is all that our Free Church tradition requires.

The moral meaning of 'Christian'

The term Christian may also be used in a *moral* sense. When it is, it describes people who take very seriously the moral example and precepts of Jesus. It describes those who, to a noticeable extent, live out the ideals and precepts highlighted in the Sermon on the Mount. It describes, that is to say, those who recognize their spiritual inadequacy; who are genuinely humble; whose greatest wish in life is to do what God requires; who are kind and merciful; who are pure in heart; who work tirelessly for peace; who are beacons of light in a dark world; who are as practically helpful in society as salt; who control their anger, sex drive, and language; who respond to animosity with generosity; who love even their enemies. In other words, when used in a moral sense, the term 'Christian' refers to those who, in their private thoughts, family life, personal relationships and involvement in society – in all their 'going out and coming in' – aim to have the spiritual attitudes, and to apply the moral teachings, of Jesus.

Are you and I Christians in *this* sense? We might like to think so while we are well aware we don't always live up to our aspirations. We echo the frustration of the would-be disciple that

Paul brilliantly describes in his heartfelt exposé of the human condition in Romans chapter 7: "I don't do what I would like to do, but instead I do what I hate". But if it's moral *intention* rather than moral *achievement* that defines the Christian venture, then we might be bold enough at least to whisper, "Yes, I am a Christian".

To be thought of as a Christian in the moral sense, then, might seem a prize to go for. There's a snag though! For moral issues can be terribly divisive. Not only do those who call themselves Christian take up opposing views on old chestnuts like capital punishment and fox hunting, but they differ on a great range of matters – over abortion, homosexual legislation, contraception, euthanasia, crime and punishment and many other big social issues. Such differences are inevitable and we have to live with controversy. What is so sad is that Christians can be among the most opinionated and dogmatic of people, often stubbornly convinced that they, and they alone, are right! And if you are totally sure you are on God's side of the argument, it's not easy to admit, just maybe, you've got it wrong. So even in its moral sense, to be called a 'Christian' may not be altogether complimentary.

To sum up so far. The term 'Christian' can be used in a *philosophical* or 'faith outlook' sense – distinguishing the believer in Jesus from, for example, the devotee of Muhammad, or the purveyor of Humanism. The term 'Christian' has a *doctrinal* connotation referring to a particular understanding of the Jesus Event. It also has a *moral* meaning.

A fourth meaning: 'Christlikeness'

There's also a fourth meaning of the term 'Christian'. It is linked to the other three but stands head and shoulders above them. It has to do with *Christlikeness.*

Of course, we can never be sure about the 'mind' of Jesus. For the Jesus of history has been overlaid with the Christ of faith and the Gospels were written, roughly speaking, between twenty-five and seventy-five years after the events. Nevertheless, the impressions of Jesus's outlook provided by the Gospels suggest he was not primarily concerned about the philosophical basis of religious faith. Nor does he appear to have had much time for religious doctrine, judging by his impatience with religious leaders who put the niggling details of Jewish teaching before important things like 'justice, mercy and humility'. Nor, even, was he sold on moral excellence especially when it was confused with respectability – 'doing the right thing' merely because it was expected of you amounted to the rock-bottom sin of hypocrisy. So what *was* Jesus consistently passionate about? It was those attributes he himself had in full measure: inner purity; transparent honesty; integrity of spirit, mind and body; and, of course, unbounded compassion.

When all is said and done, little if anything in the Gospels suggests Jesus aimed to establish a new religion or philosophy with a new set of beliefs and principles. He was more concerned with encouraging people to open their hearts and minds to God's Presence and God's ways. Clearly reluctant to define himself as 'Son of God' or 'Messiah' or any of the other categories that opponents and followers attempted to put him in, he most certainly was *not* involved with the formulation of doctrines about his status and role. Serious Christian doctrine began and developed *after* his death. Jesus never produced a moral code, preferring simply to highlight the two ancient commandments about loving God with all your heart and soul and mind and strength – and loving your neighbour as yourself. In fact, he boiled morality down to one, new commandment: "in the way I have loved you, you also should love one another" (John 15:12).

The question that ultimately matters
Are you a Christian? Am I? How *important* a question *is* it? After all, Jesus knew *nothing* of the term for it was a term applied to his followers *well after his death*. If he ever came across the earlier term 'People of The Way' I guess he would have much preferred that label – because he lived and died to show people the way to live authentically and the way to know the presence and intentions of God. Christian religious faith, Christian doctrinal beliefs, Christian moral principles, may all have their place. But what our confused and spiritually hungry world needs, far more than those, are people whose lives are seriously and noticeably influenced by Jesus – people being transformed by the 'Jesus Experience'.

So, whatever label you and I attach to our personal brand of Christian faith – 'traditionalist', 'progressive', 'committed' or 'searcher' – or even if we simply find the whole notion of God too hot to handle, isn't the question that *ultimately* matters: 'How far are you and I *Christlike?*'

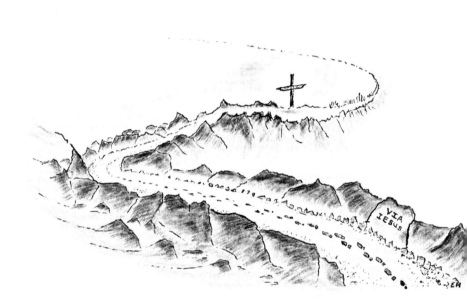

26   HERE AT LAST – THANK GOD!

A playlet about prayer

In this playlet we again eavesdrop on a discussion between four church-connected friends: Ernest Hope, Mona Gloom, Faith Wise and Frank Talker. Their friendship is platonic and developed probably more because of, than in spite of, the big differences in their personalities and views. Deciding to go on a canal holiday for a few days, they have just taken charge of their narrowboat 'Water Rat'.
Now, after a tiring journey, they are sitting on the brightly painted seats in the stern, recuperating...

Ernest Hope   Here at last – thank God!

Frank Talker   Huh, thank *Frank*, more like, for his brilliant driving!

Mona Gloom   All that traffic and all those road works! Now perhaps you can see why I wanted to travel by train. As the old lady said, 'If God had meant us to go by car he wouldn't have given us the railways!'

Faith Wise   Give us a break, Mona! Car or train, what matters, is we're here and still in one piece – and I'm thankful to Frank *and* to God.

FT   I'd be thankful for a cup of tea! Put the kettle on Mona.

MG   Put it on yourself, you lazy so-and-so – I'm just as tired as you. I hope you don't think we women are going to do all the skivvying on this blinking barge!

FT   Alright, Mona, keep your hair on!

FW   Now you two, enough arguing! *I'll* put the kettle on.

EH   And a piece of your cake, Faith, would go down a treat.

MG   You're always thinking of your stomach, Ernest. You'll get fat. These days we have to watch our calories.

FT   And cholesterol levels. I got a shock the other day when my doctor told me mine was over 8!

FW   Oh don't let's talk about such boring things as calories and cholesterol *on holiday*. Now, while I put that kettle on, the rest of you can start sorting out your luggage. I'll call you when tea's ready.

Ten minutes later

FW TEA'S UP!

EH My, that looks good, Faith. We'll all feel better after a nice cup of tea and a slice of your chocolate cake.

FT Sorry, Ernest, I was sharp with you earlier on... I didn't really mean to put you down when you thanked God for our slow but safe journey.

EH Forget it! We all felt a bit edgy. Actually – funnily enough – I've been thinking quite a lot recently about, well, God and how we think of him...her...it.

FT Same here, old boy, especially the whole business of communicating with him – prayer, in other words... Quite honestly, I really don't know *what* I believe now... I still go through the motions of praying – well, at church, and sometimes at home or in my office or just walking along – but not as often or, to be frank, anything like as confidently as I once did. Prayer can still seem real and meaningful but more often than not (if you'll pardon my bluntness, Faith) it feels more like an empty charade!

MG That's just what I find, Frank! I'm glad I'm not the only wicked one. You deserve a hefty slice of cake for that confession.

EH Seeing we're in confession mode, I must admit I also have my problems with prayer. As a serving elder, I know I should set a good example and give prayer a central place... but I don't... so feel I'm rather a hypocrite. Part of me tells me it makes sense to try and communicate with God but another part feels 'all at sea'.

FW Anyone for another cuppa?

MG As long as you don't put so much milk and water in – I can't stand dishwater.

FW Sorry, Mona. Anyhow, I don't think we should feel too guilty about our struggles. After all, you don't have to read much about the saints to discover how many of them had their problems. More recently, it's emerged, Mother Teresa had terrible worries not only with praying but even with believing in God! Judging from the fact they asked Jesus to teach them how to pray, the Twelve had their difficulties too... But *I* think that if we're ever to make head or tail of praying, we must first sort out our ideas about *God*. Just who – or what – are we wishing to address? How can we pray sensibly, intelligently – *at all* – unless we have in mind some realistic, believable notion of God?

212

EH I couldn't agree more, Faith... So what *should* we believe? What *do* we believe?

MG What *don't* we believe, more like – at least in my case. I mean, why should I praise God – as so many calls to worship, hymns and prayers assume I should – when there are so many horrible things going on... like rape, murder, wars, disease, typhoons, floods, people living in shacks I wouldn't even house a pig in, children with pot bellies and flies all over them...

FT So *much* suffering! And by people who don't deserve it any more than you or me – probably less so – yet God, who's supposed to be good and loving and in control, lets it all go on!

EH Hmm... the old, old 'problem of innocent suffering'...

MG Call it what you like, Ernest, I just don't think God's all he's cracked-up to be. To put it crudely, I find so many prayers and hymns of praise just stick in my gullet!

FW We could discuss undeserved suffering all night – though, to my mind, that, and therefore the issue of praising God, both hinge on what our idea of God actually is... If we think of God...

EH Before we explore that one, I just want to say that I think we're being very one-sided. Yes, there *is* terrible pain and evil in the world... which God appears to allow – or at least doesn't take 'direct action' to stop. But isn't there also much that *is* good... much that's amazingly wonderful in creation, in the natural world? Just look at those stupendous oaks and those magnificent pink flowers on that bank!

MG Red campion, Ernest.

EH And think about all the beauty in the human world – in music, in art – not least on this boat, just look at those arabesques round 'Water Rat' or that fine old church over there! And what about all the love there is in the world – in our families, between the four of us...

MG A rum sort of love that is!

EH And all the... co-operation! Just think of the hundreds of people – pickers on some Indian hillside, packers, shippers, distributors, shop assistants, Faith who poured it out – just think of all the chain of work that's gone into this pot of tea we're enjoying!

FT You've reminded me of the time I went to a restaurant and was discussing the menu with the waitress. Asking her what the

213

'soup of the day' was, she told me, 'It's a very special one – the chef's really *put his heart into it*'. I didn't fancy it when she said that!

EH Thank you, Frank! The point I'm making is: surely, God does deserve credit for the good there undoubtedly is. I, for one, often feel profoundly thankful and want to express my gratitude. Why not through prayer?

A brief silence ensues

FW I take it from our silence that the jury's out on whether God is 'innocent' or 'guilty'... does or doesn't deserve our praise. If so, may I again suggest the jury sort out just what its notion of God is... If we think of God...

EH Let's stick with prayer for the moment, Faith, though I do take your point. What I'm trying to argue is that, in spite of all the nasty things in life – which God undoubtedly permits, even if it's human selfishness, people's abuse of their innate, moral freedom, that causes most of the misery – in spite of the 'down' side, there's also a huge 'up' side. So I maintain there *should* be a place for praise and thanksgiving, in both public worship and personal prayer.

MG I'm still uneasy when it comes to many hymns and prayers of praise... Does God *really* want to be told, day in day out, how wonderful he is? Seems to me, he might have bit of an inferiority complex (Sorry, Faith)... But I've no doubts about prayers of *confession!* Whenever I stop to think about my life, my attitudes, my conduct, I always feel guilty... I remember all the rotten things I've thought or said or done, how ungrateful I've been, how I've grumbled.

FT *You*, Mona? Never!

EH I'm with Mona, here. While I try not to dwell too long on my failings – too much introspection, they say, being bad for the soul – I'm still glad to get things off my chest. So prayers of confession have my vote.

FT You're in good company, Ernest, when you think how many people in the Bible felt it was important to lay bare their soul before God.

FW Such as the writer of psalm 51. I had to learn it in my teens and can still remember how it starts... 'Have mercy on me, O God, according to thy lovingkindness: according unto the multitude of thy tender mercies blot out my transgressions... Wash me

214

throughly from mine iniquity, and cleanse me from my sin… For I acknowledge my transgressions: and my sin is ever before me.' Then I get stuck.

FT That's pretty impressive, even so. I wish I could quote chunks of scripture like that… but the only kind of thing I can remember, I'm ashamed to admit, are naughty schoolboy songs we sang at the back of the coach, like 'Roll me…'

FW OK, Frank – we all remember things we'd rather not and really shouldn't! Probably even 'Saint' Paul, judging from his boast to be the 'greatest sinner of all'.

EH So we're agreed… Hey-up! Look at him, he's going all over the place – he's coming straight for us, *hold tight!* LOOK OUT THERE!

The boat momentarily rocks

MG Phew! That was a close shave! He deserves to be reported. What's his boat called? I haven't got my glasses with me.

FT Er…'Sally Forth'.

MG Huh, should be called 'Silly Fool'…Ooh, I've got an idea… when he's moored and its the dead of night… I'm going to get out my paintbrush and…

FW All right, Mona… Aren't we supposed to *forgive* those who wrong us? Even when nailed to his cross, Jesus asked God to forgive those reviling him 'for they knew not what they were doing'…

MG Huh, *that bloke* certainly didn't know what he was doing!

EH As I was saying, it seems we're pretty well agreed that we do need to get things off our chest, deal with our guilt, and ask for forgiveness and help to do better in the future…

FT Yep, I think prayers of confession make sense… as long, that is, as we don't allow our confidence in God's readiness to forgive to become an excuse for 'business as usual'.

EH Don't 'sin that grace may abound'?

FW That's one way of putting it… That said, I *still* feel that our attitude to this and every aspect of praying must depend on *what our notion of God is*. If we think of God…

MG I'm getting peckish – I vote we think of *supper* and let *God* have a rest.

FT I've been wondering who's tummy keeps rumbling!

FW   Now Frank, there's no need to be personal.

EH   Hang on! I'm enjoying this discussion. In any case, there's one more aspect of prayer we really should air before we have our nosh. And that's *intercessory* prayer, prayer for others. This really does puzzle me – especially *how* it works.

MG   *If* it works, more like! When my Archie was ill – and I mean ill – slowly, painfully, wasting away – I prayed and I prayed for him to get better... until I saw it wasn't having the slightest effect. Then I prayed that God might spare him at least some of his pain... but it only got worse. Finally, I begged God just to take him and put him out of his misery... but, as two of you'll remember, he simply lingered on, for weeks. I honestly don't think my prayers – sincere, fervent and persistent as they were – made a jot of difference to the progress of the wretched disease. Nor the prayers of friends or neighbours or even the church prayer circle... Poor old Archie!

FT   I remember what you went through, Mona...vividly. And I recall how one person in particular – well-meaningly but *so* unhelpfully – claimed how *wonderfully* his prayers for his dear wife had been answered, how she had made a dramatic and full recovery, and which, he was sure, would happen in Archie's case, if you *kept on praying*... If only it were so simple! You're by no means the only one, Mona – lots of people, thoroughly devout Christians among them, have had the same, dispiriting experience. What's more, some research – with matching control groups – suggests praying for healing rarely, if ever, has any *direct* impact on the physical condition of the patient.

EH   Perhaps not on the strictly physical condition, Frank, but there's more to healing than that. Minds and emotions come into the process. Most of all, the 'innermost self' (or 'soul', if you prefer) of both pray-ers and prayed for. It's in this area, I believe, that prayer can make a difference, affecting attitudes -how people respond to the challenge. Healing is a holistic thing... No, I don't think we should dismiss the value of intercessory prayer too briskly.

FW   And we certainly shouldn't fall into the logical trap of assuming that something *cannot* happen because we don't understand *how it might*.

FT   I'm finding all this a bit beyond me. All I would add, is that when I pray really thoughtfully...

216

EH Empathetically?

FT ...For an individual, or for the victims of a tragic event, that it makes me feel I really must *do* something to help them.

FW Intercessory prayer, in other words, challenges the pray-er not just to *pray* but also to *act*?

FT Precisely!

MG Coo, the mozzies aren't half starting to bite!

EH I've got some TCP, if you'd like some, Mona.

MG I would, please – fancy that still being around, I was brought up on it!

FW We *still* haven't tackled the pivotal question: *what's our notion of God?*

FT OK, let's sort out God – then we really will deserve our supper!

FW As I see it, if we think of God mainly as a Being – up or out 'there' – essentially separate from us and who only intervenes in human matters when he chooses, then asking for God's help through prayer is perfectly reasonable. But if we think of God more as a 'universal presence'...

EH The one, as Paul put it to the crowd in Athens, 'in whom we live and move and have our being'?

FW If we think of God essentially as a universal presence – a presence the writer John characterized by such profound concepts as Spirit, Truth, Light, and Love... prayer *then* is more a matter of *opening our innermost selves to receive* this spirit-renewing, truth-revealing, light- and love-giving presence...When we pray for *others*, we express our willingness to help convey the same 'God-sourced' spiritual benefits...

EH And, it strikes me, if we think of God in Faith's kind of way, we're less likely to 'pass the buck' – as can so easily happen when we think of God 'up or out there' waiting for us to persuade him to do what we want. What's more, we won't *expect* God to 'come to heal' and then be disappointed, or resentful, when he doesn't!

MG Hmm...Thank you, that's been quite enlightening – though I'm sure we've only dipped our toes in the water, so to speak... Talking of water, just look at those magnificent swans... Mum and Dad with their five, no six, babies all in a circle!

FT That's what they call a 'cygnet ring'!

MG Push that man overboard!

FT Sorry folks! Seriously, I'm a good deal happier now.

EH I think I am, too. But whatever our hang-ups about praying, there must be *something important* about it if Jesus himself engaged in it.

FW And so regularly – publicly in the synagogue, privately in quiet places whenever he could.

MG And what was good enough for him, should be good enough for us!

EH Good for everyone, come to think of it – not just church-goers... Whoever we are, don't we need to make time... to reflect, to appreciate the truly worthwhile things in life, to realize what an amazing planet we inhabit and its infinite potential for good?

FT Time also to recognize how we mess it all up, wrecking the natural world, fouling-up even the climate... depriving, hurting, killing our own species... being horrid even to those we claim we love...

MG Time to think about the world outside ourselves – about the suffering and needs – God pity us! – of *millions* of our fellow men, women and children, and what we might do to ease their plight ...

FW In a nutshell, everyone needs: to appreciate the good in life and be thankful for it; to admit their moral and relational failings and needs; to think intently and empathetically about others that they may, in some measure, act as channels of God's spirit, God's truth, God's light, God's love...

EH And when people do these things, even if they themselves wouldn't *call* it such, I for one say they are *praying*...

MG *Please* can we have our supper now?

27   TIME AND ETERNITY

Reflections on the nature and significance of time

Have you ever thought hard and long about the strange phenomenon we call 'Time'? I'm sure you have – when you've had time! You may well reflect on it momentarily at the threshold of a new year. But whatever the extent of your past philosophising on the subject, I invite you to ponder it again now – first considering the intellectually intriguing question 'What's the *nature* of Time?' and then the spiritually important question 'What's the *significance* of Time?'

The nature of time

First, then, the *nature* of time. Whilst this is primarily a philosophical and scientific matter, it is also of theological interest since time is an integral facet of the space-time process by which, people of many faiths believe, God's creation of the universe began and continues.

So, what *is* the nature of time? Unquestionably, time is very odd. For a start, you can't touch, taste, see, hear or smell it. And yet, as a newspaper leader once put it, "we sense it around us as an intangible medium in which our minds are suspended like specimens preserved in formaldehyde".

In short supply

From the perspective of a child, a life of 'three (now more likely four) score years and ten' appears unimaginably long, yet we gradually discover that life is actually rather brief and time is something often in short supply. "Please forgive this brief letter", we write, "but it's time for the post". "It'll save time if you email your article to me", we suggest. "'Would you ring me back?" we ask, "as I'm rather busy at the moment". "Thanks for inviting me", we reply, "but I'm afraid my diary's chock-a-block just then".

Is it any wonder a busy clergyman asked: "What *is* this secret pact everyone signs to be *on* time, *up* to time, *in* time – this badge of efficiency, this standard of conduct, this key to promotion, this road to exhaustion?"

Time sometimes appears to play tricks on us. The last five minutes of an exam seem to flash by if you've not finished all the questions. Yet, when your team is only just ahead in a crucial match, the last five minutes before the final whistle can seem never-ending. In each case, the interval is the same but our perception of it is totally different.

Time and space

It's not surprising that the subject of time and its meaning is one that has fascinated philosophers for centuries. Asked whether time had a limited duration or had been around forever, St Augustine sparked off all sorts of searching questions, not least whether time can go in one direction only or can actually go backwards. If time and space are inextricably linked – so that time progresses as space expands – then, if the Universe stops expanding and starts to collapse in on itself, wouldn't time reverse?

One of the greatest living theoretical physicists, Stephen Hawking, has wrestled with this question for years. At first, he suggested that time might indeed eventually run backwards. Then, in his best-seller 'A Brief History of Time' he repudiated the idea, asserting that the laws of physics simply don't permit time travel. After other experts argued that the predictions of general relativity *did* allow the possibility of time going backwards, Professor Hawking has come round to the view that they may indeed be right!

Profoundly puzzling

So, in spite of all our reflection, discovering and knowledge, we live in a universe many of whose laws and mechanisms – not least the phenomenon of time – remain profoundly puzzling. Little could William Cowper know, two hundred years ago, just *how* apt were the opening words of his hymn: "God moves in a mysterious way his wonders to perform!"

One unsung hero of our times has been fascinated by the strangeness of time for most of his life. He has invented all sorts of useful things, perhaps most notably the thermostat that stops electric kettles boiling dry as well as saving huge amounts of energy worldwide.

But John Taylor's latest invention is the Corpus Clock, Cambridge, unveiled in September 2008 by Stephen Hawking. A mechanical, spring-driven clock, unlike any other, its distinctive features include a blinking, jaw-snapping, tail-wagging 'Chronophage' in perpetual motion. The Chronophage looks like a giant grasshopper which appears to 'eat time' – hence its Greek name. And on the hour the clock reminds observers of their mortality with the sound of a chain dropping into a wooden coffin.

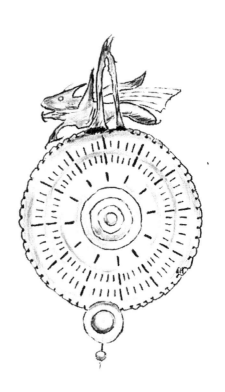

It's not only great philosophers, scientists and inventors who have been captivated by the strangeness of time. When I taught, I found my students invariably were, as this selection of definitions produced by one group of twelve-year-olds shows:

"Time is a substance with no physical form".

"Time is a space between one thing and another: you spend a lot of it at school but not a lot, maybe, in the bath".

"Time can never stop: it will always go on even if the earth disintegrates and everything dies".

"Every moment of time is unique: there will never be another day, hour, minute, second, or millisecond exactly the same as this one".

Yes, exploring the *nature* of time is a fascinating exercise and can tell us something about the nature of the world and universe we inhabit – and perhaps, even, the odd glimpse into the 'Mind of God'.

The significance of time

But what about the *significance* of time?

A social convenience

The concept of time is certainly an extremely useful one. In fact, it's difficult to imagine the modern, global human family managing without it. Contemporary society depends hugely on the idea of time and the internationally agreed method of measuring it.

Of course, the choice of units used to measure the passing of time is largely arbitrary. As we all know, the length of a year and that of a day are based on features of our planetary system. But the length of a century or week or hour or minute or second is totally artificial. So, if we had measured the number of years since the birth of Jesus in units of seven, instead of ten, there wouldn't have been anything particularly special about, for instance, the year labelled 2000 (or, more strictly, 2001).

And it's perhaps because we know the numbering system is purely arbitrary, that a part of us isn't all that excited by the arrival of a new year (or century, or millennium). We know that once the celebrations are over, life continues essentially as before.

So we can sympathise with the Biblical philosopher's thoughts on time. Life, the writer of Ecclesiastes argued, always goes on in much the same way – with a time for this, a time for that and a time for virtually anything (Ecclesiastes 3: 1-8). And at the physical level he was right. Like everything else in the natural world, we're born, we grow up, we fade, we die. The process is the inevitable outcome of the physical laws built into Creation right from the primordial explosion.

So, at the material level, when a new year (or century or millennium) is acknowledged, the world remains virtually the same. Human knowledge of it and our ability to exploit its resources – many no doubt as yet hidden from us – goes on growing, but the physical world itself remains constant. In one sense, therefore, marking the passing of time is no more than a social convenience.

An opportunity to take stock

And yet... in another sense, marking the passing of time *is* important.

Doesn't it provide us with an opportunity to take stock – to reflect on the past, be truly aware of the present, and prepare wisely for the future?

When we look back, we can trace so much that is shameful in human history. Sadly, much of the Christian Church's story is far from glorious. Virtually from its birth, it was a fractious community. Some of its early international councils degenerated into pandemonium while later the whole of Christendom split with the great East-West schism. There were the merciless Crusades which tried to evangelise by spiritually contradictory and ethically indefensible means. There was the brutal Inquisition which equally failed to realize it is morally repugnant (and ineffective) to try and force people into a state of faith. As Orthodox, Roman Catholic and Protestant leaders now readily admit, throughout its history, the 'holy, catholic and apostolic church' has, all too often, been sinful, exclusive, and introverted!

Empires and ideologies come and go

And yet, I believe we *may also* look back gratefully, unutterably thankful for so much else that has been good, for so many ways in which Christ's people *have* followed in their master's footsteps, for so many signs that the Kingdom, or Rule, of God *has* become real. Look back over two thousand years of Christendom and think how many mighty empires have been built, most in their day seeming indestructible and permanent – the Roman, the Arab, the Turkish, the Mogul, the Spanish, the French, the British – yet each of them eventually faded and collapsed. Think of the birth and rise of ideologies in the 20th Century – some (like Fascism and Naziism) horrific in both principle and practice, others (like Marxism-Leninism) worthy in aspiration but soon degenerating into cruel and inhuman systems: yet these ideologies, also, have withered. Humanism, as a conscious systematic faith, has never really caught on, the British Humanist Association (for instance) numbering only a few thousand: for all its virtues, Humanism has never been realistic about the evil element in the human condition. Even capitalism, the first genuinely global ideology, is changing, increasingly recognising its social and environmental responsibilities, finding itself pressed to consider the claims of justice and to heed Mother Earth's plea for sustainable development.

The Eternal Rock amid the 'shifting sands' of Time

The winning way of Jesus

Yes, human empires and ideologies have come and gone (or at least changed), older people having witnessed this process to a degree unprecedented in world history. The world is littered with ruins testifying to the erstwhile power and glory of this or that empire or ideology! Even American neo-imperialism, characterised by the posturing and policies of extreme Republicanism, will eventually implode and may well already be doing so, judging from the continuing turmoil in Afghanistan, Iraq and the Middle East. Meanwhile, crosses, wayside shrines, humble churches, majestic cathedrals, enlightened laws, transforming movements, and compassionate enterprises, all witness to the resilient and winning way of Jesus.

One story, among countless that demonstrate the tenacity of Christian faith at its best, began in Robben Island prison (where Nelson Mandela was once incarcerated). Because he was black, a particular prisoner was not allowed to visit the prison chapel, one more of a series of indignities he had suffered under the Apartheid regime. On release, however, he was accepted for the Christian ministry and became the talented and influential Archbishop of Cape Town. The call of Christ finally outwitted the racist ideology.

As we look around at the world of today, we see the same hotchpotch of good and evil... so much going on which saddens and appals us, so much that debases and destroys human well-being, so much that flouts God's way revealed in Jesus. Yet – in this neighbourhood, in this city, all over the nation and the world – we also see so much that is wholesome, beautiful, just and loving; so many signs that Truth, Goodness, Selfless Love *do* overcome evil and build up that rule of Love for which Jesus lived and gave his life. The God who was present to a unique degree in the wisdom and life, love and suffering of Jesus, is still alive and active, wherever people open their minds and hearts to God's 'gentle knocking'.

How will the future be shaped?

But what of the future? All sorts of forecasts can be made, some aided by ultra-powerful computer projections, and many very disturbing, such as the Stern Report on Climate Change. Predictions, however, are not certainties. The future has yet to be shaped.

How will it be shaped? The core factor will be the spiritual condition of both leaders and citizens. For it is this, which forms people's attitudes and the way they relate to each other and their environment. People's spiritual condition has always been crucial to genuine human progress. But with the technological power that our species now has – power sufficient either to destroy everything on Earth or to provide universal well-being – the health of people's innermost selves, or souls, is more vital than ever. It is this that will determine how the world responds to the choices it faces, choices which are essentially those Moses put before his migrant Hebrews over three thousand years ago – between good and evil, life and death, serving or defying God. (Deuteronomy 30:15-20)

The demands of eternity
Putting it another way, as we recognise the passing of time, so we must acknowledge afresh the demands of eternity. Which means, I submit, that those who claim to follow Jesus must go on trying to proclaim and embody the changeless, life-enhancing, attributes so amply present in his life, teaching and final self-giving... forgiveness, reconciliation, justice, trust, forbearance and, supremely, tireless, indiscriminate, love. *Somehow*, these *simply must* become the trademarks of human relationships world wide, if the human species and the entire living planet is to survive, let alone thrive.

The philosopher of Ecclesiastes thought time has an irresistible power and authority of its own. But Jesus showed humanity that people *do* have the power to shape their lives, the world they live in, and their future – though they will succeed and enjoy life 'in all its fulness', only when they follow his way... In a sentence, Christ calls us to live whatever time we have, in the context of eternity.

28   DEAD-END OR DOORWAY?

Thoughts about death and beyond

Is death a *dead-end* or a *doorway*?

According to recent surveys, if you and I are typical of British Christians and we feel free enough to be honest – which isn't always the case in church circles – roughly half of us would answer 'dead-end' and half 'doorway'.

So it is surely right for preachers to air the question – candidly but sensitively – and try to shed at least a glimmer of light on it.

Our reluctance and confusion

But we don't really like thinking or talking about death and what might follow! Mostly, we enjoy life and want it to go on for as long as we can cope. Though we concede there are people for whom life is so horrid that death is a welcome prospect. And contemporary culture, with its hedonistic materialism, reinforces our reluctance to ponder our move to the final 'departure lounge'.

Isn't a major reason, however, why we hesitate to look the 'Grim Reaper' in the face, our confusion? Many, if not most, of us are not sure what we believe about death and its aftermath.

Funeral, cremation, memorial and life-celebrating services increasingly reflect our confusion. Like it or not, the traditional service, with its familiar Bible texts and its confident affirmations, appeals and convinces less and less. Now, 'goodbye' ceremonies, with their family tributes, poems, and favourite songs of the departed, generally sideline theological reflection.

True, the subject of death and its sequel may be tackled in an Advent service but for the rest of the Christian year it rarely features. And one can sympathize with the busy, multi-church minister lacking time and energy to address such a difficult and sombre theme. To cap it all, there may well be someone in the pew just bereaved and simply not in the frame of mind to think deeply and frankly about the destiny of a loved one. If that's the case now, I hope you'll be forbearing.

Signs of serious interest

On the face of it, then, the question of death and what follows appears to be mentally marginalised, both within and outside church circles. And yet, when you look at contemporary society more carefully, I believe you *can* detect signs of serious interest.

This is undoubtedly so when someone, local or famous, dies early or tragically. Flowers are heaped at the site of the accident. Total strangers flock to the funeral. There's a palpable sense of shock and perplexity.

But many popular songs, magazine articles, novels, and episodes in TV and radio soaps, I suggest, also show that, beneath the hectic, noisy, pushy surface of contemporary life, there's a genuine and serious concern about big questions like death and its meaning. Might not the very loudness of modern living, with its cacophony of phone jingles, thumping muzak, 24/7 radio, actually be a barrier people subconsciously erect against the fears and uncertainties they *do* feel in their rare moments of silence?

And haven't we all, at some time, been challenged to make some sort of helpful answer to the question where life is heading? Out of the blue, a child asks us: "What will happen to me when I die?" Or a frazzled colleague rages: "Why on earth do I come into this office, day in and day out? Where's it all leading?" Or a friend or relative on their death bed whispers: "What will happen to me when I go?" Deep down, people *do* wonder about death and its meaning.

Ministers may have their doubts

Ministers, too, may have their doubts, even if some of them lack the confidence or humility to admit it. When I first took funerals and cremations and lead the procession into the chapel, I rang out the revered words that imply death is indeed a doorway:

> "I am the resurrection and the life, saith the Lord: he that believeth in me, though he were dead, yet shall he live; and whosoever liveth and believeth in me shall never die" (John 11:25-26).

As time went on though, I felt more and more uncomfortable. The rational 'me' increasingly battled with the 'pastoral' me. When the coffin slid quietly away towards the furnace or sank slowly down into the earth, I wondered just *how* the soul of that person could escape and survive the imminent destruction of its lifelong frame. I couldn't help feeling death was more likely a dead-end. And I wrote a service which faced up to that confusion.

Like it or not, a Christian's 'rational' self is not immune to society's general scepticism and is liable, to some extent, to share its doubts. So I don't think we should feel inadequate, or guilty, whenever we reckon death is more likely a dead-end than a doorway.

But now, let's be more positive. Can science or philosophy or religion generally, and last but certainly not least, the New Testament, help us make sense of death and what might lie beyond it?

Can science help us?
I'm not a qualified scientist, but I am confident one thing science shows us is that things in the physical world are not always what they appear to be. Something apparently solid, for instance, actually contains lots of empty space both within and between

the atoms from which it's made – though even that emptiness may well be only apparent. Might it not be that the connection between our body and our innermost essence (mind, emotions and will) is also something we cannot be too definite about?

An interdisciplinary group of scientists in New Mexico has suggested that, along with mass and energy, the concept of information should be admitted as a fundamental concept of theoretical physics. So, if information is a basic facet of the way things are, and the human 'soul' or 'essence' is defined as a 'collection of information', the notion of it existing elsewhere when the body returns to 'star dust' is a plausible one. Especially if the nature of our post-death existence is a little like radio waves, unseen and intangible yet indisputably real. That said, *how* we would recognize each other as a bundle of information or dismembered radio-like waves, makes the mind boggle! And it's not a very inviting prospect!

Near-death experiences
Some scientists believe evidence for life after death might be found in what are called 'near-death experiences'. These, may I remind you, are those in which someone, on the very brink of death or momentarily beyond it, appears, briefly, spectacularly and usually joyously, to experience a totally different reality. All sorts of people, atheists as well as believers, claim they have had such an experience and, almost without exception, have thereby become convinced there *is* life after death.

Certain medics counter that the euphoria near-death experiences generate is only to be expected when the brain is temporarily starved of oxygen. Their explanation, however, doesn't actually rule out the possibility that such ecstasy might be a feature of our journey to a further life. And we are still left wondering how some people who say they have had an 'out of body' experience, can so accurately describe scenes which require an elevated point of observation, unless some aspect of their being really had temporarily escaped and risen above their all-but-dead body.

Dr Sam Parnia of Southampton University hopes to shed light on the phenomenon. In September 2008, he announced that his team, along with others at twenty-five centres in the UK and

US, would be sharing in an investigation bearing the acronym AWARE. Over the following thirty-six months, they would carry out a combination of sophisticated brain monitoring experiments to find out whether the mind can, in truth, be 'non local to the brain'. Can those who claim to 'see' when their eyes are closed and their brain is in a 'flatline' state actually do so? Admitting that 'we know nothing about the mind itself – it really is a mystery', Dr Parnia nevertheless hopes the AWARE project will reveal whether near-death experiences are illusory or possible evidence of consciousness being able to exist outside its human frame – evidence, even, of post-death existence. Watch this space!

So scientists of integrity, I submit, will keep an open mind about the answer to our great question. They will agree that even though at present there's no incontrovertible evidence either way, there might be in the future. And they certainly won't commit the logical fallacy of assuming that something *could* not happen because we cannot currently understand or imagine *how* it might.

Might philosophy help us?
Turning to philosophy, some philosophers suggest that the way the human spirit can remain astoundingly strong, even when the body suffers intense pain or is all but wasted away, could be evidence for the ultimate independence of spirit and body. I am sure we have all witnessed remarkable examples where a person's mind, or spirit, appears to be in such control of their suffering body that the two seem virtually detached.

Other serious thinkers maintain that human mortality seems so wasteful. Can it really be that something so intricate, versatile and unique as a human being ends up as nothing more than 'earth' or 'ashes'? Wouldn't it be odd if the very species which unlocks Creation's secrets and resources ended up as nothing more than lifeless atoms? Doesn't our stunted, spiritual condition cry out for a further opportunity to grow and flourish? Of course, the feeling that we *ought* to survive may be no more than wishful, even arrogant, thinking. Yet this sense of incompleteness just might be evidence of a future fulfilment.

Leaving science and philosophy on one side, how might religion help our enquiry?

Religious beliefs
Eastern religions – such as Hinduism and Buddhism – maintain that body and soul are distinct and joined only during a person's or creature's life on Earth. When the body dies and the soul is released, it then inhabits a different body and the process is repeated. Through the cycles of birth, death and re-birth – 're-incarnation' – the soul has a chance to develop until it eventually finds release from the cycle, or achieves the transformed mode of consciousness known as 'nirvana'.

Certainly in their traditional forms, the three Abrahamic faiths – Judaism, Christianity and Islam – assert that a new soul is created when, or shortly after, a baby is conceived and that this spiritual facet of our humanity survives the death of its bodily frame. Orthodox adherents of these faiths also claim the nature of post-death life is determined by the way the individual behaves in their earthly life: be evil, and you'll end up in hell; be good, and you'll go to heaven. And these destinations have been graphically envisaged, especially in the Christian mediaeval era.

Sinister symbols

The 15th century painter Hieronymus Bosch loved to fill his minutely detailed pictures with all manner of sinister symbols. In a work called 'Death and the Miser', an animated skeleton threatens the dying man with an arrow, a grotesque devil tries to win his soul by proffering a bag of gold, while an angel touches his shoulder in a final bid to win his penitence.

But, today, we're not so sure about heaven and hell! Relatively few people believe they are real, physical places. We regard them more as symbols of goodness and evil, heaven evident in places, moments and relationships that are wholesome and beautiful, hell manifest in the conflicts and evil of the world.

And yet, even when our *minds* persuade us death could well be a dead-end, the *feeling* that our present values, attitude and conduct really might affect our destiny still lingers. Is this simply because we have been conditioned to believe death is a doorway? Or could it be because the Spirit of God, which faith assures us is ever present, is gently telling us it is true?

What might the Spirit say?

But what else might the Spirit of God say to us about our intellectually fiendish question?

I don't think we can ever distinguish absolutely between the ordinary, internal workings of our mind and what we believe are the promptings of God's Spirit within that same mind. And yet, if you will allow me to vocalize the Spirit, I believe the Spirit says to me something like this:

"Edward, use your intellect fully for it's ultimately a product of the Cosmic Intelligence you call 'God'. Don't worry if your rational self is confused and cannot, on scientific or philosophical grounds, decide whether death is a dead-end or doorway. After all, it is a metaphysical question – by definition beyond the scope of physical investigation. Remember that Jesus himself admitted it was largely a mystery – 'not for you to understand', this side of death".

Take Jesus at his word!
"So what I suggest" ('I' still being the Holy Spirit!) "is that you take Jesus at his word. Because when you *do* allow him to influence you – your thoughts, values, attitudes, speaking, doing, relationships, and involvement in the community – you know full well that Jesus 'got it right'. When you *do* take him seriously, you know that his wisdom and love, his insights and forgiveness, his understanding of the human condition and vision for the human family, all make absolute and permanent sense".

"You know full well that if people the world over – leaders, people in positions of influence generally, as well as ordinary men, women and children – you know full well that if people the world over, really took on board his teaching and manner of life, the world would be transformed! Wars would cease and the billions spent fighting them would be spent fighting disease. Everyone would have a proper home, be fully educated, have a decent job and enjoy a contented life. Even climate change would be slowed down, as everyone acted in the interests of their near and distant neighbours".

"Yes, Edward, you know Jesus makes total sense for the *here and now*... Would such a person really be 'off his rocker' when he spoke so confidently about *life beyond death*? Should you not take him at his word?"

What can separate us?
Maybe the Spirit of God said something along those lines to Paul. Like the rest of us, the apostle wrestled with the great question death thrust at him. He, too, offered intellectual arguments, not least that any after-death 'body' must be radically different from the mortal one. But what finally convinced him, I surmise, was his personal discovery that discipleship worked, and worked through thick and thin. For Paul, taking Jesus seriously in the here and now made absolute sense.

"In view of that, what can we say?" he asks. And answers with his memorable testimony recorded in his letter to the Christians of

Rome. "What can separate us from the love of Christ? Can trouble... or hardship or persecution or hunger or poverty or danger or *death*? No... there is nothing in all creation that will ever be able to separate us from the love of God" (Romans 8:31,35,39).

Our purely 'rational self' may sometimes persuade us death is more likely to be a *dead-end*. But in the light of our experience of Jesus here and now, our 'faith self' may quietly affirm that death is a *doorway*.

`

29   VISION POWER!

A celebration of the value of visions, then and now

Proverbs 29:18: 'Where there is no vision, the people perish'.

Have you ever had a vision – of a truly saintly 'you', or a radically better Britain, or a world 'fair as it might be'? Of course you have and probably repeatedly. And whenever we do have such visions, we're in good company. The Bible, for a start, is packed with visions, some grand and eloquent, others confined and simple; some explicit, others implicit – but all conveying a longing for a better, happier order.

Visions in the Bible
Early in the Bible's opening book, there's a familiar vision that looks back – to an imaginary age when the entire Earth was like the garden paradise of Eden, with its beautiful trees and luscious fruit, its starkly innocent primordial couple, and its quaint picture of God enjoying an evening stroll.

The vision described in the Christian scriptures' closing pages looks forwards – to a new and resplendent Jerusalem where, once again, God has his home, and "there is no more death or grief or crying or pain" (Revelation 21:4), the old selfish, sinful order having passed away with earth and heaven in perfect harmony.

Based on real life
Between these two highly poetic visions, there are many others. The author of our particular proverb would have been familiar with those reported in the still evolving Jewish scriptures. As a wordsmith, he – and it almost certainly would be a 'he' at the time – put the idea into an arresting and elegant form but, like other proverbs, "Where there is no vision, the people perish", was based on real-life experience. Like his fellow authors and compilers of the Wisdom Literature – writings put together in the last three centuries B.C. and comprising (in the Hebrew scriptures) Job, Ecclesiastes, Song of Songs, Proverbs and, arguably, Psalms – like his fellow writers, our proverb author (or editor) would know his people's story.

In particular, he would know the power of visions in that story. Now the word 'vision' is clearly a tricky one to translate into English. The Hebrew 'Chazon' has been rendered 'prophecy', 'guiding hand' and 'God's guidance', to mention just three attempts. So linguistic precision eludes us. Yet the underlying message is clear: without prophetic, divinely inspired ideals and goals, a community is likely to decline and fail. As the King James' version hauntingly conveys the Hebrew, "Where there is no vision, the people perish".

Perhaps our sage had in mind Moses' brave guidance which led his people out of slavery and ethnic oblivion. Or David's inspiring, if ruthless, military skill that welded the separate tribes into a nation able, at least for a while, to withstand the onslaughts of its mightier neighbours. Or the moral charter that prophets, like Amos and Isaiah, offered king, priests and subjects, to halt their social and political decay. Whoever our sage had in mind, his people's long and turbulent experience convinced him: "Where there is no vision, the people perish".

The 'Jesus Vision'
One or two centuries after the Book of Proverbs was complete, a stranger from Nazareth invited a tiny group, composed largely of descendants of the same faith community, to catch and share his life-changing, world-transforming vision. This Galilean wished to offer humanity the secret, as the Fourth Evangelist put it some seventy years later, to "life in all its fulness". His life's mission, he learnt, was to show – by word, attitude and action to anyone ready to listen and follow – what living in harmony with God truly meant. And, brought up in the Jewish tradition, he drew heavily from its scriptures, cherishing their wisdom. We may be confident that Jesus knew, and affirmed, our proverb: "Where there is no vision, the people perish".

The Early Church took up the torch Jesus had lit and spread its light. At first, Jesus's vision was too dazzling for even its leaders. It took a graphic dream about eating ritually impure food and a mind-changing encounter with a Roman soldier, to persuade Peter that Gentiles, in God's 'sight', really were on a par with Jews. It took a soul-searing vision to turn Saul the Christian terminator into Paul the Christian missionary, convinced that only the 'Jesus vision' for the world was great enough "to set creation free from

238

its slavery to decay". Leaders and members of the infant Church would have agreed, "Where there is no vision, the people perish".

In spite of the Christian Church's immaturity, the Jesus vision *was* passed on, inspiring successive generations with ideals winsome and strong enough to counter any assault on their faithfulness. Both famous and ordinary disciples caught the dream of a world in tune with God.

Modern visionaries

When visionary Nelson Mandela addressed the British Parliament in 1996, he marvelled at an earlier visionary who, nearly 200 years before, had addressed the same institution, "daring to stand up and demand that slaves be freed". Thanks to William Wilberforce's

vision of a nation and world freed from the bartering and trafficking of human labour, many thousands of men, women and children were saved from, literally, perishing – in the holds of brutally cramped ships or on the estates that still sought their muscle power. Also in the 19th century, Charles Dickens envisioned a Britain rid of destitution, an ambition which, even in his lifetime, legislation and reform began to address, allowing millions to receive a measure of education and decent sanitation. Wilberforce and Dickens were just two who, knowingly or unknowingly, espoused the truth "Where there is no vision, the people perish".

The 20th Century produced its own visionaries, not least during the Second World War. Born only the year before it started, I tend to remember more homely details – such as going with my mother to a sewing meeting where a circle of women busily knitted khaki garments like mittens and socks, or watching my father stick little flags on a map to chart the Allies' advance. But I do remember the stirring voice of Winston Churchill and his vision of ultimate victory, a vision that sparked off all sorts of wonderful welfare and rebuilding plans. Without such vision, Britain could well have lost its nerve with millions more perishing at Hitler's hands.

But plenty of other leaders – at various positions on the faith spectrum – fired their people's imaginations in the last century. People like Mikhail Gorbachev with his visionary ten historic theses of June 1988, 'perestroika' ('restructuring') and 'glasnost' ('openness') among them; or Martin Luther King with his riveting dream of an America free from racial and economic injustice. As the ten statues of 20th Century martyrs, installed in 1998 above the west entrance of Westminster Abbey, symbolize, there was a succession of men and women who saw, in their soul's eye, a better world and who were ready to give their all to bring it about.

Sometimes, visions are corporate – like the Anti Apartheid or Jubilee 2000 or Fair Trade movements. One world-challenging vision was the concept of the United Nations whose charter, at least, surely accords with New Testament hopes for humanity. Like every institution it is fallible and can only be as successful as its member states allow. Yet its achievements, I suggest, massively surpass its failures. Like me, you may have visited its offices in Vienna, a suite of buildings so huge it's dubbed United Nations City. To me, this is a monument to the organization's visionary purposes – to promote justice, prevent conflict, facilitate reconciliation, provide practical help, and devise laws and conventions of benefit to the whole human family. Without this global enterprise, many millions more would have died as a result of neglected conflict, natural disasters, starvation and disease. For "where there is no vision, the people perish".

Guarantees a **better deal** for Third World Producers

FAIRTRADE

The vision principle today
Of course, we should never suspend our God-given critical faculties simply because something is written in the Bible. Yet, I do believe a very strong case can be made for our proverb's claim. Both Testaments and history since testify that without ideals and goals, without vision, societies are likely to fragment and decline.

Now the original Hebrew puts the maxim negatively, possibly because the Jews were habitually a subservient people with low morale. In happier times the proverb might have been put positively: "Where there *is* vision, people *flourish*". Negatively or positively expressed, the question remains: is Proverbs 29, verse 18, still valid in the 21st Century?

You may remember watching a series of four programmes called 'The Choir: boys don't sing'. To me, it was a striking demonstration of the vision principle working. From its foundation, the all-boys school featured had a music department but choral singing had never taken off. On becoming a PE specialist school, it developed quite a macho ethos with singing popularly deemed 'sissy'.

So when a young, enthusiastic musician, alarmed at the widespread decline in school choral music, offered to try and introduce choral singing – of a classical style indeed – his startling vision was met with cynicism. Undeterred, Gareth Malone doggedly pressed on, little by little winning the support of staff and students alike until, within a year, he was able to take a choir of 150 boys and teachers to sing in a national competition at the Royal Albert Hall! So, certainly musically speaking, where there's *no* challenge people 'perish': but where there *is* vision, they can flourish.

Take another heart-warming story. Operation Smile was the name given to a visionary campaign begun in 1982. Building on earlier experience, a plastic surgeon called Bill Magee and his nurse wife Kathleen, felt impelled to help people, particularly children, in poorer countries who suffered the pain and stigma of hideous facial disfigurement. Since its start, the project has steadily expanded, so that now it works in over 30 countries providing life-transforming treatment for around 10,000 children a year. "Where there *is* vision, people flourish".

Yet another person whose vision has radically improved the lives of millions is Professor Muhammad Yunus. In 1976, he founded Bangladesh's pioneering Grameen (or village) Bank with $27 from his own pocket. Unlike conventional banks, this lends to the poorest of the poor, often enabling them to start up a basic business. At first, financial experts dismissed the scheme as 'a one-off' and 'too good to be true'. But the professor showed that it was the most destitute of people – downtrodden, illiterate village women – who were the most dutiful and productive borrowers. Before long, even the World Bank gave its approval. Subsequently, the Grameen Foundation has grown enormously and by 2008 had helped over 34 million people in 28 countries. The micro-credit movement has lifted huge numbers of people out of destitution. "Where there *is* vision, people flourish".

No doubt you could tell other stories demonstrating that the vision principle does indeed work.

The 'earthly city'
But how might our proverb apply directly to you and me? If, to borrow Biblical imagery, Christians belong to two 'cities', 'earthly' and 'heavenly', we should live out the vision principle or process in two, parallel ways.

As members of the '*earthly* city', people who belong to civic society, we have obligations to our neighbourhood, town or city, nation and world, to 'render to Caesar what is his', as long as he's doing his job relatively honourably. One thing this means, I suggest, is that we belong to the 'visionary element' in society.

Belonging to the visionary element may sometimes involve our taking the initiative personally – looking critically at the world around us, discerning how it might be improved, and then offering our vision to the community, hoping it might be inspired to try and turn our vision into reality.

The vision process may occur on a family scale: the lady next door leads a lonely, humdrum life – what can we do to brighten her days? It may occur at a street level: there's been a spate of crimes – could we sow the idea of a Neighbourhood Watch group? It may occur within an institution: bullying is damaging our school or pilfering is threatening our business – what might I and other concerned colleagues do to promote a caring or honest environment? It may occur in a town or city context: binge drinking is causing misery for visitors and residents alike – what should I do to try and halt the madness and at least fractionally improve the situation? The vision process may occur at the international level: as always, there's oppression, poverty, hunger, disease, cruelty, conflict and such evils, all mocking the vision of justice, compassion and peace held up by prophets and apostles, and supremely by Jesus, and which, deep down, any thoughtful, empathetic person knows is how things ought to be – what more might I do to turn the vision into reality, for at least some deprived and suffering men, women and children?

Individuals who personally manage to turn big visions into transforming reality are relatively few. For most of us, most of the time, belonging to the visionary element in society is a lower profile business – a matter of lobbying here, giving there, writing to some cabinet minister, filling in a questionnaire about a local authority strategic plan – in one way or another, helping to turn visions into actuality. Doing such may be humdrum and often dispiriting, but it is surely one vital duty of those who claim to be disciples of the greatest visionary of all.

The 'heavenly city'

But what does membership of a 'heavenly city' imply? It means, I believe, offering society a radical alternative to the futile 'golden calves' of celebrity and consumerism. It means offering society a way out of its spiritual malaise towards spiritual health. However daunting it may be in the current cultural climate, it means we must still try to introduce people to the 'Jesus Experience'. Because it is only when a person's innermost self – conscience, values, attitudes and moment by moment moral decision-making – only when a person's 'soul', is exposed and responds to the Jesus type of vision, is he or she most likely to live a vision-glimpsing, vision-radiating and vision-achieving life. Once *genuinely* moved by the living Christ, a disciple surely *must* engage in the vision process. For where Christ truly is, the vision of God's Rule on Earth becomes real.

30   "NOW *THAT* I *CAN* BELIEVE!"

My reply to 'Mr Dubious'

Sheep without a shepherd

How many of us are there here now, do you think? If this church is typical of mainstream churches in Britain, the number attending today is likely to be lower than it would have been on a comparable Sunday fifty years ago. Most of us, moreover, are likely to belong to the SAGA age band. Membership of every mainstream denomination has slumped. Now, people who worship at least once a month make up around one-tenth of the British population. And the general drift away continues. *Why?*

At the same time, judging from the busyness of helpline programmes and a wide range of counselling services, it seems a high proportion of people feel rudderless, as they venture through the choppy sea of 21st Century life. Others, whilst not exactly feeling insecure, discover a deep desire to develop spiritually, a need recognised – according to a university magazine – in the burgeoning of personal development courses. Perhaps the most telling witness to our nation's spiritual need, is its morass of social problems. It does seem that great numbers of our fellow citizens are, in the words of the Biblical simile, "like sheep without a shepherd" (Mark 6:34). Yet only a tiny fraction of them now turn to the Church for spiritual guidance and care. *Why?*

Why people reject the Church

The reasons why so few people turn to the Church are largely the same reasons why others drift away from it.

One major reason, I suggest, is *the changing cultural climate*. Fifty years ago, there was still a fairly widespread assumption that the good citizen went to church on Sunday, even if only a minority actually did so. Today though, the idea of doing what you and I are engaging in now is totally alien to the great majority of British people. As I found when teaching secondary school students, "it isn't cool" to go to church.

Isn't another possible reason for people drifting away, or not being drawn to the Christian Church, *the pull of competing world views*? Various religious faiths and non-theistic ideologies, like

Humanism or astrology, offer alternative compasses for living. At the same time, many influential people, from academics to pop singers, either implicitly or directly, rubbish the whole notion of religion, especially Christianity. Faith-wise, we live in a *far* more competitive, if not hostile, world.

A further reason for the Church failing to keep or win 'customers' lies in *the diversity of rival attractions*. For much of the year, on Sunday mornings the Rec in Bath teems with children learning rugby football. More and more shops open on Sundays. It's the day many clubs now prefer for outings and functions.

A fourth reason why there's a net outflow from most churches could be *the sheer busyness of life*. In most families, Mum as well as Dad works full-time, so that household chores have to be packed into the weekend. There really isn't time for *church*!

A fifth reason why people don't regularly make their way to the local church must, at least in some cases, be *because their one experience of it was not a pleasant one.* "'No one spoke to me", they complain, "The service was deadly", "The pews gave me backache". Even those who do give church a longer chance, may not receive what Carl Dudley called the 'three strokes' – recognition, esteem and a sense of belonging – so they soon give up their experiment.

Probably the biggest, underlying reason why people turn their backs on church worship and indeed Christian commitment must lie, as it always has, in people's attitudes. As Jesus made plain in the Parable of the Sower (better called the Parable of the *Soils*), people shy away from spiritual nurture *because of everyday human frailty.*

The crisis of faith
So, I suggest: the changed social climate, the wider choice of 'world views', the multiplicity of rival attractions, the busyness of life, the off-putting experience, and supremely innate human fragility, all undermine church attendance. But, I believe, there's another, difficult to quantify yet highly significant, reason. It's what could be called 'the crisis of faith'.

What do I mean by 'the crisis of faith'? I have met someone who can make my meaning clearer. I should like to introduce him to you. You'll have to use your imagination about what he looks like! All I will say, he's neither hunk nor wimp but just an ordinary-looking bloke, like most men! Funnily enough, over the years I've kept on bumping into him. I would meet him at Round Table meetings. I came across him in the school staff room. I taught students who had clearly been influenced by him. I've sat next to him at parties and functions. I've talked with him in conferences and on courses. He just keeps on cropping up!

So I've got to know his opinions pretty well. Once he discovered I was a Christian – a minister at that – he liked to get on to the subject of religion. He soon made it clear that he has a latent sympathy for Christianity. In principle, he respects the Bible. In particular, he regards the values and attitudes of Jesus as attractive and relevant. More than once, he's given me the impression that he's got a sneaky admiration for the Church – at least for what it's doing to help other people. My impression is that, emotionally and spiritually, he is quite drawn to the Christian faith and the Christian Church.

The unbridgeable chasm

But intellectually, he's not at all sure. He's never been aggressive let alone rude. But he has been honest, telling me he simply cannot square certain features of conventional Christian faith with either his scientific knowledge or what his mind tells him is reasonable. Once, I remember, he put his position very graphically. He said he felt there was an *unbridgeable chasm* between his scientifically informed, evidence based, understanding of the world and what he gathered was the traditional, Biblically orientated, doctrinally expressed, Christian understanding of the world.

After that particular occasion, I couldn't get his image of the 'unbridgeable chasm' out of my mind. What's more, I realised he was actually describing the kind of tension I've found quite a number of churchgoers experience. Maybe there are plenty more of them but they're a little nervous about admitting their difficulties.

Anyhow, I asked my friend – which he has now become – to be more specific. What precisely was it that put him off conventional Christianity?

Mr Dubious shares his concerns
So he told me. I think what he said was in confidence so I'd better not divulge his name. I'll call him Mr Dubious.

Mr Dubious explained that, broadly speaking, he had two main concerns, one to do with the Bible, the other with Christian belief.

His concerns about the Bible
On his concern to do with the Bible, he said he really couldn't understand why so many churchgoers he had met seemed so ready to take the Bible at its face value. (I had to admit that literalism, or near literalism, does seem to be growing as a result of Fundamentalism's spreading influence). He then focussed on some particular narratives.

"Take the story of Noah", he began, "*You* know it's essentially a yarn – a sort of parable – though perhaps based on a sliver of historical reality. But I find many of your fellow church people take it just as it stands! I can't, though," Mr Dubious went on. "In the light of what science… and logic… and ethics tell me, I want to ask those who treat the whole story as historical, all sorts of questions, like these… If matter is neither created nor destroyed – though sometimes changed into energy – *where* is all that five-miles-deep global floodwater now? Could one family *really* collect and house millions of different animals and birds in just seven days? Did God *really* wipe out the entire natural world except for one far-from-saintly family and the creatures they managed to cram into their ark, just because humanity was going through one of its moral troughs?"

Then my friend turned to the story of the Hebrew migration from Egypt to the Promised Land. "When I examine the story closely I find it really gets my goat. Is God *really* so brutal and partisan? I mean, when the pharaoh refused Moses' plea for freedom, what did God do? He told Moses to turn the Egyptians' entire water supply into blood! In my book, that's just as bad as someone today putting cyanide in Chew Valley reservoir. When that didn't budge the pharaoh, God inflicted a series of horrific disasters, conducting his attack in ways Geneva conventions have banned for yonks! Then, God took a final swipe at his enemy by slaying all the first-born children – what had they done to deserve his wrath? Later, as the Israelites approached the Promised Land, God said, 'When you reach the land of Canaan, you shall cast out many nations. You shall smite and utterly destroy them. You shall make no covenant with them and show them no mercy'! I'm sorry to be so blunt, but when I read that verse, I couldn't help thinking of human tyrants like Hitler, Stalin and Pol Pot! And what did God tell his appointee King Saul to do to the Amalekites? 'Do not spare but kill man, woman, babe and suckling!' Talk about ethnic cleansing! Sorry, Edward, but I just can't see how anyone can believe in, let alone worship, a militaristic nationalistic God like that!"

My friend moved on to the New Testament. With equal candour, he remarked, "I'm particularly puzzled about miracles, not so much the healing ones but those where Jesus is portrayed as having power over nature. The scientist in me wonders, 'Did Jesus really walk on water? Or calm a storm? Or turn water into wine?' Surely, there must be alternative explanations. To be a Christian, do I *have* to believe in occurrences which are intrinsically implausible when there are so many amazing things – true miracles, I call them – to marvel at in the *normal* workings of Creation?"

His concerns about Christian belief
At that stage in our chat, I didn't wish to get bogged down in a discussion on miracles. After all, I had asked him to do the talking. So I asked him to switch to what bugged him about Christian belief.

He paused, stroked his chin and replied. "For a start, the Creeds. Now I know they've been around a very long time – since the Fourth Century, I believe – and are still precious to millions of Christians. But I do wonder about those clauses claiming to describe the manner of Jesus's conception and birth – you know, where they say he was 'conceived by the Holy Ghost' and 'born of the Virgin Mary'? By now you know I'm seriously interested in your faith, Edward, and so I've been reading quite a bit about it. And one thing I've discovered is that neither the apostle Paul, nor the Gospel writers Mark and John, nor even Jesus himself, appears to have heard of those extraordinary claims. What's more, I gather the Hebrew quoted simply means 'a young woman' rather than 'virgin'. Apart from all that, the modern world makes it plain real humans aren't produced in that sort of way! So how *could* Jesus be 'fully human', as traditional theology affirms?"

Now really wound up, Mr Dubious continued, "Not only do you Christians claim Jesus was 'fully human' but was also 'fully divine'! I'm sorry, but my sense of logic just won't let me swallow that!"

"As for the jump in that same creed, from the clause 'Born of the Virgin Mary' straight to 'Suffered under Pontius Pilate', well! It may be historically explainable but for a key statement of faith, 1600 years later, to go on ignoring the entire ministry of Jesus, beats me! I hope I haven't offended you, but you did ask me to share my concerns!"

How do we respond?
Well!!! How *do* we respond to Mr Dubious and the many like him – people who, though drawn to Jesus and, to some extent, to the Church, nevertheless have very real intellectual difficulties with traditional Christian faith?

Should we insist that if they wish to join us they must accept both Bible and Christian doctrine pretty well as they stand? Should we, in other words, simply expect them to make the age-old 'leap of faith' over the intellectual chasm?

Or, in 'broad church' fashion, should we accept them, allowing them to join us on more or less their own terms, as long as they don't 'upset the apple cart'?

250

"Come and join us!"

My response to Mr Dubious – and to Mrs, Miss, Ms and all who share his outlook – is this. "Come and join us! Thoughtful, well-educated, morally mature people like you have always made a vital contribution to Christians' understanding of the Bible and their beliefs. Now though, we need you more than ever, if we're to withstand the growing onslaught on our faith and even its very right to exist! We need the knowledge of science, the precision of logic, the insights of philosophy, ethics, psychology and sociology – and every other potential agent of truth and enlightenment, if Christ's Church is to offer intelligent help to the beleaguered human family in its turmoil".

I would go on, "I'm not just flattering you, but I believe that thinking, knowledgeable people like you, are actually potential agents of God! For all genuine knowledge and wisdom ultimately derive from God, assuming God is, in Paul's words, "the one in whom we live and move and have our being" (Acts 17:28).

The hour has come for credible faith

Putting aside my imaginary dialogue, what I am trying to say is this. That I believe the hour has come to do what Paul did for his time and situation. This is to work out, using contemporary knowledge and understanding, what the Jesus events, teaching and experience mean for the culture and circumstances in which we live. I am convinced that we should look again, rigorously and fearlessly, at both the substance and presentation of our beliefs, and come up with a truly *credible* faith. As David Peel, when Principal of Northern (Theological) College, Manchester, claimed in his book 'Reforming Theology': "Only a thoughtful faith will satisfy the mission imperative; only a well-worked-out theology will stand up in our sophisticated world".

Having a 'credible faith' doesn't mean doing away with theological statements. They have their value, as long as we remember they are statements of *belief*, therefore fallible and provisional. At the same time, we need to note: that the Free Churches have never, *on principle*, given creeds very much weight; that the only credal condition for membership of the Early Church was the brief but potentially life-changing confession 'Jesus is Lord'; that all that *Jesus himself* seems to have asked from would-be disciples was *faith,* 'fiducia', trust, that he, the Good Shepherd, could provide all the spiritual guidance and nurture they needed.

Mystery...and confidence

Having a 'credible faith' doesn't mean saying goodbye to mystery or poetry or symbolism. Faith wouldn't be faith, if it claimed everything it focused on could be fully understood or described. By definition, faith involves uncertainty – be it the faith that underpins the quest of science for truth about the physical world, or the faith that drives religion in its quest for truth about the moral and spiritual order. As Paul concluded in his Hymn to Love, we can see no more than a 'dim image' of truth (1 Corinthians 13). But we should surely *try* to offer a faith built on *plausible* evidence and *believable* claims. Personally, I find having a faith which unites the 'spiritual me' with the 'scientific, logical me' is immensely liberating and soul-renewing. What's more, it gives me the confidence – still with sensitivity, of course – to share my faith!

Faith for mind as well as heart

If we *don't* offer a credible faith, huge numbers of people will *go on* rejecting the *essence* of Christianity *as well as* its confusing and inessential accretions. They will *go on* 'throwing out the baby' as well as 'the bath water'. But for us to *let* them throw out the baby – who is none other than Jesus – would be 'mission failure' with a vengeance!

For there are people 'out there' wearied and bewildered by life's complexity, by work and family pressures, by social and technological changes; people 'out there' lost and aimless, like 'sheep without a shepherd'; people 'out there', like you and me, with immense potential for both good and evil; people 'out there' who need, more than anything else, to be touched by the perfect love, eternal wisdom, and life-transforming companionship of Jesus.

In countless, often courageous and imaginative ways, the Christian Church – across its theological and ecclesiastical spectra – *does* offer the world Christlike love. May it *also* offer something people can embrace with *mind* as well as *heart:* a *credible* faith! Then, people such as Mr Dubious might say, 'Now *that* I *can* believe' – and gladly join us!

252